OXFORD HANDBOOK OF
Medical Ethics and Law

Published and forthcoming Oxford Handbooks

Oxford Handbook for the Foundation Programme 5e

Oxford Handbook for Medical School

Oxford Handbook of Acute Medicine 4e

Oxford Handbook of Anaesthesia 4e

Oxford Handbook of Cardiology 2e

Oxford Handbook of Clinical and Healthcare Research

Oxford Handbook of Clinical and Laboratory Investigation 4e

Oxford Handbook of Clinical Dentistry 7e

Oxford Handbook of Clinical Diagnosis 3e

Oxford Handbook of Clinical Examination and Practical Skills 2e

Oxford Handbook of Clinical Haematology 4e

Oxford Handbook of Clinical Immunology and Allergy 4e

Oxford Handbook of Clinical Medicine – Mini Edition 10e

Oxford Handbook of Clinical Medicine 10e

Oxford Handbook of Clinical Pathology

Oxford Handbook of Clinical Pharmacy 3e

Oxford Handbook of Clinical Specialties 11e

Oxford Handbook of Clinical Surgery 4e

Oxford Handbook of Complementary Medicine

Oxford Handbook of Critical Care 3e

Oxford Handbook of Dental Patient Care

Oxford Handbook of Dialysis 4e

Oxford Handbook of Emergency Medicine 5e

Oxford Handbook of Endocrinology and Diabetes 3e

Oxford Handbook of ENT and Head and Neck Surgery 3e

Oxford Handbook of Epidemiology for Clinicians

Oxford Handbook of Expedition and Wilderness Medicine 2e

Oxford Handbook of Forensic Medicine

Oxford Handbook of Gastroenterology and Hepatology 3e

Oxford Handbook of General Practice 5e

Oxford Handbook of Genetics

Oxford Handbook of Genitourinary Medicine, HIV, and Sexual Health 3e

Oxford Handbook of Geriatric Medicine 3e

Oxford Handbook of Infectious Diseases and Microbiology 2e

Oxford Handbook of Integrated Dental Biosciences 2e

Oxford Handbook of Head and Neck Anatomy

Oxford Handbook of Humanitarian Medicine

Oxford Handbook of Key Clinical Evidence 2e

Oxford Handbook of Medical Dermatology 2e

Oxford Handbook of Medical Ethics and Law

Oxford Handbook of Medical Imaging

Oxford Handbook of Medical Sciences 3e

Oxford Handbook of Medical Statistics 2e

Oxford Handbook of Neonatology 2e

Oxford Handbook of Nephrology and Hypertension 2e

Oxford Handbook of Neurology 2e

Oxford Handbook of Nutrition and Dietetics 3e

Oxford Handbook of Obstetrics and Gynaecology 3e

Oxford Handbook of Occupational Health 2e

Oxford Handbook of Oncology 3e

Oxford Handbook of Operative Surgery 3e

Oxford Handbook of Ophthalmology 4e

Oxford Handbook of Oral and Maxillofacial Surgery 2e

Oxford Handbook of Orthopaedics and Trauma

Oxford Handbook of Paediatrics 3e

Oxford Handbook of Pain Management

Oxford Handbook of Palliative Care 3e

Oxford Handbook of Practical Drug Therapy 2e

Oxford Handbook of Pre-Hospital Care 2e

Oxford Handbook of Psychiatry 4e

Oxford Handbook of Public Health Practice 4e

Oxford Handbook of Rehabilitation Medicine 3e

Oxford Handbook of Reproductive Medicine and Family Planning 2e

Oxford Handbook of Respiratory Medicine 4e

Oxford Handbook of Rheumatology 4e

Oxford Handbook of Sleep Medicine

Oxford Handbook of Sport and Exercise Medicine 2e

Handbook of Surgical Consent

Oxford Handbook of Tropical Medicine 4e

Oxford Handbook of Urology 4e

Acknowledgements

Thanks to Kate McCombe for her input during the early stages of this book.

OXFORD HANDBOOK OF
Medical Ethics and Law

FIRST EDITION

Anna Smajdor
Associate Professor of Practical Philosophy
University of Oslo, Norway

Jonathan Herring
Professor of Law, Faculty of Law, University of Oxford
DM Wolfe-Clarendon Fellow in Law, Exeter College,
Oxford, UK

Robert Wheeler
Consultant Paediatric and Neonatal Surgeon
Director, Department of Clinical Law;
University Hospitals of Southampton, UK

OXFORD
UNIVERSITY PRESS

UNIVERSITY PRESS

Great Clarendon Street, Oxford, OX2 6DP,
United Kingdom

Oxford University Press is a department of the University of Oxford.
It furthers the University's objective of excellence in research, scholarship,
and education by publishing worldwide. Oxford is a registered trade mark of
Oxford University Press in the UK and in certain other countries

© Oxford University Press 2022

The moral rights of the authors have been asserted

First Edition published in 2022

Impression: 1

Published in the United States of America by Oxford University Press
198 Madison Avenue, New York, NY 10016, United States of America

British Library Cataloguing in Publication Data
Data available

Library of Congress Control Number: 2021944928

ISBN 978–0–19–965942–5

DOI: 10.1093/med/9780199659425.001.0001

Printed and bound in China by
C&C Offset Printing Co., Ltd.

This book is dedicated to Dr Andrew Lawson.

Andrew was a consultant anaesthetist, an expert in pain management, and a man with a fascination for the ethical challenges of
medicine. In 2007, he was diagnosed with mesothelioma. His experience as a patient gave him new and poignant insights into the
workings of the health system, which he documented with charac-
teristic frankness. In 2014, he died at the age of 55.

This book was Andrew's idea. He wanted to create something that
would be accessible; a handbook that would provide practical and
effective tools for resolving conflicts while recognizing the complex-
ities of medical law and ethics. He was ultimately deprived of the
chance of seeing it completed. But without his energy and enthu-
siasm, it would never have come into existence.

Foreword

Raanan Gillon, Emeritus Professor of Medical Ethics Imperial College London, Past President British Medical Association, Honorary President Institute of Medical Ethics, Former Editor Journal of Medical Ethics

What an honour to be asked to write a foreword for such an interesting and useful handbook of medical ethics and law—straightforwardly written and helpfully combining ethical and legal reasoning with advice and at least some legal *obligations* for clinicians practising under English law—analysis and advice worth considering even by doctors practising elsewhere. This is not, it should be emphasized, a book for those seeking extensive and detailed philosophical or jurisprudential bioethical argument (though plenty of that is to be found in the sensible referencing). Instead the reader is introduced first to a clear and succinct account of the elements of philosophical medical ethics, combining accounts of virtue ethics, consequentialism, deontology, the four principles approach, care ethics, moral relativism and subjectivism and critical reasoning, showing how all these approaches have relevance in actual clinical practice—but especially the last one, critical reasoning:

> Like good medicine, good moral reasoning involves reflection and critical application of theory rather than blind adherence to rules or theory. The path by which one arrives at a conclusion should be clear and explicable to others.

The second section gives a similarly clear and helpful introduction to Anglo-American medical law in general and English medical law in particular. This includes an excellent account—and critique—of contemporary clinical negligence law. There is then a useful section in which important 'generic legal and ethical issues' are addressed—for example an extensive account of ethical and legal issues in the context of resource allocation, sections on confidentiality, honesty and candour, relationships with patients, end-of-life issues, the role of the General Medical Council, and particular issues arising in medical research and in medical education. A subsection in the relationships section headed 'What is paternalism and why has it fallen out of favour?' gives a flavour of this book's agreeably straightforward approach.

There's then the unusual and fascinating fourth section of the book in which the sort of 'ethico-legal' cases that arise in clinical practice are very succinctly summarized in terms of case 'vignettes', relevant ethical and legal considerations, and recommendations about what to do, along with one or two legal case references. These vignettes are based on Dr Wheeler's long medico-legal experience of advising clinicians. As the authors acknowledge the vignettes are admittedly somewhat 'artificial, since most focus on a singular clinical legal or ethical point. Naturally, most aspects of clinical legal and ethical practice impinge on most of the multifarious specialities that comprise twenty-first century clinical practice'. So as the authors point out readers are 'encouraged to read every vignette bearing their own speciality in mind, since as the GMC and the Nursing and Midwifery Council correctly remind us, clinical law and ethics touch all facets of clinical care'.

The vignettes are categorized alphabetically in relation to branches of practice from which they have arisen and the type of problem involved. Thus an abortion issue is categorized under 'Gynaecology: abortion' and the particular vignette concerns a doctor's conscientious objection to pre-scribing an abortifacient. The analysis reinforces the book's earlier 'generic' discussion about conscience and conscientious objection, pointing out that the doctor is legally entitled not to prescribe but is required by the General Medical Council to refer the patient to a colleague who does not have such an objection. The text makes it clear that this is 'an ethically contested area in UK society' but supports the GMC's advice. As with the earlier discussion about conscience, the legal reference is to a fascinating UK Supreme Court judgement that specifies just what is and is not legally included within the term 'participation' in an abortion in relation to the Abortion Act's con-science clause. Thus busy doctors (or nurses or midwives or anyone else involved) will have what they need in the very brief account in section four of the book. The index will remind them of the earlier longer entry; and if they have time and interest to delve further, the judgement will tell them just what degree of 'participation' in an abortion they are legally entitled to include within their legal right of conscientious objection.

I certainly found the book fascinating, enjoyed its clear disentangling of often complex medico-moral and ethico-legal issues, and enjoyed also dipping into some of the judgements to which the reader is referred. They remind me incidentally, as does the book in general, of how closely medical ethics and medical law are interwoven and also of the often superbly clear and logical analysis that is provided by lawyers and judges involved in med-ical and health care law. I'm sure that Andrew Lawson, the instigator of this handbook, whose lively no-nonsense approach to these issues was such a delightful aspect of his character, would have been extremely pleased with the authors' fulfilment of his ambition to create a clear and straightfor-wardly written handbook of medical ethics and law.

Contents

Symbols and abbreviations *xiii*

Part 1 **Ethics**

1	Introduction to ethics	3
2	The virtuous doctor	9
3	Consequentialism	15
4	Deontology	21
5	The four principles	29
6	Care ethics	43
7	Moral relativism and subjectivism	49
8	Critical reasoning	55

Part 2 **Law**

9	Introduction to the legal system	67
10	Key articles of law	75
11	Court	83
12	Law within medical practice	91
13	Negligence	97
14	Other issues of liability	109

Part 3 **Generic legal and ethical issues**

15	Resource allocation	119
16	Candour and confidentiality	131
17	Issues in the doctor–patient relationship	147
18	Issues in death and dying	177
19	Doctors and the General Medical Council (GMC)	201
20	Medical research	211
21	Medical education	219

Part 4 Ethico-legal issues by medical specialism

229   22   Ethico-legal issues by medical specialism A–M

261   23   Ethico-legal issues by medical specialism N–V

Part 5 Statutory provisions

283   24   Abortion Act 1967

287   25   Female Genital Mutilation Act 2003

289   26   Gender Recognition Act 2004

291   27   Human Fertilisation and Embryology Act 1990

299   28   Human Rights Act 1998 (European Convention on Human Rights)

307   29   Human Tissue Act 2004

323   30   Mental Capacity Act 2005

339   31   Mental Health Act 1983

349   32   Suicide Act 1961

351   33   Surrogacy Arrangements Act 1985

Index   *357*

Symbols and abbreviations

➲	cross-reference
🔗	website
A&E	accident and emergency
AMCP	approved mental capacity professional
CANH	clinically assisted nutrition and hydration
CPR	cardiopulmonary resuscitation
DNACPR	do not attempt cardiopulmonary resuscitation
DNAR	do not attempt resuscitation
DVLA	Driver and Vehicle Licensing Agency
ECHR	European Convention on Human Rights
ECtHR	European Court of Human Rights
ED	emergency department
ENT	ear, nose, and throat
EU	European Union
FGM	female genital mutilation
GMC	General Medical Council
GP	general practitioner
HIV	human immunodeficiency virus
HTA	Human Tissue Authority
IMCA	independent mental capacity advocate
IVF	*in vitro* fertilization
LPA	lasting power of attorney
LPS	Liberty Protection Safeguards
MPTS	Medical Practitioners Tribunal Service
NHS	National Health Service
NICE	National Institute for Health and Clinical Excellence
P	a person
PEG	percutaneous endoscopic gastrostomy
PVS	persistent vegetative state
QALY	quality-adjusted life year
UK	United Kingdom

Part 1

Ethics

1 Introduction to ethics *3*

2 The virtuous doctor *9*

3 Consequentialism *15*

4 Deontology *21*

5 The four principles *29*

6 Care ethics *43*

7 Moral relativism and subjectivism *49*

8 Critical reasoning *55*

Introduction to ethics

Background 4
The Hippocratic oath 5
What is ethical theory? 6
Ethical theory: sample question 7

Background

Doctors have been concerned with ethics since the earliest days of medical practice. Traditionally, medical practitioners have been expected to be motivated by a desire to help their patients. Ethical codes and systems, such as the Hippocratic oath, have emphasized this.

During the latter half of the twentieth century, advances in medical science, in conjunction with social and political changes, meant that the accepted conventions of the doctor–patient relationship were increasingly being questioned. After the Nuremberg trials, in which the crimes of Nazi doctors, among others, were exposed, it became clear that doctors cannot be assumed to be good simply by virtue of their profession. Not only this, but doctors who transgress moral boundaries can harm people in the most appalling ways.

Nazi Germany is an extreme example of how the power and privilege that doctors have can allow them to perform terrible acts of atrocity. But on a more mundane level, the traditional power and authority of doctors has been increasingly recognized as being in itself a cause for ethical concern.

Doctors are often better educated than their patients, and may occupy a higher social status than those they care for. Doctors are usually in a position of power over their patients for these reasons, as well as simply because patients are likely to be sick, suffering, and vulnerable when they seek the doctor's help. For all of these reasons, ethics has been and remains an integral aspect of medical practice.

The Hippocratic oath

Many people are familiar with the idea that doctors take a solemn oath, in which they promise to behave ethically and in accordance with the moral standards required for the practice of medicine. The existence of the Hippocratic oath is in itself an indication that medical ethics has been recognized as a central aspect of medicine since the very earliest days. The World Medical Association has sought to produce a modern version of the traditional Greek version in the Declaration of Geneva (🔗 https://www.wma.net/what-we-do/medical-ethics/declaration-of-geneva/).

How useful is the Hippocratic oath?

In terms of providing answers for the questions raised by modern medical practice, the Hippocratic oath is limited for several reasons:

- There is dispute as to what the Hippocratic oath actually *is*. There are several texts that lay claim to being the oath, but there is little consensus as to which of these texts is the 'real' oath.
- Although many trainee doctors do take an oath, the content is widely variable, and the oath is not a standard or essential part of medical training or practice, either in the UK or beyond.
- The fragments of text that are regarded as being part of the original oath are very much a product of their time. Much of the text focuses on the medical student's obligations to respect the wisdom and authority of the master.

Nevertheless, within the body of texts that comprise the Hippocratic oath, there are mentions of core tenets of medical ethics, such as *confidentiality* (➔ p. 134) and the obligation to avoid causing harm (*non-maleficence* (➔ p. 36)). While these are clearly important aspects of medical ethics, relying on the Hippocratic oath alone does not necessarily help modern doctors in navigating the ethical challenges they face.

Pros and cons of the Hippocratic oath

Pros	Universally recognized as one of the first attempts to co-dify medical ethics
	Some components that are still highly relevant to modern medicine
Cons	No consensus as to the exact content of the oath
	Not always applicable to modern medicine
	No longer a standard or universal part of medical training

What is ethical theory?

Similarity between ethical and scientific theories

Ethical theories have some characteristics in common with scientific theories. Both are tools which we can use in order to explain and classify certain kinds of phenomena. However, scientific theories aim to predict and explain events, whereas ethical theories aim to recommend or forbid certain courses of action: to provide us with moral *reasons* for doing things.

As with scientific theories, there may be a number of ethical theories that provide reasons that explain or justify certain phenomena—sometimes these theories will work together smoothly; at other times, they may conflict with one another.

Sometimes a new theory may emerge that seems to solve or reconcile some of these conflicts. One of the most difficult aspects of ethics is that in the absence of proof, we tend to look to our intuitions to verify whether a particular course of action is acceptable. However, as we know from other areas of life, intuitions are not always reliable. It is because of this that ethical analysis is so important.

Is ethical theory a necessary part of making ethical decisions?

Being able to think about your options as a healthcare professional, and provide moral reasons for your choices is fundamental to ethics in any context. Most of us engage in moral reasoning, thinking through a problem and weighing up different options, without necessarily being consciously aware that we are doing so.

Knowledge of ethical theory is not an essential part of this process. However, in situations of extreme complexity, or when disputes arise, it can be helpful to be familiar with ethical theory. An understanding of ethical theory may help in unpicking a seemingly intractable disagreement. It may clarify the questions that need to be asked. Further, it may help in identifying areas of concern, or in identifying options that might otherwise have gone unrecognized.

Ethical theory: sample question

To demonstrate how theories may be applied in practice, we will use an example to show how each theory might be interpreted in the context of a specific ethical question. Read the question and see what your initial thoughts are. During the course of the discussion of different moral theories, we will present different lines of argument. You can test your initial judgement against the various approaches we consider as we progress through this part of the handbook.

> Ten medical students are learning how to perform rectal examinations. This is important for their education. However, no one likes undergoing a rectal examination unnecessarily.
>
> To ensure that students get the necessary practice, the consultant who is teaching them is trying to decide whether to allow these ten students to practise a rectal examination on 96-year-old anaesthetized woman who is undergoing surgery for an unrelated issue.
>
> The woman, who has mental capacity, has not been informed nor has she given consent.
>
> Is this ethically acceptable?

Additional reading

Jonsen AR. A Short History of Medical Ethics. Oxford: Oxford University Press; 2000.

Loudon I. The Hippocratic oath. BMJ. 1994;309(6959):952.

Miles SH. The Hippocratic Oath and the Ethics of Medicine. Oxford: Oxford University Press; 2005.

Rachels J. Can Ethics Provide Answers?: And Other Essays in Moral Philosophy. Lanham, MD: Rowman & Littlefield; 1997.

Richardson HS. Moral Reasoning. In: Valta EN (ed) The Stanford Encyclopedia of Philosophy (Fall 2018 Edition). https://plato.stanford.edu/archives/fall2018/entries/reasoning-moral/.

The virtuous doctor

Introduction to virtue *10*
Virtue ethics in practice *12*
Virtue ethics: sample question *14*
Applying virtue ethics to the sample question *14*

Introduction to virtue

The Greek philosopher Aristotle was one of the earliest thinkers to apply a rigorous and systematic approach to the study of ethics. Aristotle drew on the work of earlier philosophers including Plato, but differed from his predecessors in many ways, not least in his treatment of ethics as a specific field of study in its own right.

Key concepts in virtue ethics

Aristotle's ethical theory revolves around a number of key concepts, including virtue, practical wisdom, and eudaimonia (human flourishing). Perhaps the most familiar of these is the concept of virtue. For Aristotle, the way to find the right course of action is to look not at the action in itself, but at the kind of person who is making the decision.

A virtuous person will make a good decision, but it is by recognizing the virtues of the person, rather than by analysing the act itself, or its outcome, that we know it is right.

In recent decades, there has been a resurgence of philosophical interest in virtue ethics, after several centuries of neglect. Philosophers such as Rosalind Hursthouse have shown how questions of virtue can illuminate seemingly intractable moral problems, including, for example, that of abortion.

Virtue ethics is now regarded as being one of the three key moral theories, along with *consequentialism* (➲ p. 16) and *deontology* (➲ p. 22).

Virtue

Virtue ethicists regard virtues as being a balance between extremes. Courage, for example, lies midway between the extremes of cowardice on the one hand, and recklessness on the other. Applying this to medical ethics, we might say that a doctor who lacks courage may not fulfil our idea of what it means to be a virtuous doctor; they might not be willing to challenge accepted practices or protocols. A doctor who is overly courageous on the other hand might be unable to recognize the risks that she is embracing. She may become arrogant in her conviction that her way is right.

Another example is that of compassion, or empathy. Empathy is often regarded as a virtue for doctors. We ordinarily expect that doctors should be able to recognize and respond to their patients' feelings. Indeed, this can be regarded as part of the healing process. A doctor who cannot understand or relate to her patients and whose manner is cold and unfeeling may increase suffering and impede the patient's recovery. Conversely, a doctor who enters so fully into his patients' pain or distress that he cannot bear to perform painful procedures, may also fail his patients. The virtuous doctor is the one who is able to find a balance between these two extremes.

Working at it

People are likely to find that certain virtues come fairly easily to them, while they have to work on others. Can one claim any merit for drinking very little alcohol if one happens not to like alcohol very much? For the virtue ethicist, the answer is no. The effort of cultivating virtue is an ongoing process: an intrinsic part of living a good life. It is not simply a question of having or not having certain properties. Rather, we are continually developing and building on our virtues.

The appeal of virtue ethics lies in the fact that it puts the person at the centre of the moral question. Intuitively, many people feel that character, motivation, and intention are important aspects of ethics, and other ethical theories are not always able to accommodate these features.

However, virtue ethics requires fundamentally that we have an idea of what the virtues *are*, and this can be difficult to establish. Certainly, Aristotle's idea of the virtues does not necessarily harmonize with twenty-first century values. (Along with many other Greeks of his time, Aristotle thought that keeping slaves was perfectly compatible with being virtuous, and believed that women were intrinsically inferior to men.)

Virtue ethics in practice

Wisdom

The most valuable of all the virtues is wisdom. It is wisdom that enables the virtuous person to recognize the appropriate balance between extremes, in any particular situation. Without wisdom, 'virtues' such as courage or honesty are mere attributes. They may be exercised in ways that are selfish, harmful, or foolish. Only when tempered with wisdom do they become part of what constitutes a virtuous person. Because of this, wisdom is of supreme importance in virtue theory.

Eudaimonia

Another important aspect of virtue ethics is the concept of eudaimonia. Some Greek philosophers, such as Epicurus, suggest that happiness or pleasure is the supreme moral goal. If this is true, it seems mean that we should pursue pleasure by the quickest and most direct means. Rather than taking time to appreciate art or poetry, if we can take a pill that makes us happy, or simply get drunk, we should do so.

Virtue ethicists adopt a much richer view of what it is that makes a person's life good. Eudaimonia is commonly translated as 'human flourishing', and it encompasses all of the capabilities that are associated with being a person: not just immediate pleasure, but long-term endeavours such as education, art, and culture. Virtue ethicists such as Hursthouse believe that developing and exercising the virtues helps us to achieve eudaimonia, and so the two are intricately connected. For Aristotle, a person lacking virtue will not live a flourishing life.

Once again, however, there may be difficulties in defining exactly what we mean by eudaimonia. If we really try to pin the concept down, it becomes rather slippery. If we cannot easily agree, it may not be helpful in reaching answers to ethical questions. Nevertheless, it can be a useful way of thinking about what we regard as a 'good' life, and in identifying the 'good' that we are aiming for in endeavours such as medicine.

Justice

A further element of Aristotle's moral philosophy to consider here is the question of justice. Aristotle famously said that justice means 'treating equals equally and unequals unequally'. From the modern-day perspective, this could be taken to show why, for example, slavery and sexism are unjust. Slaves are not intrinsically dissimilar to their masters. Therefore, the fact that they are treated radically differently is unjust. Likewise, women, although different from men, are not different in ways that are morally significant. Therefore, it is unjust to treat them differently.

Clearly, much depends on this idea of morally significant differences in interpreting and applying Aristotle's concept of justice. Given that he himself was content with slave ownership and a very subordinate role for women, it might well be that he would have claimed that the differences between men and women, for example, *are* morally significant.

One area where we do currently make distinctions between people is in the treatment of children. Young children are treated very differently in medicine, and their legal rights and protections are different from those of adults. Usually, we assume that these differences are justified, that children are unequal to adults in morally significant ways and that it would be unjust to treat them as though they were exactly the same (it is worth noting that there are some people who believe that children are an oppressed group, just as women or slaves were in the past, and who call for a much greater degree of equality between adults and children).

Pros and cons of virtue ethics

Pros	Accommodates individual personality traits intuitively re-garded as being important for doctors
	Allows for greater flexibility and nuance than some other theories
Cons	Difficulty in interpretation and application
	Dispute over what constitutes virtue
	Complex relationship between virtue, wisdom, and eudaimonia

Virtue ethics: sample question

To demonstrate how virtue ethics may be applied in practice, we will use our sample question and consider how a virtue ethics approach might help to resolve the ethical issues it raises.

> Ten medical students are learning how to perform rectal examinations. This is important for their education. However, no one likes undergoing a rectal examination unnecessarily.
>
> To ensure that students get the necessary practice, the consultant who is teaching them is trying to decide whether to allow these ten students to practise a rectal examination on 96-year-old anaesthetized woman who is undergoing surgery for an unrelated issue.
>
> The woman, who has mental capacity, has not been informed nor has she given consent.
>
> Is this ethically acceptable?

Applying virtue ethics to the sample question

Performing a medical procedure on a patient who has not agreed to this may seem deceptive. Doctors are usually expected to be honest and trust-worthy and act with integrity. These are virtues that are explicitly required by the General Medical Council (GMC).

Nevertheless, students may be well motivated in wanting to carry out the procedure: doing so should enable them to be better doctors in future. It seems reasonable to suppose that no one has ill intentions towards the patient in question; the procedure is not intended to harm her, and she need never know what has been done to her.

However, a wise consultant may be able to exercise a more discerning judgement. Although no ill intention is involved, harm *may* come to the patient. Such harm, if she was not asked for her consent, will come as a shock. Though a very low-risk procedure, a rectal examination is something that carries a strong taboo in our society. The patient if she discovers she has undergone this may feel outraged or violated. We can never be entirely sure that a patient will not discover something we would prefer was kept secret.

The patient's virtues should also be considered here. If she had been asked, and had agreed to let the students examine her, this would have been a virtuous decision on her part. However, if the students examine her without her knowledge or consent, she has no opportunity to exercise virtue.

Additional reading

Hursthouse R, Pettigrove G. Virtue ethics. In: Valta EN (ed) The Stanford Encyclopedia of Philosophy (Winter 2018 Edition). https://plato.stanford.edu/archives/win2018/entries/ethics-virtue/.

Pellegrino ED. Toward a virtue-based normative ethics for the health professions. Kennedy Institute of Ethics Journal. 1995;5(3):253–77.

Consequentialism

Introduction to consequentialism *16*
Consequentialism in practice *18*
Consequentialism: sample question *20*
Applying consequentialist theory to the sample question *20*

Introduction to consequentialism

What is consequentialism?

Consequentialism, as its name suggests, is a theory whose focus is purely on the outcome of an action. For a consequentialist, the only question to be asked when seeking a moral reason for doing something is 'What is the result?'

The most famous form of consequentialism is utilitarianism: 'an act is morally right if it maximizes the good' (the terms consequentialism and utilitarianism are commonly used interchangeably). The simplicity of this approach to ethics has a clear appeal. Once we have determined what constitutes a good outcome, we need only to establish what consequences will follow from two options to know which of them is ethically preferable.

The most famous proponents of consequentialism are Jeremy Bentham and John Stuart Mill. However, versions of consequentialism are recognizable in the philosophy of ancient Greece, and modern variations continue to emerge. Utilitarian themes are very prevalent in policy decisions related to healthcare, and in particular in the case of resource allocation. Questions about how to spend healthcare budgets usually focus on the specific outcomes of diverting money to particular treatments or procedures.

Good consequences

Consequentialism is attractive partly because once we have decided what counts as a 'good' consequence, we do not need to trouble ourselves further with morally complex principles or concepts. We can simply go out and measure outcomes. For this reason, consequentialism is often regarded as an intrinsically rational, empirical, and almost scientific approach to ethics. More fundamentally, perhaps, utilitarianism appeals to a deep intuition that is shared by many people, that the results of our choices are morally significant, and that an act that benefits many people, and harms no one, is better than an act that harms many people and benefits no one.

Consequentialism in practice

Problems with consequentialism

However, consequentialism does pose two very challenging problems for its proponents. One is the question of determining what does actually constitute a good outcome. People's interpretation of the good may differ. Perhaps still more problematic is the question of *whose* outcomes are important. Some consequentialists believe that we should include animals in our moral calculations—if so, commonly accepted practices such as the consumption of meat and the use of animals in research would look morally abhorrent. Even if we confine our moral calculus only to human beings, significant ethical questions still remain. If we are thinking about the ethics of abortion, for example, should we take into account the foetus's interests, or only those of the mother? Another difficulty relates to the question of whether we should think only of the interests of existing people, or if we should also consider future generations—people who do not yet exist.

Aside from these questions, in focusing exclusively on outcomes, consequentialism treats as irrelevant questions of motivation, of character, of intention, and of justice. Many people feel that these are highly significant components of ethical evaluation, and consequentialism's failure to accommodate them may seem unacceptably reductive, or counter-intuitive.

Acts and omissions

Consequentialism makes no distinction between acts and omissions. The outcome of choosing *not* to do something is just as significant for a consequentialist as the outcome of an act that one *has* chosen to perform. This means that the scope of our moral obligations may seem unfeasibly large. If I fail to send food to a starving person in a distant country who then dies, I may feel that this is very different from deliberately ending that person's life. Yet the consequences are the same in both cases.

Peter Singer, a renowned consequentialist philosopher, argues that we are indeed responsible for the deaths that arise from our failure to provide help to people in need. Critics suggest this makes consequentialism excessively burdensome: you would be allowed few moments of rest because there is almost always something more productive to do than resting.

Consequentialism and justice

Another counterintuitive aspect of consequentialism is its apparent imperviousness to considerations of justice. Suppose that we knew for a fact that capital punishment functions effectively as a deterrent: for each person executed, five murderers are deterred. To save resources, we might seize upon any random person, decree that they are the murderer, and execute them. Not only would this have the same deterrent effect, but it would also save police time and money since they would not need to track down the real culprit.

A consequentialist would not worry about this, since the overall outcome may be deemed to outweigh the fact that one innocent person has been killed. But for many people, the injustice committed on the innocent man outweighs the beneficial consequences.

Act versus rule utilitarianism

The idea of weighing up every possible outcome of every possible act or omission is rather daunting. In fact, if one really set out to do this, very few acts would be performed, since the calculations would be likely to take up all one's time! Even more problematic is the fact that we rarely know for certain what the consequences of an act will be, so most of the time, we are dealing with more or less remote possibilities. Is it really feasible to grapple with such complex uncertainties every time we are faced with a moral decision?

One way around this problem is the idea of rule utilitarianism. This form of utilitarianism is based on the idea that, in most cases, utility can be maximized by following certain sets of rules. We might assume that killing people or harming them is unlikely to maximize utility. So, a rule utilitarian might argue that, for the most part, we can take this as a rule to be followed, without having to go into the calculations in each case. However, where there is a genuine dilemma, the rule utilitarian will resort to a calculation.

While this system might save a lot of effort, it does raise questions about how we are to know when the rule needs to be queried. Moreover, those who are purists about consequentialism may regard rule utilitarianism as being unsatisfactory in that it fails adequately to apply the basic requirement of weighing consequences in every case.

Consequentialism and public health

Consequentialism poses challenges for the doctor–patient relationship since it explicitly requires doctors to consider the greater good—not just the interests of a specific patient. However, in the public health context, consequentialism has an important role to play. Measures such as cervical screening tend to be evaluated on the basis of how many lives they save, a broadly consequentialist approach. For example, the National Institute for Health and Clinical Excellence (NICE) uses the quality-adjusted life year (QALY) to determine whether healthcare interventions can be justified or not on the basis of cost per (quality-adjusted) year.

Pros and cons of consequentialism

Pros	Transparent: in theory, anyone with the same data should reach the same conclusion
	Systematic: no complex concepts or reasoning required, just weighing up of costs and benefits
Cons	Key concepts remain contested, e.g. what should be maximized
	Counterintuitive implications, e.g. acceptability of killing an innocent person to save others

Consequentialism: sample question

To demonstrate how consequentialism may be applied in practice, we will use our sample question and consider how a consequentialist might use the theory to solve this ethical issue (➲ pp. 28, 40, 46, 54).

> Ten medical students are learning how to perform rectal examinations. This is important for their education. However, no one likes undergoing a rectal examination unnecessarily.
>
> To ensure that students get the necessary practice, the consultant who is teaching them is trying to decide whether to allow these ten students to practise a rectal examination on 96-year-old anaesthetized woman who is undergoing surgery for an unrelated issue.
>
> The woman, who has mental capacity, has not been informed nor has she given consent.
>
> Is this ethically acceptable?

Applying consequentialist theory to the sample question

For a consequentialist, the question of whether the patient agrees to undergo the procedure is irrelevant. As long as she never finds out, no harm is done. If the action benefits ten medical students, this may be enough. Although, of course, it would be different if the procedure causes the patient harm (as it might on a 96-year-old patient), then the procedure could not be justified.

However, a utilitarian must also consider the harm that might arise if the patient *does* find out—the patient may be distressed and angry. Her negative experience could outweigh the benefit to the medical students.

There are also broader harms and benefits to consider. If patients learn that they may be 'practised on' while under anaesthetic, they may lose trust in hospitals. But if no one ever finds out, perhaps overall large numbers of patients could benefit, since students will have the chance to improve their skills.

If we could be 100% certain that the patient would never find out, the consequentialist would be completely happy to advise the ten students to proceed with their examination.

Additional reading

Oakley J, Cocking D. Consequentialism, complacency, and slippery slope arguments. Theoretical Medicine and Bioethics. 2005;26(3):227–39.

Savulescu J. Consequentialism, reasons, value and justice. Bioethics. 1998;12(3):212–35.

Deontology

Introduction to deontology *22*
Deontology in practice *24*
Deontology: sample question *28*
Deontology and the sample question *28*

Introduction to deontology

What is deontology?

The word 'deontology' stems from the Greek for 'duty'. In contrast to consequentialism, a deontologist approaches ethical questions by identifying and adhering to moral rules, or duties. Once we have established what our duty is, we must perform it, regardless of what the outcome may be. However, this does raise the question of how we establish what our duties are.

Often, deontological approaches are associated with religion (the Ten Commandments are a set of deontological rules) but religious duties cannot easily be imposed on those who do not share that religion. And if moral duties are derived simply from religious obligations, it seems to lead us into a logical difficulty. In Plato's Euthyphro dilemma, we are asked whether the gods approve of what is good, *because* it is good, or whether what they love is good because they approve it. Neither answer seems satisfactory.

Duties and reason: the categorical imperative

The German philosopher Immanuel Kant argues that we can establish our moral duty purely through the exercise of reason without having to derive them from any theological source. This is known as 'the categorical imperative'.

To achieve this, Kant urges that in all of our decisions we should always behave in such a way that we could will for what we do to become a universal law. This means that we cannot treat our own interests as being superior to those of others. It also means that moral duties are consistent and non-arbitrary—they apply to everyone equally.

Deontology in practice

Lying

Kant believed that telling the truth is a moral duty, and therefore that it is always wrong to lie. He explains that if you tell me a lie, it only makes sense to do so if you hope and expect that I will believe it. So, if you ask whether you can will your action to be a universal law, the answer has to be no. In such a world, no one would believe the lie you are about to tell! The whole point of lying is premised on the fact that people usually expect each other to tell the truth. For this reason, Kant concludes that lying is indeed morally wrong, and is not justifiable in any circumstances.

For many people, this absolute prohibition seems too extreme; what if a lie were necessary in order to save a life? If we see someone fleeing from a murderer, and the murderer asks us which direction they took, must we really tell the truth, even if it will result in the death of the victim? For Kant, although he admits this case is difficult, the answer still stands that we must not lie. More than this, he asserts that if we do lie, we become morally responsible for the murderer's actions. Whatever actions the murderer carries out on the basis of the false information that we have given, are now *our* moral responsibility. Although this is a very extreme case, a less dramatic example may help to show why Kant makes this apparently paradoxical claim.

When a doctor lies to a patient, that patient then proceeds to make decisions and acts on the basis of that false information. The doctor has gained control over what should be the *patient's* moral choices, by choosing to deceive.

Duties to whom? The importance of humanity

A key facet of Kant's deontological approach is the importance he places on humanity. For Kant, being human means that we have unique moral status and moral responsibilities. As a rational person, I am a moral decision maker. I can use my ability to reason and to discover the moral law, as described previously. In each other human being, I must recognize fellow decision makers.

This entails a crucial requirement that we do not interfere with this rational decision-making capacity in other people. Just as we wish to formulate our own decisions and judgements, without being hindered or thwarted, we must acknowledge that it is wrong to hinder or thwart others in their judgement, or in the exercise of their autonomy. In keeping with respect for humanity and autonomy, Kant famously asserts that we must always treat other human beings as ends in their own right. We must never use a human being (other people or ourselves) as a mere means to an end.

Means and ends

Exactly what it means to treat a human being as a mere means is not always easy to specify. However, Kant's instruction has a very deep resonance with many people's intuitions, especially in cases where other moral theories shed no light. For example, a consequentialist might believe that slavery is acceptable if the slaves are reasonably well treated and if the system of slavery produces benefits overall.

Similarly, a virtue ethicist might argue that if the slave owner is virtuous, slave ownership is not in itself unethical. A slave owner might keep slaves because he believes they are better off under his ownership than if they were obliged to eke a living in a hostile country.

Some people believe slavery would still be wrong even if the slaves were well fed, well housed, and given medical attention when required, and even if the slave owner simply wanted the best for the slaves. This is because slavery is regarded as being intrinsically wrong. It is often hard to articulate this intrinsic wrongness, and this is where Kant's philosophy can be useful— it helps us to identify what we feel is really wrong about slavery: the treatment of human beings as mere means to our own ends. If we accept this, it is easy to see that deontological moral theory forbids slavery.

The focus on humanity in deontological reasoning makes it very clear that slavery is unacceptable. However, in other contexts, it is not so obvious what a deontologist should believe. Kant's emphasis on humanity is based heavily on the assumption that humans are *rational*. It is this that requires respect.

Kant's philosophy does not help very much in determining the moral status of abortion, for example. Fetuses are not rational per se, so it might seem that they lack moral status on a deontological view, in which case abortion might be permissible. However, in practice, many deontologists are opposed to abortion. The emphasis on rationality also poses problems for the treatment of adults who lack capacity to consent, whether due to mental illness, cognitive impairment, intoxication, injury, and so on.

Consent and agreement

Because respect for autonomy is crucial to Kant's deontological ethics, coercion and deception are absolutely prohibited. As demonstrated by the slavery example, it does not matter for Kant how well people are treated, nor what motivations are at play. To override another human being's will is not acceptable.

However, there are many things that we do which might seem to use other people as means to our own ends. Would Kant's injunction imply that employment itself is unethical? If I go to work reluctantly, and only because I get paid for it, does this imply that I am being used as a means to the employer's ends? The essential difference between slavery and employment lies in the question of consent. If I agree to carry out work in exchange for money, on Kant's view, I am not being treating *merely* as a means to an end: my own ends are being recognized (since I have agreed to do the work and am being paid).

Dignity and human rights

Deontological morality is often associated with the language of human dignity and human rights. Because it imposes absolute prohibitions on the ways in which we can treat other people, this seems to imply that human beings are imbued with a special moral significance. This may be termed as 'dignity'. The prohibitions on what we can do to each other can be turned round the other way, and interpreted as rights. Instead of focusing on those things that we must not do to others, rights focus on what we, as individuals, are entitled to expect from others.

However, although the language of dignity and rights are appealing, they raise their own sets of problems. Dignity, again, is very hard to define. Those who are pro-euthanasia and those who are anti-euthanasia are diametrically opposed. Yet lobbyists on both sides of the euthanasia debate use the term 'dignity' in support of their cause (➲ p. 180). Likewise, the nature and interpretation of human rights can be difficult to ascertain. The 'right to life' is also cited by lobbyists both for and against euthanasia.

Pros and cons of deontology

Pros	Simplicity of absolute prohibitions
	Harmonizes with some basic intuitions
Cons	Rigidity: does not allow for individual interpretation, or adaptation to circumstances
	Counterintuitive in some cases, e.g. that lying is *never* justifiable

Deontology: sample question

To demonstrate how deontology may be applied in practice, we will use our sample question and consider how a deontologist might use the theory to solve this ethical issue.

> Ten medical students are learning how to perform rectal examinations. This is important for their education. However, no one likes undergoing a rectal examination unnecessarily.
>
> To ensure that students get the necessary practice, the consultant who is teaching them is trying to decide whether to allow these ten students to practise a rectal examination on 96-year-old anaesthetized woman who is undergoing surgery for an unrelated issue.
>
> The woman, who has mental capacity, has not been informed nor has she given consent.
>
> Is this ethically acceptable?

Deontology and the sample question

It should immediately be apparent that a deontologist would not allow medical students to practise on an unconscious patient without her consent. This would be disregarding her autonomy, as well as being deceptive.

However, would obtaining consent in advance make a difference, given that students would still be 'using' the patient for their own practice?

Given the previous points about autonomy and consent, it seems plausible that a deontologist would be happy for the students to practise on the patient if she had consented in advance. If the patient consents, she shares in the ends of the students, that is, their desire to become better doctors, and this becomes one of her own ends.

Additional reading

Garbutt G, Davies P. Should the practice of medicine be a deontological or utilitarian enterprise? Journal of Medical Ethics. 2011;37(5):267–70.

Veatch RM. Against virtue: a deontological critique of virtue theory in medical ethics. In: Shelp EE (ed) Virtue and Medicine, pp. 329–45. Dordrecht: Springer; 1985.

The four principles

Introduction to the four principles *30*
The four principles 1: autonomy *32*
The four principles 2: beneficence *34*
The four principles 3: non-maleficence *36*
The four principles 4: justice *37*
The four principles in practice *38*
The four principles: sample question *40*
The four principles and the sample question *41*

Introduction to the four principles

Background

The inherent power imbalance in doctor–patient relationships raises ethical problems. What should be done if doctors' views and values differ from those of patients? How should doctors deal with ethical problems that arise in medical practice—does the Hippocratic oath really provide all the answers we need? Or can we perhaps rely on ethical theories such as those outlined in previous chapters?

After the events of the Second World War, and in the face of shifting social and political expectations during the latter half of the twentieth century, the social or moral superiority of the doctor no longer seemed a sufficient basis on which to assume the 'doctor knows best'.

This trend continues to the extent that even doctors' skill and training nowadays have, perhaps, less cachet than they used to in the days before patients could do their own research on the internet. For these and many other reasons, a need for a new paradigm and a new set of principles arose. We needed to be sure that whatever the race or religion of the patient, and whatever the ideological convictions of the doctor, patients would be respected and protected.

The need for universal principles

One of the challenges was to identify overarching principles that could be recognized and valued by people of all cultures and communities. After the Nuremberg Trials, many nations began to feel that a universal framework was needed, to which all people could subscribe, and within which doctors could practise ethically. This has led to a range of international protocols, notably the International Council on Harmonisation of Technical Requirements for Registration of Pharmaceuticals for Human Use, Good Clinical Practice (ICHGCP), which ensures clinical trials of pharmaceuticals are rigorous and protect the rights of research participants.

Existing ethical theories did not seem to meet the need; they do not necessarily give easy answers to moral problems and, indeed, can yield counterintuitive results if pushed to their logical extremes. There is also the problem that moral values differ according to culture and context. What if the doctor is a deontologist, and the patient a consequentialist?

Increasingly, in modern medicine, doctors may be treating patients who speak a different language, come from a different country, or practise a different religion. In short, patients' values may be radically different from those of the doctor, and those of one doctor may differ from those of her colleagues. The importance of respecting diversity is frequently emphasized in UK medical practice, but it can be difficult to distinguish between cultural differences that are to be recognized and respected, and moral outrages that cannot, or should not, be tolerated. For example, a court is likely to overrule the objection of a Jehovah's Witness parent who refuses to consent to a blood transfusion for their child. By contrast, the law permits male circumcision in accordance with religious tradition.

What are the four principles?

The 'four principles' approach to medical ethics was developed partly in response to the problems just described. The four principles approach is not an ethical theory per se. Rather, it attempts to set out certain key considerations which are independent of social, cultural, or religious contexts. Since its inception in the twentieth century, the four principles approach has become extremely influential and is now the dominant framework for medical ethics teaching.

The principles in question are:

Respect for autonomy	Providing information to patients and allowing them to make their own decisions
Beneficence	Undertaking actions intended to benefit the patient
Non-maleficence	Acting so as to avoid harming the patient
Justice	Avoiding discrimination, distributing resources fairly

As suggested, these principles are not to be regarded an ethical theory in their own right. They are more properly understood as a distillation of other ethical theories, synthesized and reformatted for use in the medical setting.

The four principles 1: autonomy

What is autonomy?

Autonomy means self-governance: making and carrying out one's own decisions. The importance of respect for autonomy is implicit or explicit in nearly all moral theories. With changing social expectations and, arguably, less hierarchical social and political structures, respect for autonomy has grown in importance, and is regarded by some as the cornerstone of the four principles. Respect for autonomy is at the root of many of the fundamental requirements of good medical practice.

Autonomy and consent

Respect for autonomy entails that patients should be the ones who decide between treatment options, rather than the doctor. In earlier times, there was a far greater acceptance of the doctor's authority. The physician was expected to dictate to the patient what s/he must do, and the doctor's orders were to be obeyed implicitly.

In contrast, we now expect patients to share in the decision-making process, engaging with deliberation with the doctor, drawing on the doctor's expertise and opinion, but ultimately making their own choices. If patients are to be involved in making decisions, this of course means that they must be fully informed about the options, about the risks and benefits of particular courses of treatment, and about their prognosis.

This places an additional burden on the doctor, who must now not only have the medical expertise to diagnose and recognize appropriate treatment options, but must also be able to communicate complex medical information accurately and effectively.

How far does autonomy extend?

Respect for autonomy has become such an important feature of medical ethics that it can be hard to know where its boundaries lie. Respecting autonomy entails that we acknowledge people's different values, and accept that doctors are no better placed than anyone else to impose their values on others.

But what if patients request harmful, experimental, or expensive treatments? Claims of patient autonomy seem stronger when a patient is refusing treatment which a doctor thinks is beneficial, than where a patient is demanding treatment which a doctor thinks is unsuitable.

The principle of respect for autonomy is not absolute, but there is heated debate about how and when it should be overridden by other principles. What does seem clear is that it will inevitably clash with one or more of the other three principles at times. Resolving these clashes is one of the major preoccupations of medical ethicists and medical practitioners.

Autonomy and paternalism

When the principles of beneficence and respect for autonomy come into conflict, questions arise about which principle to prioritize. A patient may, for example, wish to undergo treatment that the doctor feels is unacceptably risky and carries a very small chance of success. Cardiopulmonary resuscitation (CPR) may be a good example here.

A patient who is already terminally ill, is frail, and has co-morbidities is unlikely to survive an arrest. If CPR is carried out aggressively, the likelihood is that if the patient survives at all, it will be for a few extra days, in the intensive treatment unit, perhaps never regaining consciousness, and possibly with broken ribs. It may seem clear to a doctor that to embark on CPR would not be beneficent while to the patient it seems equally clear that it *would*.

Those who prioritize the principle of respect for autonomy may feel that, all other things being equal, it is more appropriate to accept the patient's interpretation of beneficence. Respect for autonomy entails, after all, a recognition that people have different values, and their understanding of what is good cannot simply be 'corrected' by a doctor whose worldview and background may be completely different to that of her patient.

However, if the principle of beneficence is prioritized, the doctor may be accused of paternalism. Paternalism is, simply, the triumph of beneficence over autonomy. In the past, paternalism was regarded as a thoroughly acceptable basis for the doctor–patient relationship. In more recent decades, it has acquired a bad reputation. Nevertheless, it could be argued that paternalism still plays a therapeutic role in many doctor–patient encounters, and indeed, some patients prefer this relationship.

Autonomy and informed decision-making

In the example described earlier, where a patient feels CPR would be beneficent but the doctor does not, it can be tempting to assume that what is going on here is actually a result of inadequate communication. The doctor may feel that, if only the patient *really* understood the facts, he would be *bound* to come round to the doctor's point of view. This, of course, is a fallacy. As suggested previously, people's view of what is good or desirable may differ, so that even though the facts may be the same, people may value them differently, and so come to different decisions.

The four principles 2: beneficence

What is beneficence?

Beneficence is the act of *helping* people, or benefiting them.

The centrality of beneficence for medicine

Beneficence encapsulates what many people regard as the essence of medicine. Doctors are not here to function as servants, mechanics, shopkeepers, or teachers for their patients. Rather, their unique and special role is to *help* people, cure disease, relieve distress and suffering, prolong lives, and improve health. It has been argued that in this respect, doctors are radically different from other professionals.

An off-duty plumber has no moral obligation to fix a dripping radiator in a restaurant where he is eating. But an off-duty doctor, it is commonly assumed, *does* have a moral obligation to attend to someone who suffers a heart attack at the restaurant where he is eating. (In fact, this common assumption may be more complex on closer inspection; the ethical and legal obligations of off-duty doctors are discussed in greater depth on ⊃ p. 99.)

Differing views on beneficence

Despite its clear moral force, the principle of beneficence is not always as straightforward as one might hope. With recent developments in medical technology, many people have begun to wonder if we should regard extending a person's lifespan as being beneficent in all cases.

Should we resuscitate a patient who is dying of terminal cancer, only for them to survive another 2 days in intensive care, perhaps without ever regaining consciousness? Should we continue to provide artificial nutrition and hydration for a patient in a persistent vegetative state if there is no prospect of recovery or improvement?

Is it always beneficent to save life or cure/prevent illness?

As medical technology and life-preserving interventions have proliferated, it has become evident that patients and doctors have extremely divergent views on the beneficence of life-prolonging measures. Some argue passionately for the continuance of treatment, while others argue that there are situations in which the patient cannot be benefited by being kept alive.

Problems arise when a patient's view of what is 'beneficent' differs from that of the doctor. We have seen that respect for autonomy is an essential component of the four principles. But a doctor may find it difficult, if not impossible, to respect the autonomy of a patient whose concept of beneficence is radically different.

Beneficence and cultural values

Still more difficult than individual doctor–patient discrepancies are those disputes that engage complex social, religious, and cultural beliefs. We have commented on the fact that the four principles were envisaged as a universally applicable system of ethics, but different cultures have varying views on what constitutes health, or health benefits. Is there an overarching objective truth about what is 'good' for someone's health?

As well as the challenges of new drugs and/or technologies, problems arise when thinking about different cultural understandings of beneficence. Practices regarded as beneficent in some cultures, such as female genital mutilation (FGM), are viewed as harmful and degrading by others. Indeed, FGM is a criminal offence in England, Wales, and Scotland.

We might try to explain the wrongness of FGM by saying that it confers no direct health benefits, but causes risk and pain to those who undergo it. Yet this is precisely where things become difficult, since the elements of risk and pain can be substantially alleviated if the procedure is performed by a skilled doctor using the best medical technology available.

To further complicate matters, many of those who object to FGM are happy to participate in male circumcision which is culturally normal in much of Europe and North America.

The four principles 3: non-maleficence

What is non-maleficence?

Non-maleficence is the principle of preventing or avoiding harm to others.

The scope of non-maleficence

Non-maleficence is sometimes regarded as the primary ethical principle to which doctors should adhere. It features in the Hippocratic oath, and it re-appears in the common phrase 'primum non nocere': first, do no harm. The importance of this principle stems largely from the recognition that those same skills which allow a doctor to improve a patient's health or well-being, can in themselves cause damage, pain, or sickness.

Yet the injunction 'first do no harm' is perhaps too extreme. After all, if this really were a doctor's first and primary obligation, she would not be able to do anything at all. It is impossible to think of any medical procedure or intervention that is entirely without risk.

A simple vaccination causes harm by puncturing the skin; even screening may cause harm in the form of anxiety or a false-positive result. For this reason, it is clear that non-maleficence cannot function as medicine's pri-mary principle; rather, it serves as a balance against beneficence.

Beneficence is an active principle—it calls for doctors to intervene to benefit their patients. Non-maleficence is a passive and cautionary prin-ciple that reminds doctors to think about the harm they may cause by intervening. Only in conjunction do these principles make sense.

Understanding harm

Of all the principles, the injunction to avoid harm may appear to be the sim-plest. We may argue about what exactly beneficence means, but one might imagine that the concept of harm is rather more straightforward. However, this is not always the case as the examples of circumcision and FGM show.

Some years ago, a doctor practising in Scotland was severely criticized for his willingness to amputate healthy limbs at patients' request. Why a pa-tient would wish for a healthy leg to be amputated is a perplexing question. Some believe it indicates a psychiatric disorder, others that it is a lifestyle choice. Either way, it is clear that such requests push our understanding of non-maleficence to the extreme.

Screening programmes and harm

Questions of how to interpret harm also arise in the public health context. In recent years, some criticisms have been raised regarding breast screening. Frequently, screening programmes are justified on the ground that they save lives by detecting diseases which might otherwise have gone unnoticed until too late.

However, in the breast screening context, it has been suggested that the screening programme causes excessive and unjustified interventions. In short, it causes harm. Some patients have biopsies only to discover there was nothing wrong. Others may have cancer detected, but in circumstances where the disease would never have become symptomatic.

For example, if a very elderly patient has a very slow-growing cancer, it is highly unlikely that it will kill her. The question of whether such inadvertent harms outweigh the benefits of screening programmes is fraught. These problems, of course, also affect other moral theories that rely on concepts of harm, in particular *consequentialism* (➲ p. 15).

The four principles 4: justice

What is justice?

Justice is the principle of treating others fairly, avoiding discrimination and distributing resources equally.

Justice differs from the three principles already discussed. Autonomy, beneficence, and non-maleficence are highly patient centred. However, most moral theories recognize that the individual is not the sole ethical concern. By its very nature, ethics is a social phenomenon, meaning that questions of fairness come into play.

There are two primary ways in which the principle of justice affects ethical decision-making in medicine. Firstly, there is the issue of how other people may be affected by a particular decision. Secondly, there is the question of discrimination: do some patients receive better or worse treatment than others?

Justice and resource allocation

In a publicly funded healthcare system, such as the National Health Service (NHS), there is a limited budget. At its crudest level, this means that choosing to spend money on one particular patient will mean there may be less to spend on another. However much we might like to, we simply cannot provide all the treatments that each patient may want or need. Because of this, we need to find ways of prioritizing patients.

Justice and need

In the NHS, the first step is to establish clinical need. Some people may wish to undergo medical interventions which, in the doctor's view, are not needed. Cosmetic surgery may be a useful example to consider here. There may be no autonomy-based reason to refuse an informed request for cosmetic surgery and, following our exploration of beneficence and non-maleficence, it seems plausible that one could view the provision of cosmetic surgery as fitting within these principles, especially if we privilege the patient's interpretation of these concepts.

Yet, if every patient's request for elective surgery of this kind is met, the NHS's budget may be drained before it has met the most basic health needs of its patients. Of course, providing surgery for *one* patient would not break the budget, but justice requires that those whose needs are the same should be treated equally. Therefore, it would be arbitrary and unjust to provide some patients with elective cosmetic surgery, and refuse others.

Alternatively, to prioritize cases of greater need and therefore refuse *all* cases of elective cosmetic surgery may seem reasonable. The crucial factor here is establishing what constitutes 'need', and allocating budgets accordingly.

The four principles in practice

Challenges in defining medical need

In a needs-based system, it makes sense to prioritize the greatest need, in order to ensure that funds are distributed appropriately. This means that the concept of need can become contested, since being able to demonstrate need will help one to claim treatment. A ruptured appendix may be the paradigm of clinical need. The patient will be in pain and if they do not receive medical attention quickly, they may die.

We can compare this with a more contentious example of clinical need: a patient seeking *in vitro* fertilization (IVF), for example—she may not be in pain, and IVF is more likely to shorten her lifespan than prolong it. However, patients who seek IVF may feel strongly that they need to have a child just as much as another patient may need to have their appendix removed.

To comply with the requirements of justice, it is important that decision-making is transparent and consistent. This can be difficult in complex healthcare systems, serving patients whose needs and values vary widely. It is perhaps no surprise, therefore, that there are ongoing debates about which procedures the NHS should fund.

The deserving patient

There are also ongoing debates about how to prioritize access to treatment. As we have mentioned, the NHS takes a needs-based approach; however, some doctors feel that it would be appropriate to allow or deny access to healthcare based on other factors, such as whether a person 'deserves' treatment. On this view, smokers, for example, might be debarred from treatment.

At first glimpse, this might seem quite sensible. Not only would it reward responsible patients, but it would provide an incentive for those who engage in unhealthy pastimes to stop. However, it raises many other difficulties, including the question of how far it is possible to regard poor lifestyle choices as being freely pursued.

Children whose parents smoke are more likely to smoke themselves. Is it really fair to penalize them when they reach adulthood, and offer preferential treatment to someone who was brought up by strict parents who never smoked a cigarette in their lives? How do we decide what is unhealthy? Should obese people or those who practise unsafe sex be denied treatment because of their 'lifestyles'?

Postcode lotteries

For many people, the very pinnacle of unfairness is the 'postcode lottery'. Patients living in one part of the UK may be provided with treatment on the NHS that is not funded in another part of the country. Is this necessarily unjust? One of the problems here is that needs may differ according to location. Those living in remote rural areas may suffer from different medical problems from those living in built-up urban areas.

Because of this, some decisions are made at local, rather than national levels. The ability of local decision-makers to allocate funds according to their own judgement is what leads to the postcode lottery. To avoid this altogether, it would seem necessary that all funding and decision-making is carried out at the governmental level and that identical treatments be funded in all areas, regardless of discrepancies between populations.

Discrimination

The other facet of justice is discrimination. It is often assumed that discrimination is intrinsically wrong. Yet, if we never discriminated, we would be unable to function at all. Remembering Aristotle's injunction, 'treat equals equally and unequals unequally', it is clear that discrimination in itself is not a problem. It would be unjust to treat a patient with a broken neck exactly the same as one with a broken finger. Where needs are different, we should treat people differently. This involves discriminating: noticing those differences and making decisions accordingly.

Discrimination is only a problem when it is unjust. We have suggested it is appropriate to discriminate between patients with different needs; however, if it were decided that only dark-haired patients would be treated, this would clearly be unjust, since there is no connection between hair colour and need for treatment. The challenge, therefore, is to be able to recognize what are, and what are not, the sorts of inequalities that justify treating people differently.

Pros and cons of the four principles

Pros	Intended to apply universally, independent of religious or cultural difference
	Designed specially for issues in medicine
	They encapsulate the most valuable aspects of the different moral theories
Cons	The interpretation of the principles is open to dispute
	The principles have been regarded as embodying Western liberal values at the expense of other value systems
	The principles frequently clash with each other, and it is not always clear which should be prioritized

The four principles: sample question

To demonstrate how the four principles may be applied in practice, we will use our sample question and consider how they might help to solve this ethical issue.

> Ten medical students are learning how to perform rectal examinations. This is important for their education. However, no one likes undergoing a rectal examination unnecessarily.
>
> To ensure that students get the necessary practice, the consultant who is teaching them is trying to decide whether to allow these ten students to practise a rectal examination on 96-year-old anaesthetized woman who is undergoing surgery for an unrelated issue.
>
> The woman, who has mental capacity, has not been informed nor has she given consent.
>
> Is this ethically acceptable?

The four principles and the sample question

Clearly, performing examinations on a patient without her consent is not in keeping with respect for autonomy. However, if this is known to be a teaching hospital, perhaps we could assume that consent to training is implied by this patient's presence in the hospital. If so, then the procedure may not be deemed to breach the patient's autonomy at all.

One might argue that the procedure is non-maleficent, and could even be beneficent if by chance it picks up something that would otherwise have gone unnoticed. It could also be argued that the broader benefits of carrying out such training in terms of improving population health could be taken to outweigh the other principles, that is, justice might decree that all patients should be willing to undergo this kind of thing for the sake of a wider population benefit. However, there are a number of issues to consider here.

The first issue is whether it is reasonable to infer consent from a patient's presence in a teaching hospital. Doctors often make this argument, but it is highly questionable. Many members of the public may not be aware of whether their nearest hospital is a teaching hospital or not. Even if they are, there is no reason to assume that they will know that this means they will be exposed to students' examinations. Therefore, unless the patient has been explicitly consulted, it is not reasonable to suppose that she has somehow consented to being examined while under anaesthetic.

The arguments related to beneficence and non-maleficence likewise seem weak when probed further. It is unlikely that the examinations will cause harm; yet there is always some degree of risk and this may be exacerbated by the patient's anger and distress if she feels she's been abused or deceived. The question about beneficence is very significant here. Some patients do not wish to know if they have a particular condition, and would choose not to attend screening programmes for this reason. The knowledge of having a serious medical condition, though regarded as beneficial by many people, can be regarded as harmful by others. This is why people are offered screening, rather than being compelled to participate. If something sinister were identified in this woman, we do not know if she would be grateful or angry and upset about having been denied a choice.

Finally, it is undoubtedly an admirable thing to participate in research or training. Surprisingly many patients are willing to do this when asked directly. Their choice to be involved may be described as truly altruistic. But when no choice is given, the act is not altruistic. There may also be questions to ask about why this patient in particular is being selected for this training. This is where considerations of justice can be extremely useful in identifying hidden ethical problems. What role is this patient's age playing here? Has she been chosen as an 'easy' option?

Additional reading

Childress JF, Beauchamp TL. Principles of Biomedical Ethics. New York: Oxford University Press; 2019.

Gillon R. Medical ethics: four principles plus attention to scope. BMJ. 1994;309(6948):184.

Care ethics

Introduction to care ethics *44*
Care ethics in practice *45*
Care ethics: sample question *46*
Applying care ethics to the sample case *47*

Introduction to care ethics

What is care ethics?

Care ethics offers a more relationship-focused approach to ethics. One which takes into account emotion and interdependency—both key features of a characteristically human life.

The male bias

All of the approaches to ethical reasoning discussed in previous chapters have been formulated by men. Many of them are concerned with questions of abstract principles or justice. All of them, to various degrees, call for an ability to reason through an ethical problem. Aristotle associates reason, or wisdom, with virtue. In fact, for him, morality is intrinsically connected with man's power to be rational.

Utilitarianism clearly requires an evaluation of consequences, again a highly rational endeavour. Kant, like Aristotle, places the capacity for reason at the centre of his approach to ethics. Finally, the four principles require a reasoned, objective, and analytical approach.

But are these theories missing something elemental? Is there a male bias, and if so, could it be a problem?

Care ethics in practice

A different voice

These questions are among those that have given rise to a relatively new approach to moral reasoning: that of 'care ethics'. One of the first proponents of care ethics was a psychologist, Carol Gilligan. Gilligan was concerned that when psychologists had studied the development of moral reasoning in children, they had imposed a masculine interpretation of ethics on their studies.

Objectivity, universality, and application of principles were specifically regarded as being indicators of moral development. Psychologists had found that girls performed significantly worse on these measures than boys. Gilligan therefore undertook her own research, and found what she described as a 'different voice'. According to Gilligan, women tend to emphasize the importance of relationships, rather than seeking rational objectivity, or a universal approach to ethics.

For Gilligan, this is not a weakness but a difference, which needs to be acknowledged. Gilligan's approach has some affinity with virtue ethics in viewing the character of the person as being significant. Both utilitarianism and deontology can be atomistic, focusing on specific acts. Virtue ethics and care ethics are able to accommodate a broader view of human beings in the context of their lives and relationships.

Relationships

For care ethicists, the key to resolving a dilemma is to consider what will promote caring relationships. This will involving considering the responsibilities that have arisen as a result of the relationships to date and the impact of those relationships in the future. In complex cases, people may have competing caring obligations and it will be necessary to weigh these up.

The feminist critique

Gilligan has been criticized for what some have taken to be her assumption that women are, or should be, caring by nature, as well as for her apparent acceptance of the idea that women are less able to grapple with abstract thought or rational deliberation than men. To focus on caring as the central aspect of women's experience, and therefore of their ethics, may indeed seem reactionary. Nevertheless, Gilligan did not wish to deny that men are able to care and, hence, to incorporate an element of care ethics into their moral reasoning. However, she has argued that there are few incentives for boys and men to develop these attributes.

Pros and cons of care ethics

Pros	Accommodates important human values, especially those involved in interdependency and relationships
	Particularly relevant to questions of sickness, suffering, and medicine
Cons	Can be regarded as reactionary or essentialist in terms of its association with 'female' attributes of nurturing
	Primary focus on subjective relationships, which doesn't help in questions involving larger cohorts or formal/impersonal relationships

Care ethics: sample question

To demonstrate how care ethics might help in practice, we will use our sample question and consider what insights a care ethics approach can provide.

Ten medical students are learning how to perform rectal examinations. This is important for their education. However, no one likes undergoing a rectal examination unnecessarily.

To ensure that students get the necessary practice, the consultant who is teaching them is trying to decide whether to allow these ten students to practise a rectal examination on 96-year-old anaesthetized woman who is undergoing surgery for an unrelated issue.

The woman, who has mental capacity, has not been informed nor has she given consent.

Is this ethically acceptable?

Applying care ethics to the sample case

A care ethicist is not concerned with protocol per se, nor are they likely to worry about autonomy as much as other ethical theorists. However, the care ethicist will think deeply about the context and the relationships in question.

Although care ethics is not necessarily associated with feminism, it is more specifically female-oriented than other theories. Therefore, a care ethicist might be especially interested in why this particular patient had been selected. Are women being perceived as more accessible? Are women's bodies regarded as being public property to a greater extent than those of men?

Questions about the relationships between the consultant and the students would also be important here. It is well known that medical students often feel under pressure to perform tasks or procedures that they feel uncomfortable about. A care ethicist would want to know details about how the students felt about the proposed task, as well as thinking about the character and motivations of the consultant.

Most fundamentally, a care ethicist would be asking whether the proposed course of action is in keeping with a loving and caring relationship with this patient. While the absence of official consent may not in itself be a problem here, the question of whether this patient is being taken advantage of would be significant.

Within a certain type of relationship, a care ethicist might not object to the examinations. For example, if the consultant has a very close relationship with her, and perhaps if he has discussed this kind of thing with her in the past. However, on the basis of the scenario given, we simply do not know these details. This is crucial to care ethics, which is concerned with specifics, rather than the application of abstract principles. In the absence of information about the detail of the relationship, the care ethicist would be likely to view the proposed examinations with scepticism.

Additional reading

Gilligan C. In a different voice: women's conceptions of self and of morality. Harvard Educational Review. 1977;47(4):481–517.

Slote M. The Ethics of Care and Empathy. New York: Routledge; 2007.

Moral relativism and subjectivism

Introduction to moral relativism and subjectivism *50*
Moral relativism and subjectivism in practice *52*
Moral relativism and subjectivism: sample question *54*
Applying relativism and subjectivism to the sample question *54*

Introduction to moral relativism and subjectivism

Many of those involved in teaching and studying ethics have asked themselves if there is any 'real' truth about ethics, or if the answer to ethical questions is simply a matter of personal taste, or context. Moral relativism and subjectivism are, properly speaking, not ethical theories at all. However, they are both significant, not least because they pose a challenge to ethical decision makers and political decision makers.

What is relativism?

A moral relativist holds that there are no strict truths about what is ethically right or wrong. Rather, those questions that appear to be about right or wrong are in fact questions that relate more accurately to what is normal or accepted for that particular time or place. In this way, the relativist can explain why an English person may be horrified at the idea of eating a dog, while someone in Korea may feel very differently. For the relativist, the way to handle this anomaly is not to ask which is right, but to accept that both are right, according to local custom.

What is subjectivism?

Subjectivism is similar to relativism, but instead of answering moral questions by referring to accepted custom, a subjectivist asserts that it is all a matter of individual taste. This takes into account the fact that we may observe differences of moral opinion within as well as between cultures. Suppose that one person believes it is morally wrong to eat meat, while another feels it entirely acceptable.

The subjectivist feels no obligation to delve into the details of the reasons or justifications in either case, but simply accepts that what is right for one is wrong for another. According to this view, therefore, each of us constructs a moral framework, whose external validity is irrelevant, but which is meaningful to the person who holds it.

Moral relativism and subjectivism in practice

Tolerance and diversity

Both relativism and subjectivism have some appeal. There clearly are many judgements which are informed by context and culture. And likewise, many of our most deeply held values are, at the same time, deeply personal. In today's multicultural and diverse environments, there are strong pragmatic pressures on all of us to recognize and respect other people's values.

The difficulty with relativism and subjectivism, however, lies in the challenge of setting boundaries. To an extent, most of us are probably relativists: there are some things we would regard as wrong, but we are happy to live with people who think differently. When we are talking about vegetarianism, or eating dogs, this seems reasonable. However, pushed to extremes, relativism and subjectivism can lead to some unpalatable conclusions.

Limits to relativism and subjectivism

Suppose, for example, that we are considering whether the Nazis were morally correct to exterminate Jews in concentration camps. A relativist would not simply be able to say 'no'. S/he would have to consider whether this kind of behaviour was acceptable in that particular time and place.

This is where most relativists break down. There are few people who are willing to argue that the holocaust *would* have been right if a few more people had thought so at the time. Similarly, there are few subjectivists who would be willing to accept that if a Nazi guard's personal moral framework allows for the gassing of Jews, that this would render their conduct ethically unobjectionable.

The illusory nature of the homogeneous society

Another problem for relativism is that cultures and contexts are diverse, as the Nazi example shows. Of course, there were Nazis, and perhaps other members of society at the time, who believed that the gassing of Jews was morally acceptable. However, there were many people within Germany and the rest of the world, who did not.

The idea of a homogeneous society, whose members all concur with a particular belief, is simply a fiction. Even in the most cohesive of societies, in the days preceding multiculturalism, there has *always* been dispute about morality. This, indeed, is how the discipline of ethics arose.

Ethics as a social endeavour

Similarly, while the individual nature of moral reflection cannot be denied, the fact is that our moral decisions invariably have an impact on others. It is precisely here that the need for analysing, exploring, and evaluating ethical problems becomes necessary. A subjectivist may believe, for example, that it is ethically acceptable for her to steal my car. A true subjectivist would need to be able to accept that the fact that, for another person, to shoot a car thief would be morally right. Viewed in this way, subjectivism seems to lead to anarchy.

The social nature of ethics is absent from subjectivism, while the deliberative element seems lacking in relativism. Perhaps more fundamentally, neither approach has much to say about the resolution of ethical conflicts, which is our concern here. It may be highly speculative to wonder about the existence of objective ethical 'truths'. But on a far more basic and pragmatic level, we have to grapple with ethical questions, and the decisions that we and others make will have profound effects on all of our lives.

Pros and cons of relativism and subjectivism

Pros	Reflect values of secular and tolerant societies
	Avoid prescribing one set of absolute values
Cons	Problem of how to manage conflict between individuals or cultures
	Lack of coherent basis from which to strive towards consensus

Moral relativism and subjectivism: sample question

To demonstrate how moral relativism and subjectivism might be interpreted in practice, we will use our sample question and consider what insights they can provide.

> Ten medical students are learning how to perform rectal examinations. This is important for their education. However, no one likes undergoing a rectal examination unnecessarily.
>
> To ensure that students get the necessary practice, the consultant who is teaching them is trying to decide whether to allow these ten students to practise a rectal examination on 96-year-old anaesthetized woman who is undergoing surgery for an unrelated issue.
>
> The woman, who has mental capacity, has not been informed nor has she given consent.
>
> Is this ethically acceptable?

Applying relativism and subjectivism to the sample question

What would a relativist or subjectivist say about whether it is acceptable to perform rectal examinations on a patient without consent? The relativist would look around and take note of what is normal practice.

Thus, the answer would vary from one hospital to another, and possibly even from one ward to another. However, if there was disagreement among the group as to whether the practice is acceptable, the relativist would be at a loss to know how to reconcile this disagreement.

The subjectivist, likewise, would find this a difficult matter. Each individual student, as a subjectivist, might take their own view as to whether the examination is ethically acceptable or not. Yet this would not help in telling us whether or not the practice should be allowed.

Additional reading

Rachels J. The challenge of cultural relativism. In: Jecker NS, Jonsen AR, Pearlman RA (eds) Bioethics: An Introduction to the History, Methods, and Practice, pp. 616–23. Sudbury, MA: Jones and Bartlett Publishers; 2007.
Wong DB. Relativism, moral. In: LaFollette H (ed) International Encyclopedia of Ethics. Oxford: Blackwell; 2013.

Chapter 8

Critical reasoning

Critical reasoning and combining theories 56
Critical reasoning: sample question 58
Applying critical reasoning to the sample question 60

Critical reasoning and combining theories

As we have seen, most moral theories focus on certain aspects of moral decision-making, to the exclusion of others. A deontologist is most concerned about duty, and respect for the person, but does not care about consequences. A consequentialist will think about what results might follow from an act and does not care about motivations, while a virtue ethicist is only interested in what a particular decision implies about the nature of the person who makes it, rather than anything directly related to the decision itself.

But for those who are interested in morality and moral reasoning, all of these concerns are important in some senses, though some may seem more obviously central to a particular ethical question than others.

Dealing with complexity

Life would be simpler if there were one simple rule to follow in all cases. However, just as medicine is infinitely complex, so is morality! When doctors seek to diagnose a patient's condition, they draw upon a wide variety of knowledge, skill, and experience, selecting the approach that seems best for the job in hand. They will make and test hypotheses, and if they make mistakes, they will be able—if they are good doctors—to retrace their steps of reasoning, and identify the point at which they went wrong.

The same is true of moral reasoning. Moral reasoning is complex, and draws upon many areas of knowledge, skill, and experience. Like good medicine, good moral reasoning involves reflection and critical application of theory rather than blind adherence to rules or theory. The path by which one arrives at a conclusion should be clear and explicable to others.

This is important in medical ethics, where moral decisions may have a significant impact on patients, as well as affecting policymaking, or in setting precedents for accepted behaviour in an institution. If a doctor is challenged on his or her decisions, or judgements, s/he may need to show why this judgement was reached, and be able to provide reasons for it. The GMC states:

> You are personally accountable for your professional practice and must always be prepared to justify your decisions and actions.

Critical reasoning

Critical reasoning is the skill of being able to think through one's options, and deliberate on their merits. Following from this, a decision should be able to be expressed in the form of an argument—that is, a set of reasons in support of a claim. In the context of ethics, critical reasoning will involve recognizing that there is an ethical question to be faced and working towards an answer. A moral question may be answered without recourse to moral theory, but it cannot be answered without critical thinking, especially in medicine. Doctors have to be answerable for their decisions.

Right answers or right reasoning

It is commonly suggested that there are no 'wrong answers' in ethics. It is certainly the case that right answers cannot always be proven—but again, the same is often true of a choice of treatment for a patient. In the absence of certainty, we have to do the best we can with the knowledge and tools at our disposal. In fact, in ethical deliberation based on critical reasoning, there may very often be wrong answers, and it is very important to bear these potential wrong answers in mind.

Good moral reasoning

Critical reasoning on an ethical question is likely to involve the following steps:
1. You identify and account for your own interests in your argument.
2. You identify the ethical principles or values that are in conflict in the issue.
3. You recognize and question the assumptions that play a part in your argument.
4. You identify all of those whose interests are involved.
5. You consider the strongest possible counterarguments to your position.
6. You scrutinize your reasoning for mistakes.
7. You show clearly how your conclusion was reached.

Poor moral reasoning

Conversely, poor moral reasoning is likely to result from one or more of the following:
1. You fail to recognize the role that self-interest plays in your analysis.
2. You fail to identify the ethical conflicts involved.
3. You fail to recognize the assumptions that you have made.
4. You fail to recognize all of the people who have interests at stake.
5. You fail to take counterarguments into account.
6. You fail to recognize a logical fallacy in your argument.
7. You fail to show how your conclusions were reached.

Critical reasoning: sample question

To demonstrate how reasoning might be applied in practice, we will use our sample question and consider what insights it can provide.

Ten medical students are learning how to perform rectal examinations. This is important for their education. However, no one likes undergoing a rectal examination unnecessarily.

To ensure that students get the necessary practice, the consultant who is teaching them is trying to decide whether to allow these ten students to practise a rectal examination on 96-year-old anaesthetized woman who is undergoing surgery for an unrelated issue.

The woman, who has mental capacity, has not been informed nor has she given consent.

Is this ethically acceptable?

Applying critical reasoning to the sample question

Common pitfalls

Here is a set of very basic statements put forward to answer the question of whether to perform a rectal examination of an elderly patient while under anaesthetic. Each sentence consists of a conclusion and with one reason given to support the conclusion. Each one falls foul of one or more of the points listed previously.

- 'We should do this because we need the knowledge to pass our exams.'
- 'The examination should be done because I have to fulfil my teaching duties to these students.'
- 'We should go ahead, as this is normal practice.'
- 'There is no major ethical dilemma here, because the outcome is good for all concerned.'
- 'We should not do this, because anyone can see this is unacceptable.'
- 'This is a bit unpleasant, but on balance it is acceptable because she will never know about it.'
- 'The examination is ethically OK because it can't possibly cause any harm.'
- 'The only people involved in this will either be benefited or at least will not be harmed, so there is no problem.'
- 'We should not undertake this procedure unless there is some benefit to the patient.'
- 'Any procedure undertaken without consent is unethical.'
- 'This procedure will have no effect beyond benefiting these students.'
- 'Either we teach students in this way, or we send out newly qualified doctors who have no knowledge of how to perform these examinations.'

It is clear that poor arguments may be advanced on either side of the question. Now, let us see if we can create an argument that will put forward a solution to the problem by going through the steps of good reasoning outlined earlier. Firstly, the question of self-interest. The students and consultant in the scenario have an interest in carrying out the examination. This means that they need to be extra careful in weighing up its ethical benefits: they will be biased, because they have a conflict of interest.

Seeking advice from others

One solution might be to take the question to someone else who is not so closely tied up in the matter. (This is one reason why clinical ethics committees can be a valuable resource.) However, if this is not possible, the safest option is to consciously try to reason through the case without giving undue weight to one's own preferences. This step will clearly diminish some of the weight on the side in favour of performing the examination, since by far the strongest reason is because it will be helpful to the students, and will make the consultant's life easier!

Identifying values

The next step is to identify the principles or values at stake. It is here that moral theory might come in. We can see that the ethical reasons in favour of carrying out the examination—once we have discounted self-interest—are not based on any direct benefits for the patient. We are thinking more about broad, general benefits for medicine, and medical practice, and ultimately for patients.

In contrast with this, we have the principle of autonomy. We are thinking about sacrificing the autonomy of one individual patient in order to gain benefits for a wider group of people, which may not include the individual in question. This is a very problematic ethical situation. The willingness to impose risk on one person in order to benefit someone else is troubling. It raises questions of justice, which are difficult to answer from the consequentialist perspective.

The moral issue seems, therefore, to be primarily a conflict between consequentialist values—the importance of securing a wide-spread benefit, and Kantian autonomy—respecting individual choices. There are, of course, other moral considerations that could play a part, including the question of honesty, and care, but the main arguments on both sides are likely to be of the nature outlined earlier.

Resolving ethical conflict

Having recognized the key conflicts, it becomes possible to deliberate as to the best way to resolve them. If we regard the consequentialist benefits as outweighing the issue of autonomy, we might ask how great we expect those benefits to be, and whether there is any prospect of achieving the same results without sacrificing the patient's autonomy. It is here that the third point of good reasoning is likely to come in. Frequently, those who make use of consequentialist arguments will make claims about the anticipated benefits of a particular course of action. In this case, we might initially assume that medical training is simply not possible without this kind of procedure. This is especially likely to be assumed if it has been routine practice.

Identifying and evaluating assumptions

However, recognizing that this is an assumption means that we can go ahead and consider whether it is a justified assumption. The answer to this is likely to be 'no'. Clearly, medical training can take place in many ways that do not require examination of anaesthetized patients without their consent.

Some of these ways may be less effective than others, for example, using models. Others may be just as effective, for example, asking patients' agreement in advance. Another assumption that is likely to appear in this context is that the patient will never find out. This kind of assumption is at the root of many scandals and mishaps in medicine. Often, patients won't find out, but sometimes they will! Relying on an assumption that someone won't find out is a dangerous thing to do, and is often in itself a strong signal that there is an ethical problem.

Whose interests are at stake?

The next step is to recognize and consider all those whose interests are at stake. In this particular case, this includes the patient herself, the students, the consultant, and then the hospital's patients more broadly, and the other hospital staff. Thus, the ethical problem extends beyond just those who are present in the room.

If they continue with unconsented examinations of anaesthetized patients, this further entrenches the practice, and it will affect more patients. If the practice continues, the likelihood that it will be found out increases. This in turn will affect staff, students, and patients. A worst-case scenario might be a public scandal of the sort that arose at Alder Hey Children's Hospital. In cases such as these, the apparent consequentialist benefits of a practice may be reversed in the event of a significant loss of public trust.

Coming to a conclusion

We can now see that the balance seems to swing in favour of not undertaking the examination. We therefore need to consider the strongest possible arguments against this position. We have already identified the strong consequentialist position: being willing to undertake examinations without consent is beneficial to many people, and the chances of harm are small. Perhaps we can also think about counterarguments from the autonomy perspective. If we were to ask the patient's consent to undergo the examinations, perhaps she would feel coerced and suffer undue influence, or flustered, in which case it might not really be true that we are respecting her autonomy.

Possible mistakes in reasoning

Here, we can identify a possible mistake in reasoning. It is certainly true that an insensitive request might fluster a patient, and that some patients might feel pressurized if suddenly asked to consent to an unexpected procedure. However, this is not a necessary aspect of asking consent. She could be asked in advance, or by the consultant alone. And, of course, she can be offered the opportunity to refuse. Thus, although if undertaken badly the process of gaining consent might fail to adequately respect patient autonomy, the point is that if done well, it would not.

Other issues to consider

What other points of our reasoning do we need to examine here? Have we leapt to the conclusion that patients would consent if given the opportunity? It is interesting to compare this with research, where participants are often willing to undergo often painful, embarrassing, time-consuming procedures without any expectation of personal benefit. It may be surprising that so many patients are willing to put themselves through this, but it seems to indicate that in fact many people are happy to experience some discomfort if they are convinced that it is in a good cause, and if they trust those involved in the research.

Ethically, the argument seems to lead towards a decision not to perform the examination without consent. However, this will depend partly on the way that one weighs up the potential harm of the patient discovering what has happened.

In practice, there might be many other contextual considerations to take into account, and for this reason, it is very rarely the case that one can apply exactly the same argument from one situation to another case. It might well transpire that even after having argued the case through, people still diverge as to their idea of what should be done. However, those involved might be more willing to agree to a shared decision if the case has been worked through conscientiously—and we can at any rate be sure that any obvious fallacies have been dismissed.

Do you disagree with the suggested outcome, or the reasoning in this case? If so, think about how you could construct a well-argued case to support your view, taking into account all the suggestions given. You are now engaging in moral reasoning!

Additional reading

Daniels N. Wide reflective equilibrium and theory acceptance in ethics. The Journal of Philosophy. 1979;76(5):256–82.

Thomson A. Critical Reasoning in Ethics: A Practical Introduction. New York: Routledge; 2002.

Part 2

Law

9 Introduction to the legal system *67*

10 Key articles of law *75*

11 Court *83*

12 Law within medical practice *91*

13 Negligence *97*

14 Other issues of liability *109*

Introduction to the legal system

Basic legal principles *68*
Civil and criminal cases *70*
Contract and tort *71*
Hierarchy of courts *72*

Basic legal principles

England, Wales, Northern Ireland, and Scotland

This handbook focuses on English law. The law in Wales and Northern Ireland is generally the same as in England, although the Welsh and Northern Irish assemblies have the power to enact law which applies just to Wales or Northern Ireland, respectively. The Scottish legal system is completely different. Some resources on Scottish law are listed in the 'Additional reading' at the end of this chapter (➲ p. 73).

Sources of law

There are three primary sources of law:
- UK legislation: this can be Acts of Parliament or statutory instruments. Statutory instruments are used to provide detailed regulations, rather than establishing general principles. Some Acts of Parliament only apply to England, or Scotland or Wales; while some apply to all countries in the UK.
- European Union (EU) law: this emanates from Brussels. Sometimes EU law is automatically binding in the UK (if it has 'direct effect'); sometimes it requires UK legislation to put it into effect. With Brexit, EU law ceased to have direct effect, unless there is an Act of Parliament saying it will (European Union (Withdrawal) Act 2018).
- Case law: the legal systems in England, Scotland, and Wales rely on the doctrine of precedent. When a court hears a case, it uses principles established from earlier cases to apply to this case. In controversial cases, much time is spent by lawyers arguing over which previous case provides the closest analogy to the case at hand. Lawyers will try and distinguish previous cases, arguing there are important ways in which the current case is different from the previous ones.

There are two main kinds of law:
- Statute.
- Common law.

Statute law comes from Acts of Parliament or statutory instruments. Common law relies on established legal principles which have been developed by the courts over the years. If there is a conflict between the two, statutes will normally prevail. However, a court may decide to interpret legislation in line with common law principles so that there is no conflict.

Interpretation of statutes

In some cases, it is clear whether a statute applies to a case or not. In others, the statute may be ambiguous. For example, if a statute refers to a vehicle, does this apply to bicycle? If a previous case has interpreted the statute, then all lower courts will be bound to follow that interpretation. If, however, there are no previous cases, judges will rely on the following principles of interpretation:
- The literal rule. Normally judges will apply the literal meaning of the words.
- The golden rule. Judges will not apply the literal meaning if that will lead to an absurd result.

- The purpose rule. The judge will seek to ascertain what the 'mischief' was that the statute was trying to deal with and seek to ensure that the statute is interpreted in a way which achieves that purpose, if that can be done without stretching the meaning of words too much.
- The context rule. The judge will look at the words in issue in the context of the whole piece of legislation.

Civil and criminal cases

Criminal and civil cases

A major distinction can be drawn by lawyers between criminal cases and civil cases. Criminal cases are brought by the state against an individual who, if found guilty, will receive punishment. Civil cases are brought by one person against another, and if the case is proved, the victim will receive compensation.

It is possible that there will be civil and criminal law consequences as a result of the same incident. For example, imagine a nurse in a fit of temper threw a cup of tea over a patient. This could result in the police becoming involved and a prosecution for the criminal offence of battery or an assault occasioning actual bodily harm. If convicted, the nurse will be punished and, for example, be required to pay a fine or even sent to prison.

The patient may also seek to bring a civil claim against the nurse and seek damages for the losses she suffered. Here the nurse would pay the money to the patient (not the state, as with a fine) and the patient would need to bring their own claim, rather than relying on the state to do that.

Keeping with that example, a few key points can be made:

- The first is that a criminal case does not need the permission of the victim to go ahead. So, in this case, even if the patient has forgiven the nurse and does not want them to get into trouble, the Crown Prosecution Service (which oversees prosecutions) might still decide to bring a prosecution (◗ p. 84).
- The second is that the patient does not need to pay for legal costs if a criminal case is brought, but might if a civil one is. So, in this case, unless the injuries are serious, the patient may decide it would not be a good use of money to bring a civil claim.
- The third is that a criminal case requires proof beyond reasonable doubt that the defendant is guilty, while a civil case requires just proof on the balance of probabilities. That is why sometimes a civil claim will succeed, while a criminal prosecution fails.

When looking at the name of a case you can normally tell if it is a criminal case or a civil case. A criminal case will be in the form, for example, *R v Smith*, with R being short for Regina (the Crown, representing the state) and Smith being the surname of the defendant. A civil law case will be in the form, for example, *Jones v Ahmad* with the family names of the two parties being used.

Contract and tort

There are two main claims that can be brought in civil law: a claim for breach of contract and a claim under the law of tort.

Contract

To bring a claim in the law of contract it is, obviously, necessary to show that there was a contract between the parties. A contract need not be in writing, although it often is, but it should involve an offer from one party, which is accepted by another.

In the medical context, contracts can be found between patients and doctors in private medicine, but it is generally accepted there is no contract between a doctor and patient in the context of NHS care.

If a patient can show there is a breach of contract, they are entitled to damages which will be assessed as the sum needed to put the parties in the position they would have been in had the contract been correctly performed. Many written contracts will seek to limit the circumstances in which a party will be liable to pay damages.

Tort

To bring a claim in the law of tort there is no need to show a contract between the parties. The most common tort is the tort of negligence and this is the one that is normally used in cases involving doctors and patients. It will be described at ➲ p. 97, but it can only be used where a there is a duty of care which has been breached in a way which causes harm to the patient. Damages under the law of tort are designed to put the victim of the tort in the position they were before the tort was committed.

Hierarchy of courts

The hierarchy of the English and Welsh courts is as follows. It should be noted that the Supreme Court was recently introduced to replace the House of Lords as the highest court in the land.

Fig. 9.1 slightly simplifies the situation, but gives a generally accurate picture. Magistrates' courts are presided over by lay magistrates (Justices of the Peace (JPs)) who are respected members of the public. They hear minor criminal cases and some family matters. County courts only hear civil matters and are presided over by a district judge or a circuit judge. There are three branches of the High Court: Family Division, Queen's Bench Division, and Chancery Division. The Family Division deals with cases involving family breakdown and disputes over children. Within the Family Division sits the Court of Protection which deals particularly with cases involving people who are thought to lack capacity. The Chancery Division deals primarily with disputes over wills and property. The Queen's Bench Division covers a broad range of cases including disputes over contracts and torts.

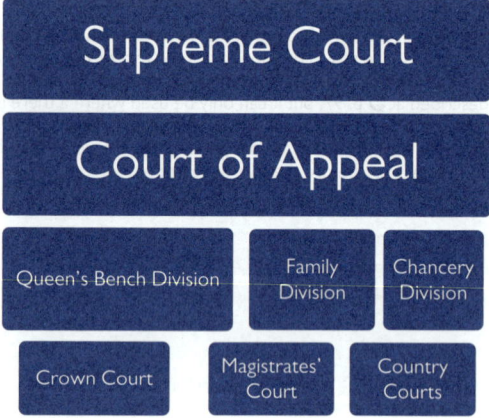

Fig. 9.1 Hierarchy of courts.

European courts

We have not included the two European courts here. The European Court of Justice (ECJ) interprets only European law. Since Brexit, the European courts do not have jurisdiction over the UK, save that their interpretation of EU law will be relied on in cases where EU regulations have been adopted into English law.

The European Court of Human Rights (ECtHR) can hear a complaint that a signatory state (including the UK) has failed to comply with its obligations under the European Convention on Human Rights (ECHR). Even after Brexit, the UK remains a signatory to the ECHR and so can be subject to rulings of the ECtHR.

Coroners

In certain circumstances, a coroner is required to investigate deaths. This can lead to an inquest, which is a legal inquiry into the causes and circumstances of a death. The coroner is a doctor or a lawyer can arrange for a postmortem if necessary.

If death occurs in any of the following circumstances, the doctor may report it to the coroner:

- After an accident or injury.
- Following an industrial disease.
- During a surgical operation.
- Before recovery from an anaesthetic.
- If the cause of death is unknown.
- If the death was violent or unnatural, for example, suicide, accident, or drug or alcohol overdose.
- If the death was sudden and unexplained, for instance, a sudden infant death (cot death).

If the deceased was not seen by the doctor issuing the medical certificate after he or she died or during the 14 days preceding the death then the death must be reported to the coroner. Anyone is entitled to inform a coroner about a death if they have concerns. Normally, however, it is a doctor or the police who inform the coroner.

Additional reading

Donald A, Gordon J, Leach P. The UK and the European Court of Human Rights. Manchester: Equality and Human Rights Commission; 2012.

Goldberg R. Medical Malpractice and Compensation in the UK. Chicago-Kent Law Review. 2012;87:131.

Herring J. Medical Law and Ethics, 8th edition. Oxford: Oxford University Press; 2020.

Jackson E. Medical Law: Text, Cases, and Materials. Oxford: Oxford University Press; 2019.

Laurie GH, Dove E. Mason and McCall Smith's Law and Medical Ethics. Oxford: Oxford University Press; 2019.

Morgan D. Issues in Medical Law and Ethics. London: Routledge-Cavendish; 2001.

Slapper G, Kelly D. Law: The Basics. Abingdon: Routledge; 2012.

Key articles of law

Human Rights Act 1998 *76*
Different kinds of human rights *77*
The rights under the European Convention 1: article 2 *78*
The rights under the European Convention 2: article 3 *79*
The rights under the European Convention 3: article 5 *80*
The rights under the European Convention 4: article 8 *81*
The rights under the European Convention 5: article 9 *81*
The rights under the European Convention 6: article 10 *82*
The rights under the European Convention 7: article 14 *82*

Human Rights Act 1998

Human rights have come to play a major role in law generally and especially medical law. Although UK law had its own understanding of human rights prior to the 1998 Act, these have largely been subsumed within the understanding of rights in the ECHR. For now, the ECHR is part of English law though the Human Rights Act 1998.

It is important to realize that you cannot bring a claim in a court against an individual simply based on a breach of human rights. So a patient cannot sue a doctor on the basis the doctor infringed his or her rights to bodily integrity. However, you can bring an action against a public authority which interfered with your human rights under the 1998 Act.

Generally, human rights are used to shape and develop the existing law, rather than create new causes of action. In particular:

- In interpreting legislation, courts, so far as is possible, should interpret the legislation in way which is compatible with the ECHR (Human Rights Act 1998, section 3).
- In interpreting and developing the common law, courts, so far as is possible, should interpret the law in a way which is compatible with the ECHR (Human Rights Act 1998, section 6).
- If a public authority infringes someone's human rights, they can be sued under Human Rights Act 1998, sections 6 and 8.

Different kinds of human rights

Absolute, qualified, and limited rights

It is necessary to distinguish:

- absolute rights
- qualified rights
- limited rights.

Absolute rights are rights which can never be violated whatever the circumstances. Under the ECHR, the right not to be subject to torture is an absolute right. Whatever good might be said to come from it, torture can never be justified.

Qualified rights are rights which can be infringed if there are sufficient reasons to do so. This must be more than a simple claim that a greater good will arise if the right is infringed. There are normally two issues to be considered when deciding if an interference with a right is permitted, namely:

- justification.
- proportionality.

Justification requires it to be shown that so much good will arise that the interference is justified. Proportionality requires proof that the interference is necessary: that there is no other less rights-infringing way of achieving the good.

Limited rights are rights which are only available in certain circumstances. For example, as we shall see shortly, there is a right to liberty protected in article 5 of the ECHR, but that does not apply to prisoners.

Positive and negative rights

Most rights are negative: they are intended to tell the state or other people what they can or cannot do. Many rights operate in the form 'Thou shalt not'! The state must not torture citizens, interfere in family life, deprive people of their liberty, and so on. But the courts have recognized that these rights can operate in a positive way and require the state to actually do something.

So not only must the state not torture its citizens, it must put in place laws and take reasonable steps to protect all citizens from torture at the hands of other citizens. Similarly, respect for private and family life means that the state should not intrude in family life unnecessarily. But it may also require the state to act positively to ensure that other institutions and individuals behave in ways that support this respect.

Rights against the state and against fellow citizens

Most human rights claims are brought against the state or state bodies. As mentioned previously, section 6 of the Human Rights Act 1998 allows a claim to be brought against a public body which has infringed someone's rights. However, section 6 cannot be used against a fellow citizen. Human rights can be used to assist a claim against a fellow citizen but have to be used alongside an established legal claim (e.g. a claim for negligence in tort).

The rights under the European Convention 1: article 2

Wording of article 2

- 'Everyone's right to life shall be protected by law. No one shall be deprived of his life intentionally save in the execution of a sentence of a court following his conviction of a crime for which this penalty is provided by law.
- Deprivation of life shall not be regarded as inflicted in contravention of this article when it results from the use of force which is no more than absolutely necessary:
  - (a) in defence of any person from unlawful violence;
  - (b) in order to effect a lawful arrest or to prevent escape of a person lawfully detained;
  - (c) in action lawfully taken for the purpose of quelling a riot or insurrection.'

Positive and negative interpretations

Article 2 has been interpreted in both a positive and negative way. Not only must the state not deprive someone of their life, they must put in place laws to protect the wrongful taking of life. This article is clearly relevant in the context of end of life decisions (➡ p. 180). It requires the law to ensure people's right to life is protected.

This is why there is a prohibition on euthanasia. However, the courts have not been willing to interpret article 2 so that all treatments which might keep someone alive must be provided. There is considerable debate over whether or not exceptions to the general prohibition on euthanasia could be made which would protect the right to life of those who did not genuinely wish to die, but allow those who wished to die to do so.

The rights under the European Convention 2: article 3

Wording of article 3

- 'No one shall be subjected to torture or to inhuman or degrading treatment or punishment.'

Positive and negative interpretations

This article has also been interpreted in both a positive and a negative way. The state must not torture someone or treat them in an inhuman or degrading way and it must also take reasonable steps to ensure one person does not treat another in that way.

This requires the state to put in place laws to protect patients from abuse at the hands of medical professionals. This is partly why forcing treatment on a patient who has capacity without their consent is generally unlawful. It may also mean that a patient cannot insist on being treated in an inhuman or degrading way (e.g. by refusing to be washed or given basic hygiene).

Absoluteness

It is worth noting that article 3 is an absolute right, meaning there are no circumstances in which a breach is justified. This may be particularly relevant in cases where a patient is resisting treatment. Forcing treatment on a patient can be permitted in limited circumstances (→ p. 269), but there comes a point where coerced treatment will infringe article 3 and become unjustifiable.

The rights under the European Convention 3: article 5

Wording of article 5

- 'Everyone has the right to liberty and security of person. No one shall be deprived of his liberty save in the following cases and in accordance with a procedure prescribed by law:
  - (a) the lawful detention of a person after conviction by a competent court;
  - (b) the lawful arrest or detention of a person for non-compliance with the lawful order of a court or in order to secure the fulfilment of any obligation prescribed by law;
  - (c) the lawful arrest or detention of a person effected for the purpose of bringing him before the competent legal authority of reasonable suspicion of having committed and offence or when it is reasonably considered necessary to prevent his committing an offence or fleeing after having done so;
  - (d) the detention of a minor by lawful order for the purpose of educational supervision or his lawful detention for the purpose of bringing him before the competent legal authority;
  - (e) the lawful detention of persons for the prevention of the spreading of infectious diseases, of persons of unsound mind, alcoholics or drug addicts, or vagrants;
  - (f) the lawful arrest or detention of a person to prevent his effecting an unauthorized entry into the country or of a person against whom action is being taken with a view to deportation or extradition.
- Everyone who is arrested shall be informed promptly, in a language which he understands, of the reasons for his arrest and the charge against him.
- Everyone arrested or detained in accordance with the provisions of paragraph 1(c) of this article shall be brought promptly before a judge or other officer authorized by law to exercise judicial power and shall be entitled to trial within a reasonable time or to release pending trial. Release may be conditioned by guarantees to appear for trial.
- Everyone who is deprived of his liberty by arrest or detention shall be entitled to take proceedings by which the lawfulness of his detention shall be decided speedily by a court and his release ordered if the detention is not lawful.
- Everyone who has been the victim of arrest or detention in contravention of the provisions of this article shall have an enforceable right to compensation.'

Applicability of article 5

This article is most relevant for patients who are detained due to their mental disorder or because they lack capacity. The Article makes it clear that persons of 'unsound mind' can be detained, but there must be lawful authority for doing so. Notably, it also permits the detention of those with infectious diseases, those of 'unsound mind', 'alcoholics', 'drug addicts', and 'vagrants'.

The rights under the European Convention 4: article 8

Wording of article 8

- 'Everyone has the right to respect for his private and family life, his home and his correspondence.
- There shall be no interference by a public authority with the exercise of this right except such as is in accordance with the law and is necessary in a democratic society in the interests of national security, public safety or the economic well-being of the country, for the prevention of disorder or crime, for the protection of health or morals, or for the protection of the rights and freedoms of others.'

Applicability of article 8

For medical lawyers, the significance of this article lies in the fact that it bolsters the rights of parents to be involved in decisions about their children. However, the courts have said that parents do not necessarily have the right to be consulted in cases where mature minors are consenting to receiving medical advice concerning abortion or contraception. It also gives family members a right to be involved in decisions about patients who lack capacity (➔ p. 152). The reference to the right to respect for private life also bolsters claims to protection of confidentiality (➔ p. 134).

The rights under the European Convention 5: article 9

Wording of article 9

- 'Everyone has the right to freedom of thought, conscience and religion; this right includes freedom to change his religion or belief, and freedom, either alone or in community with others and in public or private, to manifest his religion or belief, in worship, teaching, practice and observance.
- Freedom to manifest one's religion or beliefs shall be subject only to such limitations as are prescribed by law and are necessary in a democratic society in the interests of public safety, for the protection of public order, health or morals, or the protection of the rights and freedoms of others.'

Significance of article 9 for conscientious objection

Article 9 is significant because it bolsters the right of freedom of conscience for doctors who have ethical objections to morally controversial procedures, for example, abortion. It also means that patients in hospitals have the freedom to manifest their religious beliefs. Notably, however, this is not an absolute right and the interests of others might justify an interference in that right in some cases.

The rights under the European Convention 6: article 10

Wording of article 10

- 'Everyone has the right to freedom of expression. This right shall include freedom to hold opinions and to receive and impart information and ideas without interference by public authority and regardless of frontiers. This article shall not prevent States from requiring the licensing of broadcasting, television or cinema enterprises.

- The exercise of these freedoms, since it carries with it duties and responsibilities, may be subject to such formalities, conditions, restrictions or penalties as are prescribed by law and are necessary in a democratic society, in the interests of national security, territorial integrity or public safety, for the prevention of disorder or crime, for the protection of health or morals, for the protection of the reputation or the rights of others, for preventing the disclosure of information received in confidence, or for maintaining the authority and impartiality of the judiciary.'

Significance of article 10

This article protects the famous freedom of speech. Patients' freedom of expression should not be restricted unless doing so is justified under paragraph 2.

The rights under the European Convention 7: article 14

Wording of article 14

- 'The enjoyment of the rights and freedoms set forth in this Convention shall be secured without discrimination on any ground such as sex, race, colour, language, religion, political or other opinion, national or social origin, association with a national minority, property, birth or other status.'

Discrimination

This is a very important article which prohibits discrimination. There are several points to notice:

- The first is that article 14 cannot be used on its own. It can only be used in conjunction with another article. So a person cannot claim simply 'I have been discriminated against on the grounds of my sex', but they could say 'My right to respect for my family life has been infringed in a way which discriminates on the ground of my sex'.

- Second, the list of discriminatory grounds is not exhaustive (notice the words 'such as'). Already, the ECtHR has added sexual orientation and age.

- Third, where discrimination contrary to article 14 is shown, it will be very hard, although not impossible, to justify that discrimination.

Additional reading

Brahams D. UK: impact of European human rights law. The Lancet. 2000;356(9239):1433–4.
Horton R. Health and the UK human rights act 1998. The Lancet. 2000;356(9236):1186–8.

Court

How a criminal case proceeds *84*
How a civil case proceeds *86*
Expert witnesses *88*

How a criminal case proceeds

Criminal cases

Criminal cases normally start with an investigation by the police. They will seek to gather relevant evidence and determine whether the matter should be referred to the Crown Prosecution Service. The police may decide that there is insufficient evidence of a crime and then take no further action. Another possibility is to issue a formal caution. This can only be done where the individual agrees to accept a caution. It should be noted that a caution will form part of a criminal record, although no formal punishment will follow. A caution will normally only be used where only a minor criminal offence has occurred.

If the police are convinced there is sufficient evidence that someone has committed the crime, the file will be sent to the Crown Prosecution Service who must determine whether a prosecution should be bought. They will take into account two factors:

• The likelihood that a prosecution will be successful.
• The public interest in pursuing a prosecution.

In deciding whether there is a reasonable prospect of a prosecution being successful, the Crown Prosecution Service will take into account the fact that the jury will need to be persuaded beyond reasonable doubt that the defendant is guilty before conviction. If, therefore, the evidence does not clearly point to the guilt of the defendant, a prosecution will not be brought.

Public interest

The Crown Prosecution Service must also consider whether it is in the public interest to bring a prosecution. If a crime has been committed but it is a very minor offence or there were exceptional circumstances justifying what the defendant did, it might be thought not in the public interest to bring a prosecution.

Minor cases will be heard in the magistrates' court before lay magistrates, who are respected members of the public. They are assisted by the clerk to the court, who will have formal legal training. Serious cases will be heard in the Crown Court where a jury will determine the guilt of a defendant. Intermediate-level cases are 'either-way' offences and the defendant may select which court the case can be heard at, although if they choose the magistrates' court, the magistrates are entitled to decide the case is sufficiently serious to be heard at the Crown Court.

At the court, the charge will be read and the defendant may plead guilty or not guilty. If they plead guilty the court will proceed immediately to sentencing and the court will hear arguments for a low sentence (mitigation) from the defendant's lawyer as well as the arguments from the prosecution as to what they think the appropriate sentence is.

Guilty pleas and sentencing

A guilty plea will normally lead to a lower sentence being granted than had the defendant entered a not guilty plea. If the defendant pleads not guilty then the prosecution must present its evidence to the court. In the Crown

Court, the judge is entitled at that point to decide there is insufficient evidence for any jury to convict and immediately acquit the defendant. More commonly, the defendant will then be required to present their evidence, before the jury determines whether the defendant is guilty or not guilty. If found guilty, the judge will hear from the lawyers for the prosecution and defence as to what sentence is appropriate before deciding how the defendant should be punished.

How a civil case proceeds

Civil cases

Civil cases are brought by the claimant, against the defendant. The old language of a plaintiff and respondent is no longer used. The procedure for civil cases is complex and will only be briefly summarized here. The law is governed by the pre-action protocol This can be found at ℘ https://www.justice.gov.uk/courts/procedure-rules/civil/protocol/prot_pic.

There is a different procedure depending on whether the case is a small claims case (normally involving claims for under £5000); a 'fast track case' (for those involving between £5000 and £15,000), and a 'multi-track case' (for those which are particularly complex or for claims over £15,000). Small claims and fast track cases are generally heard at the county court, while the High Court will hear the multi-track cases. Although the County Court Jurisdiction Order 2014 allowed the county court to hear cases valued up to £350,000.

Cases will be started by the claimant issuing what is known as a part 7 claim form. This sets out the detail of the allegation being made, a statement of the facts setting out the details of the claim, and a statement of the amount of damages claimed. The defendant then has 14 days to reply. They may accept the claim and pay the amount, or file a defence. In the defence, the defendant may reject the claim altogether or accept that some compensation is due, but dispute the sum. An offer to settle may be made.

The court will then determine which track the case has to be allocated to. Small claims cases tend to be heard without lawyers and in an informal way. With fast track and multi-track cases, the court will require parties to disclose the evidence they have and make directions about what evidence must be prepared for the trial. These are often designed to encourage the parties to settle before the hearing. At the trial, the evidence on either side is heard, typically supported by the evidence of expert evidence, and the judge will need to decide on the balance of probability whose case is more convincing.

Expert witnesses

Medical professionals are sometimes invited to appear in court as an expert witness. This is an important role, which must be undertaken with care and a proper appreciation of what is involved.

The role of an expert witness

In court, the highest standards of honesty and truthfulness will be expected. Making false statements in courts or in documents in preparation for court hearings can lead to a criminal conviction. It is therefore crucial to be completely open in preparing reports, describing your expertise, and giving evidence.

Even technically true, but in fact misleading statements will be taken seriously. Do not, therefore, leave out relevant facts from reports or giving evidence. If you have agreed to provide a report or give evidence, make sure you are capable of doing so. If, in court, you are asked a question outside your expertise, you should make that clear. Similarly, if you are asked to prepare a report and you are not clear what matters you are being asked to address, seek clarification. You should make sure you have all the information you need before preparing an accurate report or evidence.

Duty to the court

The official role of the expert witness is to assist the court on a technical or specialist matter. It is crucial to realize an expert witness's duty is to the court and not to the person who instructed the expert. An expert witness should never be influenced in the evidence they give by the person who asked them to given evidence.

Independence

An expert is meant to be independent and not favour one side or the other. An expert should only give evidence on matters about which they have expertise or knowledge. Tempting as it may be, an expert should not express a view on an issue about which they have no direct knowledge or expertise. Nor should an expert be tempted to take on the role of mediator or even judge. They should seek to give evidence, not decide what the outcome of the case should be.

Deadlines are normally taken very seriously by a court. If you are required to produce a report by a particular time, then it is important that you do so.

Giving evidence

When giving evidence, an expert may be asked to explain the facts on which the assessment is based. An expert needs to be prepared not only to explain the conclusions they have reached, but to set out why they reached those conclusions. It is, therefore, important not to state conclusions which cannot be justified. When giving evidence, an expert should remember that their evidence will be heard by people who do not necessarily have medical knowledge. Therefore, technical terminology and jargon should be avoided or explained.

Changes of opinion

Sometimes an expert will have expressed a view, but in the light of new evidence or a reconsideration of the issue, change their mind. In such a case, the expert should inform both parties (normally through their lawyers) and the judge as soon as possible.

Confidentiality

If, in the capacity as an expert, a medical professional received confidential information, this must not be disclosed outside the context of the litigation, unless there is a legal justification. For example, if the patient consents to their medical information being disclosed, then it may be.

Additional reading

Schwartz R, Furrow BR, Johnson SH, Stoltzfus Jost T, Greaney TL. Bioethics: Health Case Law and Ethics (American Casebook Series). St. Paul, MN: West (Thomson Reuters); 1991.
Series H, Herring J. Doctor in court: what do lawyers really need from doctors, and what can doctors learn from lawyers? The British Journal of Psychiatry. 2017;211(3):135–6.

Law within medical practice

Medical indemnity *92*
Law within the NHS *93*
Law and private medicine *94*

Medical indemnity

Indemnity in the NHS

Many medical professionals dread being sued for medical negligence. For those working for the NHS there is some comfort in the NHS indemnity scheme. This will cover the costs and damages awarded in relation to a claim for medical negligence arising from their NHS work. It does not cover matters such as professional regulatory procedures or internal disciplinary proceedings. It is restricted to:

> [A] breach of duty of care by members of the health care professionals employed by NHS bodies or by other consequent on decisions or judgements made by members of those professions acting in their professional capacity in the course of their employment, and which are admitted as negligent by the employer or are determined as such through the legal process.

Private practice

Notably, the NHS indemnity scheme does not cover private practice or things done by a professional outside the course of their employment. The indemnity applies to a wide range of professionals including hospital doctors, dentists, nurses, midwives, health visitors, pharmacy practitioners, ambulance personnel, and laboratory staff. It does not cover general practitioners (GPs), pharmacists, or self-employed practitioners. They are expected to make their own arrangements for indemnity cover.

It only covers those working in the course of their employment. It would not cover a person acting for a private hospital, or someone acting outside the scope of their employment. It does, however, apply where the healthcare professional, while not under a contract of employment, 'was contracted to an NHS body to provide services to persons to whom the NHS owed a duty of care'.

The indemnity applies when a medical professional is treating a patient:

> [W]henever they are receiving an established treatment, whether or not in accordance with an agreed guideline or protocol; whenever they are receiving a novel or unusual treatment which, in the judgement of the healthcare professional, is appropriate for that particular patient; whenever they are subjects as patients or healthy volunteers of clinical research aimed at benefitting patients now or in the future.

Where the indemnity applies, the NHS will meet the following expenses:
- The legal and administrative costs of defending the claim and, if appropriate, of reaching a settlement, including the cost of any mediation.
- Where appropriate, the plaintiff's costs, either as agreed between the parties or as awarded by a court of law.
- The damages agreed or awarded whether as a one-off payment or a structured settlement.

Law within the NHS

NHS contracts

All employees of the NHS will have a contract of employment. This will set out the rights and responsibilities of the employee and the employer. Usually within the NHS, standard forms of contract are used for groups of employees. For example, there is a standard contract of employment for GPs. These contracts will set out the payment and the obligations of the employee.

Disciplinary proceedings

All NHS trusts will have a disciplinary code which sets out what will happen if there is a concern about the conduct of an employee. It will set out the steps that are to be taken in the investigation of any complaints about an employee and how any hearings concerning an employee are to be conducted. Where a doctor faces charges that could lead to him or her being struck off, they will normally have a right to legal representation at any hearing. For less serious matters, normally it is expected that an individual will represent themselves or be represented by a friend or professional body.

Law and private medicine

Contracts and private medicine

The legal relationship between a medical professional and a private patient is primarily governed by the law of contract, as well as the law of tort and unjust enrichment. All private medicine should be performed after a contract has been agreed, which will set out the parties' obligations. It is good practice for a contract to be in writing, but that is no requirement for it to be so. An oral contract can still be binding. The existence of the contract means that if something goes wrong, it is the individual practitioner who should be sued, not the NHS.

This is true even if normally the medical professional is an NHS employee and even if the treatment is offered in an NHS hospital. Difficulties might arise if the patient is injured by a member of the NHS staff in the hospital who has not entered into a contract with the patient. In such a case, the NHS may be liable to pay under the law of tort. This is because under the principle of vicarious liability the NHS is liable for the acts of its employees when they are acting in the course of their employment.

The terms of the contract

The detail of the contract will vary very much from individual to individual and patient to patient. The kinds of action which might arise might be very different from those available to an NHS patient. A private hospital might, for example, promise to perform the operation within a given time limit, in which case if it fails to do so it could be sued for breach of contract. Similarly, the contract might specify which doctor is to perform the operation and if a different doctor does the operation, then a legal claim may be brought.

In such a case, a successful claimant would need to show that the private hospital had promised to do the operation at a particular time or with a particular doctor, rather than simply offering a time, with no intent to guarantee it. No NHS patient could ever sue the NHS in contract for not performing the operation at an agreed time or the operation being performed by a different doctor. However, there is a county court case, *Jones v Royal Devon & Exeter NHS* [2015], where it was accepted that an NHS patient has not consented to an operation when it was not performed by the doctor promised to the patient. That was a claim in tort (battery) and would probably require proof the patient had only consented on condition a particular doctor would perform the operation.

Guaranteeing success

Although it would be unwise to do so, a doctor may warranty the outcome of a certain procedure. In such a case, if the operation fails to produce the desired outcome this will amount to a breach of contract and the patient will be entitled to damages. This will only be possible where there is a clear contractual promise that the procedure will achieve a desired result. If the contract is simply a contract for, say, the performance of a vasectomy, that will not be taken as a warranty that as a result the man will be sterile. Very clear wording would be required to produce such a warranty.

In any contract for medical services, a term will be implied in as a matter of law that the doctors will exercise reasonable care and skill in diagnosing, advising, and treating the patient. Where that does not happen, the patient will be entitled to damages for breach of contract so that he or she is put in the position as if the doctor had acted properly.

Additional reading

Bowles R, Jones P. Medical indemnity insurance in the UK: a public choice approach. Geneva Papers on Risk and Insurance. Issues and Practice. 1990;14(54):27–40.

Kessler DP, Summerton N, Graham JR. Effects of the medical liability system in Australia, the UK, and the USA. The Lancet. 2006;368(9531):240–6.

Negligence

Introduction to negligence *98*
A duty of care *99*
Breach of the duty *100*
Breach of the duty caused the loss *104*
Consequences of negligence *106*

Introduction to negligence

This chapter will set out the circumstances in which a medical professional can be found negligent and therefore liable to pay damages to a patient. Remember, a medical professional who behaved negligently might also face prosecution for a crime or disciplinary proceedings before a professional body. This chapter will simply consider the consequences under the law of tort. That is the law which will lead to the payment of compensation.

For a patient to claim damages under the law of tort against a medical professional, three things need to be shown:

1. The medical professional owed the patient a duty of care.
2. The medical professional breached the duty of care.
3. The breach of the duty caused the patient a loss.

A duty of care

This is normally not a controversial issue in medical cases. A medical professional will owe a duty of care to all patients they are looking after and those they are responsible for. A medical professional may not owe a duty of care to a stranger they pass by, but they will if they undertake any kind of medical care for them.

The main area where the concept has proved controversial is whether a doctor owes a duty of care to the relatives or friends of a patient. For example, lawyers have debated whether a doctor who diagnoses a patient as being human immunodeficiency virus (HIV) positive owes a duty to the patient's sexual partner to inform them. The general view is not, although the matter is not beyond doubt, especially if the patient poses a risk to an identified individual. The issue may be particularly relevant where a doctor is aware a patient poses a danger to other people. If the doctor is aware there is a particular person whose life is in danger as a result of the patient's condition, there may be a duty of care to that person. But a doctor will not owe a duty of care to the general public simply because they are aware a person is in general dangerous.

In *ABC v St George's Healthcare NHS Foundation Trust* [2017], it was held that a doctor who had diagnosed a father with Huntingdon's disease could owe a duty of care to disclose that diagnosis to his children, so that they could be tested. The doctor would know that the diagnosis of the father provided relevant information to the children and was aware of their existence.

It is not only doctors who may owe a duty of care. In *Darnley v Croydon* [2018] UKSC 50, receptionists at an accident and emergency (A&E) department were said to owe a duty of care not to mislead patients about how long they could expect to wait before being seen. A patient, who was negligently told they would need to wait a very long time, decided to go home rather than wait to be seen by a triage nurse. They later died at home and the hospital was told it was liable to pay damages for negligence.

It has been held that a private clinic carrying out tests on behalf of the NHS owes a duty of care to the patient. Even though there may be no direct contact between the patient and the private clinic, it should be aware that it could harm the patient if there was a mistaken diagnosis.

Breach of the duty

Normally in the law of negligence a breach of a duty is established if the defendant failed to act as the reasonable person would. However, a special test has been developed for cases involving medical professionals making medical decisions. This has become known as the *Bolam* test.

The Bolam test

In *Bolam v Friern Hospital Management Committee* [1957] 1 WLR 582, it was held:

> A doctor is not guilty of negligence if he acted in accordance with a practice accepted as proper by a responsible body of medical men skilled in that particular art.

Although that case involved doctors, it has been held to apply to any healthcare professional. What this means is that if a healthcare professional can show that the way they acted would be seen as proper by even a small group of responsible experts, there will be no negligence. That is true even if other experts, even a majority, would view it as negligent. This means it is, in fact, often not difficult for doctors to defend a case of negligence. If they find one respected expert who will state that what they did was proper and that evidence is accepted by a judge then they will win. There is one important area where the Bolam test will not apply and that is disclosure of risk, which will be discussed shortly.

It is important to realize that in order to be found not negligent the doctor only needs to show that a responsible body of medical opinion would say that they conduct was 'proper'. The expert may accept that what the doctor did was not ideal, but as long as it was of an acceptable standard that will be sufficient to mean it was not negligent.

The Bolitho development

In the House of Lords decision of *Bolitho v City and Hackney* [1998] AC 232, it was emphasized that if a case comes to court, a judge will not automatically assume that an expert is representing a responsible body of medical opinion and will need to be persuaded there is a logical basis for their views. However, only in a handful of cases has a court decided that the view of an expert is not susceptible to logical analysis. In such a case, it will be found that the view cannot be said to represent a responsible body of medical opinion.

Criticism of Bolam

The Bolam test has been criticized in some quarters, but the courts have now been using it for nearly 30 years. The argument in support of it is that if a judge is faced with the conflicting views of two medical experts, he or she is not in a position to choose between them. The claim of negligence should, therefore, be found not proved. An alternative argument is that we want to encourage doctors to try out new ways of treating patients and so they should be encouraged to use unconventional methods of treatment, as long as there is some expert backing for them.

Bolam and current knowledge

When applying the Bolam test, the court will judge a medical professional on the state of knowledge at the time of the incident, not the time of the hearing. So, if at the time of the incident, a form of treatment was acceptable that will not be negligent, even if by the time of the trial it is no longer regarded as acceptable. In determining 'the state of knowledge', a medical professional will not be expected to have read every piece of medical research, just that which has become generally known about.

Bolam and specialism

A medical professional will be judged by the standards expected of those in their profession or specialism. So a GP will not be judged by the standards of a specialist consultant in a particular area. Similarly, a nurse will be judged by the standards expected of a nurse. Whether they are inexperienced does not matter, they must live up to the standards of the job they are required to do, even if it is their first day on the job.

Although not expected to have the skills of a specialist consultant, a nurse might be found negligent for not bringing their concerns about a patient to a doctor, or a GP for not referring a patient to a specialist, if it would be reasonable to expect them to do so. Of course, for a medical professional to attempt a procedure for which they are unqualified amounts to a breach of duty.

Bolam and emergencies

In determining whether a medical professional has acted negligently, the court will take into account the situations they are in. If faced with an emergency situation requiring an immediate response, a doctor will not be expected to notice everything they could have spotted with a longer time to examine the patient. Similarly, a doctor will not be to blame if they act reasonably on the information given to them, but are misled, be that by the patient or another professional. Although it is just possible that a doctor would be found negligent in not realizing they had been misled.

Bolam and professional guidance

In deciding whether a medical professional has been negligent, the court will play attention to the guidance issued by professional bodies and any official protocols provided by their trust. If there has been a clear breach of a code of practice or protocol, it is going to be difficult for a doctor to show they have acted in accordance with a respected body of medical opinion. Difficult, but not impossible, especially if there are good reasons why the official line was not followed.

Res ipsa loquitur

At one time, the doctrine *res ipsa loquitur* (the thing speaks for itself) was commonly relied upon in clinical negligence cases. This doctrine suggested that some results spoke for themselves and would inevitably lead to a conclusion of negligence. An example might be the fact that a surgical instrument was left inside a patient after surgery. Recently, the courts have denied this is some kind of special doctrine. It is simply that in such cases common sense tells us there was negligence. There is no need to dress that up with a fancy Latin label.

Disclosure of risk and breach of duty

Following the *Montgomery v Lanarkshire Health Board* decision, the Bolam test does not apply in cases where the negligence is said to result from a failure to disclose a risk. In such a case, the clinician must disclose material risks. A material risk was defined as arising where:

> [A] reasonable person in the patient's position would be likely to attach significance to the risk, or the doctor is or should reasonably be aware that the particular patient would be likely to attach significance to it.

Notice that this includes two categories of risks:
1. Those a reasonable patient would attach risk to.
2. Those the clinician should reasonably be aware a patient would attach significance.

The second category means, for example, that if the patient is a musician, they should be informed of risks of inhibition of movement in the fingers, even if that would not concern most patients. This means that doctors need to try and find out what matters to patients so they can determine whether the risk would be significant to that patient. Note, however, that the doctor will only be found to be negligent if it was reasonable to expect them to know the risk would be material to the patient. So, using the earlier example, if the doctor asked the patient if they had any hobbies and the patient failed to mention their music then it is unlikely that the doctor could be said to have been unreasonable in not knowing about that.

Note the Bolam test does not apply here. A risk must be disclosed even if you can point to an acceptable body of opinion which says the risk does not need to be disclosed. In *Montgomery* itself, the doctor had failed to disclose the risk of shoulder dystocia and the potential ensuring complications if the patient continued with a vaginal delivery. The severity of the harm and the likelihood of its occurrence meant it was a material risk that should have been disclosed.

There are two circumstances in which it would not be a breach of duty to fail to disclose the risk. The first is that the patient has specifically asked not to be told of the risks attached to a procedure. The second is that the 'therapeutic privilege' applies, which is when the distress caused to the patient by informing them of the risk is greater than the benefit of giving them the information. This is unlikely to apply unless the level of distress would be very high indeed.

It should be noted that there may be cases where a patient insists that they do not want to be told about the risks attached to an operation. Care must be taken in such a case but as long as a patient is clear they are willing to consent to a procedure whatever the risks, it seems that would be sufficient to constitute consent. A careful note should be taken as to why the specific risk was not disclosed in such a case.

Breach of the duty caused the loss

If a patient wishes to sue a doctor, it will not be enough just to show that the doctor was negligent. It must be shown that the negligence caused an avoidable harm or injury. A failure to diagnose a terminal illness may be negligent, but if there was no treatment that would have been available had the diagnosis been correctly performed then no damages will be paid. There was negligence, but it did not lead to any loss for the patient: they were in the same position they were in had the diagnosis been performed appropriately.

'But for' causation

The key test the court uses in determining whether there is causation is the 'but for' test. This involves asking what would have happened if the medical professional had not been negligent. If the patient would have been better off had the professional acted properly then the negligence caused the loss; but if the patient would be in no better position had the professional acted properly then no damages will be paid.

In some cases, applying the 'but for' test will be straightforward. In others, it will be far harder. For example, in one case a child was blind, but it was unclear whether this was caused by negligence in his care or by his premature birth. In such a case, the question will be whether the negligence was, on the balance of probabilities, the cause of the harm. In other words, whether it was more likely than not that the negligence was the cause of the avoidable harm. In some recent cases, it has been suggested that it might be sufficient if the negligence was a material contribution to the loss, even if it was not the only cause of the loss.

Causation and multiple causes

There can be tricky cases where several medical professionals were negligent. In one case, a GP negligently failed to refer a patient to a hospital, although he did so several days later. On referral, the hospital was also negligent in failing to diagnose the condition and the child suffered injuries as a result. When the GP was sued, his defence was that even if he had referred the patient when he should have, the hospital would have been negligent and not spotted the condition and so the patient was not worse off by his late referral. The court was not willing to accept his argument. In guessing what would have happened if the GP had referred the patient at the correct time, it would not be assumed that would not be negligent and would have treated the condition, avoiding the injury.

In cases involving a failure to disclose a risk, to succeed the claimant will need to show that had they been told of the risks they would not have consented to the operation or would have had the operation at a different time. They might, for example, persuade a court that had they known of the risk, they would have sought a second opinion and that would have delayed the timing of the operation. However, there have been many cases where the court has concluded that even if the patient had been told of the risk, they would have agreed to the operation anyway and so any negligence has not caused a loss.

Consequences of negligence

Loss of a chance cases

One of the most complex areas of clinical negligence are the so-called loss of a chance cases. These arise where as a result of the negligence of a medical professional a patient has been denied the chance of treatment. Most cases involve a failure to diagnose a condition for which a treatment is available. For example, a patient has cancer and had a 60% chance of recovery had it been correctly diagnosed. Due to a negligent diagnosis the cancer was not recognized and by the time it is, the patient has a 30% chance of recovery.

The approach taken by the courts to these cases has proved controversial. In short, the courts have taken a somewhat crude approach that if a patient's chances of recovery were more than 50% had they been correctly diagnosed, it will be assumed they would have got better and so are entitled to damages if there is a negligent misdiagnosis and they go on to develop cancer. However, if their chances of recovery were less than 50% then it is assumed they would have developed cancer even if properly diagnosed and so no damages can be recovered. In a decision in which the House of Lords was sharply divided, this approach was approved by a narrow majority, with the minority preferring an approach which would have awarded the patient a proportion of their loss, reflecting the loss of chance of recovery caused by the misdiagnosis.

Damages

Once a patient has shown that they were owed a duty of care, which was breached in a way which caused a loss, then they will be entitled to damages. The court will seek to give the patient damages which will put them in the position they would have been in before the negligence was committed.

It is important to appreciate that damages are designed simply to compensate for loss. They are not used to reflect the gravity of the wrong or to punish the medical professional. The professional may have acted in an appalling way, but if only a minor loss was caused, then the damages will be very limited.

This is normally not problematic in cases where financial losses have been caused by the negligence, such as loss of income. However, it is harder in cases where there is a physical injury. The courts have set a tariff for particular kinds of injury. So, for example, there are set sums for an injury to a finger, the loss of a limb, and so forth. These will be the same for everyone. They tend to be in the nature of a few thousand pounds. Relatively small sums can be ordered for pain and suffering and for loss of amenity. Large awards tend to be made in cases where there is a loss of income as a result of the injury or there are considerable costs in the care or treatment of a patient.

Damages will be reduced if the loss was exacerbated by the failure of the patient to take reasonable steps to minimize them. For example, if a patient refused all further treatment after an injury was caused by clinical negligence, they may fail to recover the increased loss which resulted from their decision.

Secondary victims

Lawyers use the term 'secondary victims' to refer to people who are not directly affected by the negligence but suffer harm as a result of someone else being injured. In medical cases, this most commonly arises where a relative of the patient suffers a psychological distress on learning of what has happened to their family member. Generally speaking, the law is very reluctant to award damages in such cases. However, it will do in cases where the relative has actually witnessed the patient in great pain or where a relative has been informed in a particularly callous way about what has happened to the patient. For example, a parent who suffers a psychological illness because they have been told that their child has died during a routine operation might be able to recover damages. It is worth noting that if a woman is in labour, she will be the 'primary victim' and so if negligence means the child is born with horrific disabilities which cause the woman severe distress, she will be able to claim as a 'primary victim'.

The limitation period

This an extremely important part of the law on clinical negligence in practice. Any claim for personal injury, including clinical negligence, must be brought within 3 years of the date of the negligence, or the date by which the claimant should have realized that an action could be brought. This will require asking at what point in time the claimant could reasonably be expected to know the information which would be necessary for them to bring a legal action. For minors, the limitation period starts at their eighteenth birthday and so any claim must be brought by their twenty-first birthday (unless it was not reasonable for them to know they could bring an action until after their eighteenth birthday). For those who lack mental capacity, the limitation period starts when they have capacity. That means for those in permanent incapacity, the limitation period will never start. Only very rarely will the court allow an action to be brought once the limitation period has passed. The reasoning is that medical professionals should not have the fear of potential litigation hanging over them for years.

Who will be sued?

Normally this is a straightforward issue. The patient will sue the medical professional whose negligence caused the harm. However, they may have other options. They could sue the NHS trust or hospital. This can be done under the doctrine of vicarious liability, under which an employee is liable in the law of tort. However, that doctrine only applies where the employee is acting in the course of their employment. It would not apply if the medical professional was embarking on an enterprise of their own. Because the patient is much more likely to recover damages from an NHS trust rather than an individual doctor, most patients choose to sue the relevant NHS trust rather than the medical professional.

An NHS trust might be sued if the claim was that the negligence resulted from the general way the trust was managed. This might be appropriate where the essential claim was that there were an inadequate number of staff at the hospital, rather than that a particular individual acted wrongly. In some cases, the court might conclude that there was a combination of fault at the level of the management of an NHS trust and an individual doctor. This will not affect the level of damages that might be awarded

Who will pay the damages?

In theory, if the NHS trust is sued, it can recover the money from the medical professional concerned. However, this is unheard of in practice and the NHS has indicated that it has a general policy of not doing so. Similarly, if an individual member of staff is sued, the NHS will meet the cost of litigation and pay any damages awarded. GPs, however, are required to meet their own costs and maintain insurance cover.

Where two medical professionals have acted negligently towards a patient and this has caused a loss, then the court will attempt to apportion blame between the two. Due to the fact the NHS will pay the damages however the blame is allocated, this is not an issue of practical significance, although it might be to the medical professionals concerned. It will also be relevant if either professional was acting in private medicine.

Other issues of liability

Good Samaritanism *110*
Vicarious liability *112*
No-fault liability *114*

Good Samaritanism

Liability for failure to rescue

Some countries require people to offer assistance to those in peril. However, English, Welsh, and Scottish law does not recognize a general duty to rescue those who are in danger. You are permitted to walk past a child drowning in a pond without breaking the law, unless there is a particular duty to act. Before A can be shown to be legally liable for failing to act in a particular way to protect B, three things need to be shown:

• A owed B a duty of care.
• A breached the duty of care.
• A's breach of duty caused an injury to B.

A duty to act can arise in the following circumstances:

• There is a statutory duty to intervene. There are wide range of statutes that require officials to act in particular ways to protect others.
• Police officers have an obligation to assist members of the public who are in danger.
• A person is under a duty under a contract to help others. This is particularly relevant for medical professionals whose contract may provide them to act in a way which protects their patients' interests.
• If a person has voluntarily taken another into their care, be that in a professional or informal role, they may come under a duty to protect that person.
• If a person has acted in a way which puts another in danger, they are under a duty to act to promote that person's well-being.

Causation in omissions cases

If a person is being held legally liable in civil or criminal law for an omission, it would be necessary to show that they owed the victim a duty of care. Not only that, it would need to be shown that they breached their duty of care. This means that they had failed to act in the way reasonably expected. So a doctor who did not offer a patient a treatment might have owed that patient a duty of care, but not breached the duty if it was not reasonable to provide that treatment, for example, because the patient was refusing to consent to it. It must also be shown that a person's breach of duty caused the injury to the patient. In other words, that if the person has acted as they should, the injury would not have occurred. You can imagine a case where a nurse failed to check up on a patient as they ought, who then died. Although the nurse would have breached their duty of care, if the patient would have died even if the nurse had checked up on them there would be no criminal liability.

To summarize, so far as the law is concerned, there is only a legal obligation to intervene to protect others where there is a legal duty to do so. Medical professionals will inevitably owe a duty of care to patients they are looking after. However, they may not to strangers they come across in the street.

Even if there is not a legal obligation, professional bodies may require a medical professional to offer assistance in emergency situations, even where strangers are involved. For example, the GMC's 2012 'Good Medical Practice' (paragraph 23) states:

> You must offer assistance in emergency situations, taking account of your own safety, your competence and the availability of other options for care.

Note the obligation is restricted by the circumstances. Medical professionals will not be expected to assist if doing so puts themselves in real danger or other people are better placed to offer help.

Vicarious liability

Generally, in law, a person is only responsible for his or her own actions. A good example of this principle is a criminal case (*R v Kennedy*) where a drug dealer gave a client some drugs. The client injected the drugs and died. The drug dealer was prosecuted for manslaughter, but the House of Lords explained it could not hold that he had caused the death. The client was responsible for the consequences of his own actions. Notably this is true even though it was perfectly foreseeable that the client would act in this way. The same is true in civil law. Generally, you are responsible for the harms that you cause, but are not responsible for the acts of your colleagues. Although this is a general principle, it is subject to some important exceptions:

Accomplice liability in criminal law

A person can be liable under criminal law if they assist or encourage another person to commit an offence. They will be liable under common law if the other person actually commits an offence, or under the Serious Crimes Act 2007 if the other person does not.

Criminal liability for failing to supervise

A person can be criminally liable for their failure to supervise. Notice that the liability is not for the act of another, but for the defendant's failure to supervise. For example, a gross negligence manslaughter charge would lie if the defendant failed to supervise a junior colleague in a grossly negligent way and that led to death.

Corporate liability

Following the Corporate Manslaughter and Corporate Homicide Act 2007, a company or NHS trust can now be found guilty of manslaughter. It would be necessary to show that there was a serious management failure leading to a gross breach of a duty of care. For an NHS trust to be convicted, it would be necessary to show that there was a management failure. An error by an individual within the organization is unlikely to be sufficient.

Vicarious liability in tort

Under the principle of vicarious liability, an employer can be liable for the negligence of an employee if there is a sufficiently close connection between the employment and the wrongdoing that it is fair and just to hold the employer liable. Crucially, the principle applies even if the person, company, or trust was unaware of the wrongdoing of the other person. The doctrine only applies if the acts of an employee were sufficiently closely connected to the employment.

This means that an NHS Trust, for example, would not be liable in damages if harm was done by one patient to another. It would be liable if harm was caused by a medical professional in their employment. That, however, would only cover cases where the employee was acting in the course of their employment. That test has generated considerable case law. Where the employee is 'on a frolic of their own', to use one judge's memorable phrase, there is no liability. This would mean that an NHS trust would be vicariously liable for a doctor who negligently performed an operation, but might not be liable if a nurse injured a patient while practising a gymnastics routine during a break.

The Supreme Court in *Armes v Nottinghamshire County Council* [2018] UKSC 60 held that a local authority running a children's home was vicariously liable for the sexual abuse of children by the warden of the home. This was because his abuse was closely connected to performance of his duties. It is, therefore, likely a trust would be vicariously liable if a doctor or nurse who sexually abused a patient in their care would be liable. However, there may be no liability if a gardener abused a patient.

No-fault liability

There are few people, if any, who would agree that the current approach to clinical negligence is in a good shape. Clinical litigation is slow, costly, stressful for all concerned, and fails to meet the needs of the NHS or patients. The only people who seem to gain much from the current system are the lawyers! The following passage from the Bristol Inquiry Report sets out the case for moving away from clinical negligence and putting in its place a no-fault scheme:

> The system of clinical negligence litigation is now ripe for review . . . [W]e take the view that it will not be possible to achieve an environment of full, open reporting within the NHS when, outside it, there exists a litigation system the incentives of which press in the opposite direction. We believe that the way forward lies in the abolition of clinical negligence litigation, taking clinical error out of the courts and the tort system. It should be replaced by effective systems for identifying, analysing, learning from and preventing errors.

Not surprisingly, there has been much debate over the alternatives. The problem is that the alternatives seem to have as many problems as the current system. One popular alternative to the current law is no-fault liability.

No fault

Many people support a no-fault system of liability in medical cases. This would give compensation to patients injured following medical procedures, whether this was as a result of negligence or not. All those suffering unexpected consequences of medical treatment would receive compensation. The argument is made that proving negligence can be so difficult and, in a way, it can be a matter of luck whether or not the evidence of negligence can be uncovered. It will also take the heat out of events when a patient suffers unexpected consequences, an honest evaluation of what happened could be undertaken without fear that it would give evidence to one party over the other.

Perhaps the major argument against a no-fault system is that it is extremely expensive to run. There are other arguments against a no-fault system separate from its costs. One is that it draws no distinction between those medical professionals who behave badly and those who do not. It fails to deter bad treatment and acknowledge the wrong done in cases where a patient has suffered as a result of negligence. Supporters of no fault may try and argue that these issues can be dealt with under professional regulation and need not be tied to compensation payments.

No-fault systems in other countries

New Zealand has probably the best-known system of no fault. The scheme is administered by the Accident and Compensation Corporation and offers payment to anyone who suffers a personal injury due to an accident or, in the medical context a 'treatment injury', defined as injuries caused by medical treatment which are 'not a necessary part, or ordinary consequence of the treatment'. So, compensation could not be claimed for a scar following surgery, as that would be an expected consequence of surgery. But unexpected paralysis could be covered, even if that could not be shown to be the result of any wrongdoing by the surgeon.

There are considerable advantages to the New Zealand scheme because patients do not need to prove negligence. While there certainly have been difficulties with the cost of the New Zealand scheme and the contributions made to it have increased dramatically over the years, it is reasonably efficient. The money largely ends up in the hands of those who need it, rather than lining the pockets of lawyers.

The NHS Redress Act 2006

The NHS Redress Act 2006 has been passed to create a new way of dealing with complaints against the NHS. However, it is yet to be implemented in England. It has, however, been implemented in Wales. The scheme is intended to apply to claims of less than £20,000. Importantly, it is seen as an alternative to court-based litigation, rather than a substitute for it. The aim is to provide a speedy and appropriate response to allegations of clinical negligence. At its heart is a belief that when something goes wrong, the patient may be more interested in matters such as an apology and an explanation, than they are in money. Indeed, there is some evidence in support of such a belief.

Under the scheme, when a patient makes a complaint it would be assessed by the relevant NHS trust to determine the appropriate remedy. This may be an apology, an explanation of what happened and an assurance that steps have been taken to ensure it does not happen again, an offer of remedial care, or a payment of compensation. The government's hope is that such a scheme will move away from a culture of attributing blame, but move towards an approach which is focused on understanding what has happened, learning from any mistakes, and makings things right for the patient.

Apologies

It is well worth remembering that even where a patient has been harmed as a result of a mistaken, few take the matter to court. A sincere apology, an honest explanation of what happened, and a reassurance that lessons have been learned may be sufficient to avert a potential claim.

Even though a formal redress scheme is not in place in England, NHS trusts will have a formal procedure to deal with complaints. Typically, this will involve a complaints manager handling the complaint and investigating the best way of responding to it.

Part 3

Generic legal and ethical issues

15 Resource allocation *119*

16 Candour and confidentiality *131*

17 Issues in the doctor–patient relationship *147*

18 Issues in death and dying *177*

19 Doctors and the General Medical Council (GMC) *201*

20 Medical research *211*

21 Medical education *219*

Resource allocation

Introduction to resource allocation *120*
Raise taxes? *122*
Managing budgets better *122*
Triage *123*
Needs and desires *124*
Rationing by desert *125*
Entrenching health inequalities *126*
Freedom of choice *126*
Mixing retributive with distributive justice *127*
Discriminating between different types of risk-taking *128*
Social value and/or dependents *128*
Dependents *129*
Quality-adjusted life years *129*
Postcode lottery *130*

Introduction to resource allocation

The NHS is an enormously expensive institution. Increasingly, patients, doctors, NHS managers, and politicians are having to grapple with questions related to funding. The big question here is: where resources are limited and needs exceed those resources, whose needs should be met? How should we prioritize patients, and what is the best way of making use of those resources that we have?

Aristotle said that justice requires treating equals equally, and unequals unequally. This is the central challenge of resource allocation—and the allocation of *healthcare* resources is particularly fraught. Rhetorical statements often emphasize the fact that we should treat all humans as equals. In theory, there are two ways in which people could be treated with exact formal equality in terms of NHS healthcare resources. Firstly, to offer no resources to anyone at all. In this way, no one receives anything, but no one would have grounds to compare herself unfavourably with others. Secondly, resources could be divided out equally among the population at birth, so that every individual receives an identical proportion of what is available. That amount would depend on political and economic factors— if the overall pool is very limited, people will receive a tiny share; but at any rate, there would be no discrimination, and everyone would start with exactly the same benefits.

However, for most people, neither of these suggestions is acceptable as an approach to NHS healthcare resource allocation. Both scenarios, despite treating everyone equally, would result in a particular group being disadvantaged. In the first example, where no one receives anything, people who are rich would still be able to access healthcare, whereas the poor would not. In the second scenario, where everyone receives exactly the same proportion of resources, those who have very severe healthcare needs would be disadvantaged relative to those who are naturally healthy, since they would run through their share of resources quickly, and perhaps have to forego further care, while people lucky enough to be born healthy would be able to conserve their healthcare ration and might even not need to use it at all.

In these two examples, although people are being formally treated as equals, the system is blind to the fact that they are *not* equals. Some are rich, some are poor; some of them may have urgent needs, and others may be the 'worried well'. Because of this, a system of resource allocation needs to do more than just treat everyone equally. To engage fully with Aristotle's dictum, we need to identify the ways in which people are *un*equal, and work out how that should affect their access to resources.

So, if we are convinced that complete equality is not an option, it is necessary to think about what *aims* a healthcare resource allocation strategy should have. It could seek to:

• extend life expectancy
• improve quality of life
• reduce the overall burden of disease
• encourage healthy behaviour
• reduce health inequalities
• prevent illness
• improve medical knowledge
• express social values.

The common analogy used to discuss resource allocation is that of a cake. The cake is the resource that people want—but there may be more people who want a piece than there are pieces to go round.

We can think of medical resources as the cake, and the global population as the partygoers clamouring for their share. How should the cake be shared out? The 'cake' is inadequate to meet the needs of everyone who might want a piece. Therefore, it is necessary to develop a strategy of prioritization which requires thinking about its possible aims as outlined previously. There are several ways that one might approach this, all of which raise complex ethical considerations.

When the NHS was founded, it was intended to be available for everyone, irrespective of their ability to pay, social status, or any other factor other than their clinical need for treatment. It was recognized that this would be a costly endeavour at the outset. However, the expectation was that eventually, with effectively free healthcare, costs would dwindle, as the population became healthier. Access to good-quality, timely healthcare, it was thought, would reduce the overall burden of disease and the costs of treating it. However, things did not work out in quite this way. The sum of medical need did not diminish as predicted and, in fact, seemed to increase. At the same time, the progress of research meant that new techniques and treatments were continuously becoming available—but often they were costly. At its inception, the NHS aimed to provide the highest standard treatment for patients, but as that bar kept moving higher and higher, it has struggled to keep pace with its own goals.

Raise taxes?

One way of addressing the mismatch between patients' needs and healthcare resources might be to increase the resources available. To revert to the cake analogy, why not simply bake a bigger cake if we know that a lot of people are coming the party? Of course, this is not usually an attractive solution to politicians, or voters, because it involves raising taxes. Yet if we want a better healthcare service, perhaps this is precisely the bitter pill that we must swallow. Many of those who complain about the failings of the health service may be unwilling to contemplate this.

Another possibility—if we are reluctant to spend more on increasing the resources available—is to reduce the number of claimants, somehow. England already limits claimants to NHS services on the basis of nationality. But if this still leaves us with too many people to treat, we could reduce the pool still further: if the cake is insufficient for the guests at the party, and we can't afford a bigger cake, perhaps we should have a smaller party! In essence, this is precisely what current approaches to healthcare resource allocation attempt to do. By defining eligibility for treatment narrowly, we exclude some people from treatment. Yet this is highly controversial: for many people, medical treatment is regarded as something morally special, even something to which people have an intrinsic right.

Managing budgets better

Some would argue that we would not need to increase taxes *or* to limit the pool of claimants if we could just manage the budget better, and waste less money on poor administrative and management structures. Undeniably, savings can be made by using resources more efficiently. However, even if taxes were raised, or savings were made in other ways, it seems likely that the problem would remain.

What has been learnt since the NHS began—and has become evident in other health services—is that people's need for treatment will not diminish as care becomes available. There is an analogy here with road traffic planning. It is now commonly claimed that building new roads to reduce congestion eventually has the opposite effect: the improved roads make driving more pleasant and attract new drivers, ultimately leading to an increase in traffic. Some suggest that healthcare works in a similar way: providing more leads to more demand. If that is correct, it is not a problem that is ever likely to be fixed however much money we throw at it, and however rigorous our management strategies. Rather, an ethically acceptable way of prioritizing patients has to be found, and this is immensely challenging.

Triage

If the aim is to use resources to extend people's lifespans, one of the most obvious ways of approaching resource allocation is to prioritize those who are most in need, and stand to benefit most from treatment. In this way, resources are not wasted on those who are not very sick, or on those who are so sick that they will not recover. Primary care is often the place where these assessments are undertaken. This may sound a rather brutal approach but it is very effective, especially in emergency situations when quick decisions have to be made and strategic thinking may be challenging.

Incorporating triage into a resource allocation strategy seems sensible: those who are suffering most may be deemed to have most need. This is the basis on which patients seeking cosmetic surgery may be denied NHS treatment, whereas a patient with a broken leg or a ruptured appendix will not. A&E departments are there to provide urgent treatment for people in a situation of extreme need. When people attend A&E who are *not* deemed to need urgent treatment, they may be sent home, or end up waiting a very long time to be seen. This is a form of triage in action. An additional advantage of a triage system is that it does not usually raise conceptual problems in the ways that other systems may do. Urgent needs for treatment such as broken limbs, respiratory failure, or cardiac arrest do not pose questions about the validity of the patient's clinical *need* for treatment in the way that cosmetic surgery or elective procedures might do.

However, the use of triage as the sole way of managing a healthcare budget is problematic. Triage responds to extreme situations and urgent need. However, treating emergency cases is often expensive. When less urgent cases get sent home from A&E, they may reappear later when the condition has become acute. Perhaps it would be cheaper to treat them earlier on, thus preventing them from eventually becoming emergencies at all.

A further difficulty lies in the fact that because a triage system prioritizes immediate need, it may have no inbuilt way of providing for public health programmes that are not directly connected with need per se, but promote health and avoid expensive treatments later on. Vaccination, for example, would not be a priority for a purely triage-based system, since it involves spending money on healthy people. And there would be no budget for research, since there are always people with more immediate needs on whom to spend the resources.

Because of this, even though most healthcare resource allocation systems, including the UK's, incorporate elements of triage, healthcare budgets usually also make allowances for public health programmes, preventive health measures, and research, so these elements *are* incorporated. However, other treatments that do not obviously correlate with immediate need are not routinely provided. IVF, cosmetic surgery, and gender reassignment are all examples of procedures that patients can and do seek, but will not necessarily receive.

Needs and desires

Underlying the distinction between treatments that are and are not provided is an assumption about what constitutes genuine medical need. Those who seek cosmetic surgery or IVF may believe passionately that they *need* these interventions—as much as other patients *need* cancer treatment. They may suffer just as much as other patients do from their conditions, and yet their claims are sometimes denied. For this reason, the question of what a health service will and won't pay for is always fraught, and is often subject to change.

One factor that makes this question especially difficult is that medical intervention can sometimes enable people to meet their aspirations without any clear correlation between a clinically diagnosable pathology and the intervention to be undertaken.

In the case described in Box 15.1, the surgery was paid for privately. It would be very controversial for the NHS to expend its funds on such procedures. Nevertheless, some people make very strong arguments to support the provision of this kind of treatment. At the furthest end of the spectrum, these arguments take it that there is no objective or scientific way to determine what constitutes a genuine medical need, and there is no reason to deny patients a medical intervention that could satisfy a deeply felt desire, even if this seems bizarre or outrageous to some. Clearly, however, the extremes of this sort of reasoning could prove very costly for a state-funded health service.

Box 15.1 Case A

In 2000, the BBC reported on a case where a surgeon had amputated a patient's leg at the request of the patient. There were no physical or medical problems related to the leg that would normally constitute medical grounds for such an invasive procedure. However, the surgeon in question argued that the patient *was* suffering from a medical condition—a psychiatric problem known as body dysmorphic disorder. Therefore, although physically the patient did not 'need' treatment, he was regarded as having a psychiatric need for it.

Rationing by desert

Rationing by desert involves a move away from the health need itself to think about whether the patient deserves the treatment. The aims of a desert-based approach to healthcare resource rationing might be to encourage healthy behaviour and discourage risk-taking.

Factors to consider might include the following:

- *Responsibility*: penalizing people for risky behaviour, smoking, taking drugs, and so on.
- *Dependents/loved ones*: prioritize people with spouses, children, who are caring for elderly relatives, and so on.
- *Value to society*: prioritize high earners, prime minister, NHS staff, and so on.

NICE has made it clear that blame should not be a factor in denying a patient treatment. However, a patient's predicted behaviour may be a reason for denying treatment on clinical grounds. There is undeniably a common-sense truth to the fact that some patients' ill health is a matter of pure misfortune while that of others is connected with actions, choices, and decisions that the individual has made. A patient who has suffered a ruptured appendix may simply be unlucky, while some would say that a patient who requires bariatric surgery for obesity has a greater degree of responsibility for her predicament. However, that is to oversimplify the issue. The causes of obesity, for example, are complex and controversial.

Aside from thinking that one patient is more deserving of treatment, there may also be a sense that, if we continue to provide medical interventions for conditions that arise from bad lifestyle choices, people will be less likely to make sensible healthy decisions. Some would argue that people will have no incentive to change their eating habits if they can get a quick surgical fix. Could it be that, if people *knew* that bariatric surgery would be withheld, they would be less likely to become obese in the first place? If so, there would be two powerful arguments in favour of desert-based rationing. Firstly, its potential for direct cost savings in reducing the pool of eligible claimants, and secondly, its potential to reduce the sum of health need by improving people's lifestyle choices and decisions. However, it may be thought questionable whether people would choose to become unhealthy, just because they knew there were treatments available.

Entrenching health inequalities

The complex relationships between our understanding of medical conditions and socio-economic factors in determining people's unhealthy choices, make rationing by desert a much more problematic approach than it might first appear. It is well known that people in the lower socio-economic brackets are at greater risk of lifestyle-related health problems such as addiction. This means that in addition to the financial and economic disparities that exist in our society, there are health disparities that persist, despite the availability of universal healthcare, and that manifest themselves along socio-economic lines.

Some might argue that this is not the concern of healthcare providers, and that it does not matter that those who are 'less responsible' are also more likely to be less well-off. However, for those who are interested in achieving equality, the correlation between these disparities may be deeply worrying.

Freedom of choice

If cultural and economic factors affect lifestyle choices, such as eating habits, smoking, and seeking healthcare, it is not so easy to say that an individual is entirely free to choose her health status in relation to these considerations. Affluent people may be raised in households where healthy eating is the norm; they may be accustomed from an early age to seek health advice when they encounter problems, and to participate in screening programmes. Others may be raised in households where unhealthy behaviour patterns are a cultural norm, and where seeking medical advice is unusual. We know that children of obese parents are at greater risk of being or becoming obese themselves. It would seem bizarre suddenly to hold these individuals responsible for their choices the minute they turn 18.

Establishing freedom of choice in these circumstances is very difficult. Our choices are, if not determined, then strongly influenced by the environment in which we develop. It may be unfair to hold people equally responsible for their unhealthy behaviour if they have different backgrounds and cultural influences. Yet if we were to enquire into the background of patients in order to establish their 'worthiness' for treatment, this might seem problematic too. It is undeniable that among the most privileged classes, some people struggle with unhealthy behaviours. Conversely, while lifestyle-related illness is strongly associated with low socio-economic status, not everyone is predestined to follow a certain path. Smokers' children do not always smoke themselves, though they are more likely to than children of non-smokers. We simply do not yet understand the factors behind these 'choices' well enough to be sure who—if anyone—can be held responsible for their own poor health.

Mixing retributive with distributive justice

One of the problems that arises from rationing by desert is that it mixes two different sorts of justice. When resources are limited, and claims exceed what is available, it is necessary to consider distributive justice. That is, to ensure that we have a fair means of providing these resources to those who are entitled to them.

However, when we decide to provide or withhold medical resources in order to punish or reward people for their behaviour, this engages a different sort of justice: retributive justice. The kind of justice involved in sending a murderer to prison is retributive justice.

When the two sorts of justice are combined into a rationing strategy, we can see that there are some conceptual difficulties. Firstly, while murder is clearly a crime, the behaviours that might give rise to punitive measures in the health service, such as overeating, smoking, being unfit, and so on, are *not*. We might regard them as being foolish or undesirable, but they are not *crimes*. Yet those who commit them will be punished as though they *were* crimes. Still more troubling is the fact that if the punishment involves withholding medical treatment, it could literally result in the death of the patient.

Another aspect of conflating distributive and retributive justice is that of course our society includes people who *really are* criminals. Rapists, murderers, and thieves also have healthcare needs. If we adopt a desert-based system, it would appear that *these* are the first people who should be turned away. Yet a society that refuses medical treatment to its criminals and prisoners may not be the kind of society that we wish to be part of.

Discriminating between different types of risk-taking

Often, when people think about desert-based rationing, they focus on the stereotypical poor choices such as those described in previous sections: obesity, smoking, drinking, and so on. Underlying these is an assumption that taking unnecessary risks with one's health is the primary issue. Smokers do not *need* to smoke; obese people do not *need* to overeat. These are risks that people court in their pursuit of more immediate pleasures.

However, there are many activities that might be categorized as courting unnecessary risk, which can have direct impacts on people's need for medical treatment. It is important to note that these tend to be treated very differently in these debates. For example:

- mountaineering
- horse riding
- not wearing seat belts
- motorcycling ... without a helmet
- rugby
- drinking alcohol
- smoking
- poor diet
- lack of exercise
- cycling
- drug use
- getting pregnant.

Social value and/or dependents

If the possibility of adopting punitive measures to save resources is not palatable, perhaps we could look at the positive side of desert-based rationing. Rather than attempting to punish people for their poor choices, we could seek to reward those who make valuable contributions to our society.

One of the difficulties here might be defining whose concept of value should be emphasized. In liberal Western democracies, we usually expect people to have diverse values, and see this as a good thing. But it makes values-based policymaking rather tricky. Some might say that earning a high salary or running a business are the things we should reward. Others might say that charitable works are important. Gifted individuals, such as artists, musicians, actors, and athletes, might seem to offer the kind of value to society that we deem important. Alternatively, perhaps some professions could by default be prioritized for medical care. Medical professionals themselves, teachers, military personnel, police, and so on.

Any selection of categories carries with it assumptions and values that may not be shared by others.

Dependents

One way round the difficulty of specifying exactly who we regard as socially valuable, might be to prioritize instead those who have dependents. Suppose two 35-year-old women seek treatment for life-threatening conditions. One is the mother of three young children; the other has no offspring. Intuitively, we might think that offering treatment to the mother is more sensible, since the welfare of four people is at stake, rather than just one.

However, there are some concerns with such an approach. It seems to emphasize the importance of parenthood above other forms of dependency. In the example given, although one woman is not a mother, she could be caring for her elderly parents. Or perhaps she might be the CEO of a large company, and thus have many thousands of employees/dependents who might be adversely affected by her death. If one is to consider the impact on denying treatment not just on the patient but on all those who will suffer as a result, the calculation may simply become too difficult.

Thus, the question of desert-based rationing raises a plethora of social and political questions, as well as ethical questions about the degree that we can really be held responsible for appetites and habits that may have been formed in childhood.

Quality-adjusted life years

In the UK, the NHS attempts as far as possible to treat patients on the basis of clinical need, rather than enquiring into their past, or the number of their dependents. The key strategic aims of the health service are to use resources so as to increase lifespans, while also improving quality of life, for as many patients as possible. These two aims are brought together in a single measurement called the quality-adjusted life year (QALY) and are used to determine which treatments are likely to be cost-effective.

Potential medical treatments are reviewed in the UK by NICE to ascertain whether or not they are effective and provide adequate value for money. NICE then publishes guidance as to the treatments that should be provided, along with clinical indications for identifying eligible patients. Once the cost analysis is done, provided a patient meets the clinical criteria, there are no additional criteria that they have to meet. NICE explicitly states that it does not consider the social or ethical worth of particular patients.

However, in practice, some healthcare providers employ additional measures in order to limit the numbers of patients. So, for example, sometimes obese patients are refused joint replacements, and smokers may be denied surgery for certain conditions. In some instances, it may be that the risks involved are too great, such as where a very obese patient is unlikely to survive surgery. However, in other cases, it seems that rationing by desert is being employed as an additional means of reducing the financial burdens faced by healthcare providers. Political interventions make the issues all the harder.

Postcode lottery

It seems self-evident that local funding priorities should reflect local values and needs. For example, some health conditions are likely to be more prevalent in some places than others. In a rural farming community, needs will be different from in highly urbanized areas. Ethnicity and socio-economic variables will affect health needs. Because of this, although Clinical Commissioning Groups are required to provide treatments recommended by NICE, beyond that they have a degree of discretion as to which treatments their local areas need the most. Inevitably, this results in discrepancies across county borders, which are regarded with disfavour by patients, and pilloried in the media.

The 'postcode lottery' is not popular … indeed, it is often taken as self-evident that local discrepancies in access to treatment are unfair and wrong. But we cannot have local decision-making without resulting in a postcode lottery. The alternative to the postcode lottery is to have centralized decisions that apply across the entire country. At one level, this might seem fairer to those who are outraged to find that people in the next county have access to treatment which they themselves are denied. However, a heavily centralized system might raise its own challenges. Perhaps there are better ways of addressing this balance between centralized decision-making and local variability; but in the meantime, the postcode lottery looks set to stay.

Additional reading

Boyd KM. The Ethics of Resource Allocation in Health Care. Edinburgh: Edinburgh University Press; 1979.

Cookson R, McCabe C, Tsuchiya A. Public healthcare resource allocation and the Rule of Rescue. Journal of Medical Ethics. 2008;34(7):540–4.

Candour and confidentiality

Candour *132*
Introduction to confidentiality *134*
Professional guidelines for confidentiality *136*
Practical limitations on confidentiality *137*
Confidentiality and the law *138*
Data Protection Act 2018 *140*
Confidentiality after death—case studies *142*

Candour

At the heart of patient safety must be the idea that we learn from mistakes. Only if we know what mistakes have happened can we discover why they have happened and what processes can be put in place to ensure they do not happen again. However, fear of blame, litigation, and loss of reputation are strong incentives not to disclose a mistake has been made. These have discouraged 'whistle-blowers' in the past and have been seen as a significant barrier to promoting safety and hence a legal duty of candour was created in regulation 20 of the Health and Social Care Act 2008 (Regulated Activities) Regulations 2014.

Regulation 20 requires 'registered persons' to act 'in an open and transparent way' with patients. In particular, if there is a 'notifiable safety incident' they must notify the patient and inform them of 'all the facts the registered person knows about the incident as at the date of the notification' and 'include an apology'. The patient must be informed as soon as possible after a notifiable safety incident has occurred. The NHS Standard Contract requires that to be within 20 working days.

That notification must be given in person and explain to the best of the health service body's knowledge all the facts. It must advise what further enquiries are appropriate, issue an apology, and keep a written record. Regulation 20 defines a notifiable safety incident as including incidents that in the reasonable opinion of a healthcare professional could result in death, moderate harm, severe harm, or prolonged psychological harm.

Introduction to confidentiality

Background

Confidentiality has been recognized as an important aspect of the doctor–patient relationship from the earliest days of medical practice. In fact, though many other ethical values in medicine have changed considerably over time, the weight given to confidentiality has remained remarkably constant. The Hippocratic oath requires that: 'All that may come to my knowledge in the exercise of my profession or outside of my profession or in daily commerce with men, which ought not to be spread abroad, I will keep secret and never reveal.'

More than 2000 years later, the GMC confirms the relevance of confidentiality in modern medical practice: 'Patients have a right to expect that information about them will be held in confidence by their doctors.'

What is confidentiality?

A duty of confidentiality arises from a promise made, either implicitly or explicitly, not to divulge certain information. In the medical context, this promise is often implicit. Members of the public usually believe that doctors will keep information about them private. Many patients regard medical confidentiality as being akin to that of the confessional: never to be breached in any circumstances.

In practice, of course, this is not the case. There are a number of situations in which the law requires doctors to disclose information about their patients, and many other situations in which they are permitted (though not required) to do so. We will go into this in more detail later on in this chapter.

As well as information *about* patients, considerations of confidentiality also apply to patients' identity per se. A patient may not wish his/her friends, colleagues, or relatives—or anyone else—to know that they are sick. This means that the patient's identity needs to be protected. Doctors are expected to refrain from discussing their patients by name when not on duty. When medical researchers involve people in research, they are expected to ensure that participants' names and other identifying information are concealed.

Why is confidentiality important?

Given the difficulties involved in maintaining absolute confidentiality, we might well ask ourselves why we should try so hard to keep patient information private. What is the harm, if any, of breaching confidentiality? And if there is no harm in breaching confidentiality in a particular situation, does that mean it is morally acceptable?

In ethical theory, the importance of confidentiality may depend on what moral approach one takes. The four principles approach (➲ p. 29) would seem to protect confidentiality on several grounds. A patient chooses to disclose private information, only to be used for medical purposes and so confidentiality is protected as a component of respect for autonomy. Ordinarily, we expect the principle of respect for autonomy to harmonize with beneficence. In the context of confidentiality this would mean that, on the whole, maintaining confidentiality benefits the patient *and* respects their autonomy. However, there may be cases where the opposite seems to be the case. In such circumstances, the doctor may be faced with a question of whether to breach autonomy, in order to benefit the patient, or to respect the patient's wish for confidentiality, even though this may appear detrimental in the doctor's view. We will explore a case study related to this conflict later on in this chapter.

A utilitarian (➲ p. 16) will believe that maintaining confidentiality is only required if doing so is beneficial overall. A doctor who jokes with his wife about a particular patient may not harm that patient—the patient may never find out. However, from the perspective of virtue ethics, we might feel that a doctor who would breach confidentiality in this way would lack some of the characteristics we expect from a good doctor. A deontologist (➲ p. 24) would object to the breach of confidentiality *regardless* of whether the patient is harmed, since it would mean that the doctor had effectively broken a promise. And breaking promises is a dereliction of duty.

The main moral arguments in favour of breaching confidentiality are likely to draw on utilitarian themes. This means thinking carefully about the kind of harm and benefit that may arise from a breach. In fact, even if the individual patient is not harmed, if doctors are lax about confidentiality, broader problems may arise.

From a utilitarian perspective, it is important to be aware that the expectation of confidentiality is not only of benefit to patients. It also, indirectly, benefits doctors themselves. Patients who know that their privacy will be carefully maintained are likely to be happier to divulge information to the doctor. In turn, where patients are able to be open and honest with doctors, it means that the doctor is in a better position to be able to treat the patient.

In an environment where neither party trusts the other, the very practice of medicine is undermined. Because of this, if doctors are to benefit patients at all, confidentiality has to be assumed.

This does, however, raise the question of why patients might want information to be kept secret. What is so special about medicine that means it has to be private, whereas other information seems to be public property? It may be that medical information *is* overprivileged in comparison with other data. Nevertheless, it is fairly easy to see why divulging medical information could be detrimental.

Medical information concerns us much more directly than information about our cars, or houses, for example. We *are* our bodies and cannot separate ourselves from them or buy new ones. What someone knows about my body therefore is far more intimate, far more intrusive than what they may know about anything else. The body I take to see the doctor is the same one I use to do my work and live my life. Because of this, medical information can have a bearing on almost every conceivable aspect of one's life. It may affect one's ability to get a job, to be able to drive, to hold down a relationship, to enter certain countries, and to obtain insurance.

We all therefore have an interest both in maintaining control over our own information—and in accessing the information of others. I might not want my own life choices to be restricted by the fact that others have access to medical information about me. But I would not want to fly with a pilot whose narcolepsy may mean he will lose consciousness unexpectedly at any moment. Nor would I want to conceive a child with a partner who carries a devastating genetic disease. This means that a careful balance has to be struck between our individual interests and those of others.

Professional guidelines for confidentiality

The GMC has produced a helpful guide on confidentiality entitled: 'Confidentiality: good practice in handling patient information' (⌖ https://www.gmc-uk.org/ethical-guidance/ethical-guidance-for-doctors/confidentiality). It sets out eight key principles underpinning its advice:

- *Use the minimum necessary personal information.* Use anonymized information if it is practicable to do so and if it will serve the purpose.
- *Manage and protect information.* Make sure any personal information you hold or control is effectively protected at all times against improper access, disclosure, or loss.
- *Be aware of your responsibilities.* Develop and maintain an understanding of information governance that is appropriate to your role.
- *Comply with the law.* Be satisfied that you are handling personal information lawfully.
- *Share relevant information for direct care* in line with the principles in this guidance unless the patient has objected.
- *Ask for explicit consent* to disclose identifiable information about patients for purposes other than their care or local clinical audit, unless the disclosure is required by law or can be justified in the public interest.
- *Tell patients* about disclosures of personal information you make that they would not reasonably expect, or check they have received information about such disclosures, unless that is not practicable or would undermine the purpose of the disclosure. Keep a record of your decisions to disclose, or not to disclose, information.
- *Support patients to access their information.* Respect, and help patients exercise, their legal rights to be informed about how their information will be used and to have access to, or copies of, their health records.

Practical limitations on confidentiality

Both in general practice and hospital medicine, the systems involved in providing modern healthcare require the sharing and transmission of data. It is easy for patients to assume that all their information is entirely confidential. But medical care is increasingly provided by multidisciplinary teams.

Patients are unlikely to object to their doctors sharing information with other medical team members involved in their care. But what about non-medical staff? Receptionists may of necessity have access to patient information, as may cleaning staff, hospital porters, medical secretaries, and many others.

On an even more basic level, where patients are physically present for treatments or appointments, they may be recognized and identified by anyone who happens to know them. There is no guarantee of absolute confidentiality. The car park attendant may be one's neighbour, and recognize one's licence plate. The person serving in the hospital shop may spot you as the person whose child goes to the same school as theirs.

The fact that we're visiting the doctor or attending a hospital appointment cannot be guaranteed to be kept secret. However, perhaps what concerns people more is the question of whether the *reasons* for their attendance might be made known. Sometimes the reason is easily inferred from the location. For example, if I see my next-door neighbour at the STD clinic, I am likely to make more specific inferences about their condition than if I simply saw them in the waiting room at the GP surgery. (And of course, they would be making similar inferences about me!) It is hard to see a way round this, aside from attending appointments in disguise.

Confidentiality and the law

Confidential medical care is recognized in common law as being in the public interest. Confidentiality, or the right to privacy, is also protected by the Human Rights Act 1998.

Article 8

- 'Everyone has the right to respect for his private and family life, his home and his correspondence.
- There shall be no interference by a public authority with this right except as is in accordance with the law and is necessary in the interest of national security, public safety ... for the prevention of disorder or crime, for the protection of health or morals ...'

The right of confidentiality is also protected by the law of tort and the law of equity. However, most legal proceedings involving breach of confidence are attempts to prevent someone (often a newspaper) revealing confidential information. If the material has already been produced, it is usually difficult to prove that there has been a financial loss as a result which might lead to a claim for damages, in which case there will be little point seeking damages.

When can confidentiality be overridden?

If confidentiality is to be breached, there must be a good reason for doing so. The most common justifications are as follows:

- The patient consents explicitly. The patient might well, for example, consent to their doctor informing a relative of their diagnosis.
- The patient consents implicitly. Generally, a patient is taken to explicitly consent to their information being used in line with normal medical practice. So, for example, if a patient agrees to be referred to a consultant, they will be taken to have implicitly consented to the GP passing on medical information to the consultant. This exception can also apply to local clinical audits and similar standard hospital practice.
- If the patient lacks mental capacity, then confidentiality can be breached if it is in their best interests to do so.
- The disclosure is required by law. For example, doctors must register births and deaths: the patient has no right of opt-out. Likewise, patients who receive fertility treatment or abortions must be registered. Doctors are also required by law to inform the Health Protection Agency if their patients are suspected to be suffering from any of the conditions included in the list of 'notifiable disease'. These include cholera, legionnaires' disease, rabies, and whooping cough. A complete list is available online (ℛ http://www.hpa.org.uk/Topics/ InfectiousDiseases/InfectionsAZ/NotificationsOfInfectiousDiseases/ ListOfNotifiableDiseases/).
- *NB*: it is worth noting here that HIV/AIDS is *not* a notifiable disease, although it is often mistakenly assumed to be.
- The disclosure can be justified in the public interest. This might be used where a patient poses a risk to others and disclosure is needed to protect other people from harm.

- Police who are investigating a crime may obtain a judge's permission to access medical notes. In such cases, the doctor is legally obliged to provide the information requested. Doctors are also required to disclose information that may prevent an act of terrorism, or that may help police in identifying the perpetrator of a driving offence.

Disclosing confidential information

Even where confidential information can be disclosed, it does not follow that there are no restrictions on how it is disclosed. The GMC in their guidance set five principles that should be followed if there is to be disclosure of confidential information:

- Use anonymized information if it is practicable to do so and if it will serve the purpose.
- Be satisfied the patient:
  - has ready access to information explaining how their personal information will be used for their own care or local clinical audit, and that they have the right to object
  - has not objected.
- Get the patient's explicit consent if identifiable information is to be disclosed for purposes other than their own care or local clinical audit, unless the disclosure is required by law or can be justified in the public interest.
- Keep disclosures to the minimum necessary for the purpose.
- Follow all relevant legal requirements, including the common law and data protection law.

Consent must be obtained for any case presentation (other than for clinical purposes) in the absence of the patient when the patient's details are disclosed.

Data Protection Act 2018

The Data Protection Act 2018 (which has superseded the Data Protection Act 1998) implements the General Data Protection Regulation (GDPR) (which originates in EU law). This area of law is complex and only a brief overview can be offered here.

The legislation covers 'personal data'. Personal data is any information relating to an identified or identifiable natural person. It includes names, addresses, telephone numbers, dates of birth, and hospital numbers.

At the heart of the legislation are the 'data protection principles' which must be complied with by everyone responsible for using personal data. These principles seek to ensure that the information is:

- used fairly, lawfully, and transparently
- used for specified, explicit purposes
- used in a way that is adequate, relevant, and limited to only what is necessary
- accurate and, where necessary, kept up to date
- kept for no longer than is necessary
- handled in a way that ensures appropriate security, including protection against unlawful or unauthorized processing, access, loss, destruction, or damage.

There are particularly strong legal protections for information of certain kinds including:

- race
- ethnic background
- political opinions
- religious beliefs
- trade union membership
- genetics
- biometrics (where used for identification)
- health
- sex life or orientation.

To process personal data, a medical professional must have one of the six justifications in law. The one that will most often be used is explicit patient consent; that the processing is necessary for the provision of healthcare for the person concerned; or that the processing is in the vital interests of the person. If consent is relied upon it must be unambiguous, positive (i.e. not relying on the fact a patient had not objected), and freely given.

Access to medical records

Under the Data Protection Act 2018, a patient has the right to find out what information an organization, including the NHS, holds about them. The specific rights include to:

- be informed about how their data is being used
- access personal data
- have incorrect data updated
- have data erased
- stop or restrict the processing of their data

- data portability (allowing them to get and reuse their data for different services)
- object to how their data is processed in certain circumstances.

Normally patients seek access to their summary health records through their GP and increasingly they are available online.

Confidentiality after death—case studies

Patients and their relatives may assume that doctors' duties of confidentiality change after a patient's death. There are some good reasons for this assumption. Once the patient is dead, it is less clear what benefit is achieved by maintaining his or her privacy. And relatives may feel that they have a greater right to access information about their loved one after their death. In most cases, the duty of confidentiality remains unaltered after a patient's death. However, there are situations in which the relationship between confidentiality and other obligations may be challenging (Box 16.1).

Box 16.1 Case A

A GP has a patient with HIV. This patient has become very sick and is likely to die very soon. The patient's wife is estranged, but he has three adult children and an elderly mother still living. He is very concerned because his family do not know about his HIV status. He asks the doctor to maintain his confidentiality by ensuring that his condition is not revealed to his next of kin.

Helpful guidance can be found in the GMC guide on confidentiality: ✆ https://www.gmc-uk.org/guidance/ethical_guidance/confidentiality.asp.

What should the doctor say to the patient?

One might argue that a person no longer has interests after they die. If so, confidentiality might no longer be relevant after a patient's death. The patient cannot be harmed since they are already dead. However, this is contentious, and to be consistent, anyone who argued this would have to accept that wills need not be adhered to, or a person's wishes about cremation, burial, and so on, or organ donation … There is not scope to enter into these questions fully here, but it is worth noting that UK law *does* recognize ongoing interests after death. The death of the patient does not absolve the doctor from his/her duty of confidentiality.

In this case, therefore, the most obvious answer is that confidentiality should be maintained, as in any situation where a patient does not wish to share information with family members. Although there may be ethical or legal reasons to breach confidentiality, it is not obvious that any such reasons apply here.

It is of course true that a patient might cause distress or harm to their family/partner if they fail to reveal information to which family members feel entitled. However, this is an ethical failing on the part of the patient; it is not the duty of the doctor to ensure that patients always behave in a morally commendable way! See Box 16.2.

Box 16.2 Case B

The doctor reassures the patient that he will not disclose his HIV status to his next of kin when they arrive. However, the patient is still concerned and asks the doctor to promise that there is absolutely no way that his next of kin will find out.

Should the doctor make this promise?

Given the points made earlier, one might be inclined to answer yes. However, making any absolute promise can be risky. Can we really assume we are in a position to control for every eventuality? If not, it may be fairer to assure the patient that one will do one's best but that there can be no absolute guarantee.

However, in this specific situation, there is a major problem in promising absolute secrecy to a patient dying of HIV. That is, the doctor will have to fill in the death certificate, and the death certificate is a public document! See Box 16.3.

> ### Box 16.3 Case C
> The patient asks about the formalities of what will happen when his relatives arrive, and whether they will see the death certificate. He requests that the doctor should protect his confidentiality by not including HIV as the cause of death.

Harms in promising confidentiality

From an ethical perspective, the doctor might consider what harm might arise from a failure to respect the patient's wishes. The patient might become distressed; the relatives might also be distressed. It could alter the dying man's experience and destroy his trust in his carers just when he most needs it. These are very significant harms, and may seem to go entirely against a doctor's ethical instincts, which are to support and benefit the patient.

However, some of these harms would be mitigated if the doctor is able to communicate sensitively with the patient, to explain the importance of the death certificate.

It is also important to consider what harm might arise if the patient's wishes *were* respected. If the relatives found their loved one's HIV status from other sources, they might feel misled, or deceived. If there is any subsequent problem or issue, and the doctor is found to have deliberately recorded wrong information, his integrity and professionalism could be called into question. If the doctor does omit to mention HIV on the death certificate, is this tantamount to deceiving the relatives? Is it the same as if they asked 'Does he have HIV?' and the doctor said 'No'?

Lying

A direct lie is often felt to be morally worse than merely omitting some of the truth but an omission may be equally deceptive, depending on the expectations involved. If the relatives asked directly whether the patient had HIV, the doctor would not need to lie: he would need to explain that he is bound by confidentiality, and cannot disclose a patient's condition without their agreement.

In the case of the death certificate, the relatives are very likely to expect that it will tell the truth, that is, that if it doesn't mention HIV, that means the patient didn't have HIV. So, if that expectation turns out to have been wrong, they may feel misled and deceived, even though the doctor has not written anything that was actually false on the death certificate.

Death certificates

On a broader level, the point of a death certificate is to provide a public record of what people die of. It is not intended to be the property of, or to serve the interests of, individual patients or their relatives.

The importance of this lies in the fact that it is a precaution against crime. By ensuring that every death is recorded legally, we can look into the circumstances, and take steps if there is anything suspicious. Doctors are part of this system; if they cannot be relied upon to record accurate information, it could have very wide-reaching consequences for society.

It might be argued that in an individual case such as this, where there is no suggestion of foul play, a doctor should have discretion to omit information from the death certificate. However, doctors are not police officers, and this would be introducing a new dimension to the doctor's role. Would this be desirable? If doctors have discretion to write what they see fit, some patients will have their wishes met, while others will not. Does this cause a problem in regard to the principle of justice?

If doctors did begin to omit information routinely from death certificates, relatives would not necessarily regard the certificate as giving accurate information—and nor would others who have occasion to consult the information in death certificates. Again, the potential consequences might be very wide-reaching. Indeed, it would become questionable whether there is a point in having such documents if it is agreed that they can be fudged, falsified, or filled in incompletely.

Nevertheless, there is clearly some latitude in what can or should be recorded on a death certificate. A death may be caused by any number of conditions in combination. The doctor cannot be expected to record every single occurrence in the patient's medical history—so where can the line be drawn? A patient who dies of HIV, actually dies of some other illness caused by HIV. So, couldn't the other illness, such as pneumonia, be listed instead? The law and the GMC recognize that doctors cannot list every conceivable factor that might have contributed to a patient's death. Doctors are not obliged to list things that are trivial, or irrelevant.

Again, the answer lies in the expectations laid out in the law and by the GMC. The GMC states: 'If serious communicable disease has contributed to the cause of death, you must record this on the death certificate.'

Because expectations are important in this context, it is useful to turn this round and consider the patient's expectations. Do patients know that the cause of death is written on the death certificate, which is then in the public domain? If not, they may feel betrayed and misled when they realize. But it is not necessarily the doctor who is responsible for this deception.

Summary

To summarize, confidentiality is ethically and legally protected in most circumstances, but there are occasions when other factors override it. In this particular scenario, the legal and ethical considerations point towards recording HIV status on the death certificate.

Additional reading

Hilton C. Whistle-blowing and duty of candour in the National Health Service: a 'history and policy' case study of the 1960s and 2010s. Journal of the Royal Society of Medicine. 2016;109(9):327–30.

Kottow MH. Medical confidentiality: an intransigent and absolute obligation. Journal of Medical Ethics. 1986;12(3):117–22.

Rogers WA, Draper H. Confidentiality and the ethics of medical ethics. Journal of Medical Ethics. 2003;29(4):220–4.

Wheeler R. Candour for surgeons: the absence of spin. Annals of the Royal College of Surgeons of England. 2014;96(6):420–2.

Issues in the doctor–patient relationship

Introduction to the doctor–patient relationship *148*
Introduction to consent *150*
Consent and mental capacity *152*
Ensuring patients are sufficiently informed *156*
The treatment of patients who cannot consent *158*
Advance decisions *160*
Decisions that cannot be made on behalf of a person without capacity *164*
The best interests assessments *166*
The use of restraint or force *168*
Consent and children *172*
Conscience and conscientious objection *174*

Introduction to the doctor–patient relationship

Paternalism

Trust between doctors and their patients is an essential part of medicine. Patients expect doctors to be highly trained, to be both knowledgeable and caring, and above all, to have the patient's best interests at heart. This is a lot to expect of doctors working in the modern NHS. With restricted consultation times, the need to meet targets, and balance books, the pressures on the doctor–patient relationship are as great as they have ever been.

Not only this, but with social, economic, and political changes, people's expectations change too. Medical teaching these days encourages students to view paternalism—the backbone of the doctor–patient relationship in previous decades—as being outmoded, if not downright sinister.

What is paternalism and why has it fallen out of favour?

Paternalism is based on the relationship a father has with his children—as the word implies. A wise and benevolent father knows best what is in his child's interest, and has the power and authority to override the child's own wishes. Similarly, a paternalistic view of healthcare would suggest that a medical professional knows best and should make decisions about what is best for the patient. Viewed in this way, paternalism is not sinister at all. However, the doctor–patient relationship is rather different from the parent–child relationship. Adult patients are not children, and although doctors are imbued with a certain degree of power and authority, patients nowadays tend to believe that their own perceptions of what is best for them should prevail.

Underlying the decline of paternalism is the increasing weight given to the importance of individual values and choices. This can lead to conflict: doctors who went into medicine to benefit patients may find their idea of benefit challenged by the very people they are trying to help. As discussed in the ethical theory section (➔ p. 29), the principles of autonomy and beneficence often come into conflict in modern medicine. In the past, it might have been assumed that beneficence should win the day: the power balance was weighted in favour of the doctor. Now, the balance has swung the other way, and patient choice has more weight than ever before.

Patient choice means little, however, without accurate, comprehensible information. This creates a challenge for doctors: where once a doctor could simply tell the patient what to do, she must now outline the various options, their implications, side effects, and chances of success.

New understandings of the doctor–patient relationship

Nowadays it is common for doctors to see the doctor–patient relationship as a mutual one. They make decisions together. The best decisions will be made with the doctor bringing medical knowledge, with the patient bringing their values and knowledge of their lifestyle and what is important to them. The Supreme Court in *Montgomery v Lanarkshire Health Board* [2015] UKSC 11, para 81, said that the days of paternalism were past. Instead, patients were to be treated as adults who should be given the information they needed and helped to make decisions with the medical professionals. This required the doctors to inform patients of all suitable treatments and to be informed of the material risks of each. This requires disclosure of risks a reasonable patient would want to be told about and risks that the particular patient might reasonably want to know about.

Trust in modern medicine

Doctors and nurses have traditionally been regarded by the public as being the most trustworthy of all professions. Yet over past years, this trust has been tested to its limits as a series of scandals in the UK's health service have come to light.

The most extreme case is that of Harold Shipman, a GP who was discovered to have systematically killed around 250 of his patients, although the true figure will probably never be known. Dr Shipman was regarded by many of his patients as an exemplary and trustworthy doctor. The catastrophic betrayal of that trust, and the extensive media coverage of the case, during which the extent of Shipman's crimes began to emerge, struck horror into the British public.

There was also much publicity surrounding Mr Ian Patterson, a consultant surgeon who undertook unnecessary and dangerous procedures on many women after falsely telling them they needed surgery for cancer (ℜ http:// www.bbc.co.uk/news/uk-england-40815668). These cases are, of course, exceptional. However, they do highlight both the degree to which patients tend to trust their doctors, and the vulnerability that this entails for patients. One way of addressing this vulnerability is to emphasise on the importance of fully informed consent.

Introduction to consent

Introduction

A fundamental principle of medical law is that a patient with capacity cannot be given medical treatment without their consent. Even if a doctor believes that a particular treatment will benefit a patient or they will suffer serious harm without it, if the patient refuses to consent, the treatment cannot be provided. The Court of Appeal in *R (Burke) v GMC* [2005] 3 FCR 169 made that clear:

> Where a competent patient makes it clear that he does not wish to receive treatment which is, objectively, in his medical best interests, it is unlawful for doctors to administer that treatment. Personal autonomy or the right of the self-determination prevails.

A doctor who touches a patient, administers medication, or causes things to touch a patient's body without the consent of that patient could be committing the criminal offence of battery. They could also be committing a tort of battery and be liable to pay damages.

Forms of consent

There is no need for consent to be provided in writing. A verbal consent is sufficient, but for surgery it is common for signed consent to be obtained. This can ensure there is no dispute whether the patient consented to the procedure or not. The signed form can also list the dangers associated with the surgery and the fact the patient has signed will provide strong evidence that the patient was informed of the material risks. Where oral consent is relied upon, it is wise to make a note that oral consent was obtained.

Implicit consent

A doctor is entitled to rely on implied consent. For example, if a doctor shakes a patient's hand in greeting, or gives them a reassuring pat on the shoulder, this will not be a criminal offence, providing the touching is in line with 'everyday touching' such as is common between people. This is on the basis that consent to everyday touching can be implied. The courts in a case involving a police officer trying to get someone's attention held that a tap on the shoulder was not an offence, but grabbing someone's shoulder to turn them around was.

Implied consent can also be inferred from conduct. So, if a doctor said that an injection was necessary and a patient rolled up her sleeve, such behaviour may indicate a consent. Of course, it is normally preferable to obtain express consent, rather than rely on implied consent, in all but the most trivial of procedures.

Withdrawal of consent

A patient has the right to withdraw consent at any time. That might even be during a medical procedure. If a patient has capacity and withdraws consent, the doctor must cease treatment and, if appropriate, seek to acquire a new consent.

The nature of consent

For a patient to give valid consent it is not enough that the patient simply says 'yes'. The patient must give a valid consent which means:

- they have the necessary mental capacity
- they are sufficiently informed
- they are not subject to undue influence or coercion.

We shall look at each of these separately.

Consent and mental capacity

Mental capacity: the general test

The test for mental capacity is found under the Mental Capacity Act 2005. The Act sets down some key principles:

- A person is to be assumed to have capacity unless there is evidence she does not.
- If there is a dispute about mental capacity, it needs to be shown on the balance of probabilities (i.e. more likely than not) that a patient lacks capacity.
- Capacity is an 'issue-specific' matter. So patients are assessed on their abilities to make a particular decision. A person may be able to make a decision about what food to eat, even though they lack capacity to decide what should be in their will.
- Capacity is 'time specific'. So an assessment of capacity needs to be undertaken each time a patient is making a decision about capacity. Just because a patient lacks capacity on one day does not mean they necessarily will lack capacity the next day.
- All practical steps must be taken to enable a patient to make a decision. So if a doctor determines that a patient lacks capacity, they should consider whether there is anything that could be done to help a patient gain capacity. That might include, for example, using visual aids, using sign language, offering a translator, or asking a family member or IMCA to help explain the issue.
- It should not be assumed that merely because a decision is an unwise one that therefore a patient lacks capacity. The lack of wisdom of the decision can be used with other evidence to find capacity, but cannot be used on its own.
- Doctors must beware of the dangers of using discriminatory attitudes in assessing capacity. The Act specifically warns against making an assessment based on a person's age, appearance, or condition. For example, it should not be assumed that because a patient has dementia they therefore lack capacity to make any decisions.

These are important principles, but do not get to the heart of the question: what level of understanding does a person need in order to have capacity to decide an issue? This is found in section 2(1) of the Mental Capacity Act 2005:

> A person lacks capacity in relation to a matter if at the material time he is unable to make a decision for himself in relation to the matter because of an impairment of, or a disturbance in the functioning of, the mind or brain.

This test can be separated into two elements:
- The diagnostic test.
- The functional test.

Mental capacity: the diagnostic test

Under the diagnostic test, it must be shown that the person had an impairment or a disturbance in the functioning of the brain. A straightforward example of that would be a diagnosis of dementia or paranoia. It could also include learning difficulties. However, the law is not limited to impairments from medical conditions and could include an impairment caused by, for example, intoxication or concussion. It would not, however, cover a patient who is regarded as eccentric or who makes a decision based on unusual religious beliefs.

Mental capacity: the functional test

Under the functional test, it must be assessed whether as a result of that decision the individual is unable to make the decision. This is explained a little more under section 3(1):

'[A] person is unable to make a decision for himself if he is unable to do any one of the following—

- To understand the information relevant to the decision
- To retain that information
- To use or weigh that information as part of the process of making the decision, or
- To communication his decision (whether by talking, using sign language or other means).'

Each of these needs to be looked at in more detail.

What needs to be understood if a person has capacity?

Macur J in *LBL v RYJ* [2010] EWHC 2664 (Fam) has held that in order to have capacity it is not necessary for the patient to comprehend 'every detail of the issue ... all the peripheral details'. However, they need to understand the core issues. They need to understand in broad terms the nature of the procedure and its purpose. If, therefore, the patient does not realize (or accept) that they are ill, that may indicate a lack of capacity. Similarly, if they cannot understand the essential nature of the proposed treatment, that too would indicate a lack of capacity. However, a failure to understand some of the intricacies of the surgery would not lead to a lack of capacity.

Cases where a patient is actively deceived about a procedure are more likely to be found to be ones where the patient did not consent. In one case (*R v Tabassum* [2000] Ll Rep Med 404), women agreed to breast examinations on the understanding they were part of a research/education project, whereas in fact the defendant had asked the women for his own sexual purposes. It was found there was no consent because they had been misled as to the nature of the act.

Ability to retain the information

A patient who is able to understand the information but immediately forgets it will lack capacity. A medical professional seeking to rely on this ground for lack of capacity will need to be sure that there is no way of enabling the person to retain the information.

The ability to weigh the information

Not only must a patient be able to understand the information, they must be able to weigh the information to make a decision. One example of where this criterion may be relevant is a case of needle phobia, where a patient withdraws consent to treatment at the sight of the needle. Their panic on seeing the needle prevents them from weighing the information. A more controversial example may be a patient who has anorexia nervosa. In some cases, the courts have been persuaded that an 'obsessive fear of weight gain' prevents a patient from weighing up the advantages and disadvantages of treatment. That example, however, is subject to ongoing debate.

A patient's consent is valid even if it is given as a result of pressure. It is not uncommon for a patient to give consent to a procedure somewhat reluctantly, but realizing this is the best hope, given their prognosis. For pressure to invalidate consent it must in some sense be improper. Care must be taken if a medical professional is seeking to encourage a patient to consent to treatment the patient feels uncomfortable with. Particular care should be taken in cases where a patient is vulnerable to undue influence. Far more likely than a patient being improperly influenced by a medical professional is that a family member is exerting undue pressure on a patient in relation to a medical decision. In one case, a wife who refused to consent to continue her regime of contraceptive treatment was said to lack capacity as her husband dominated her completely.

Inability to communicate

A person who is able to make a decision but cannot communicate it will lack capacity. It will be very rare that this will arise, but it might apply to patients in a coma.

The link between the diagnostic and the functional test

Incapacity can only be found if the person's impairment or disturbance of the brain caused them to be unable to make the decision. It is possible to imagine a case where a patient fails to understand an important piece of information, but that is not a result of their mental disturbance. For example, if a patient with learning difficulties refused treatment because their religious beliefs led them to think that God would answer their prayers and so they did not need treatment, they might not lack capacity for the purposes of the Mental Capacity Act 2005. Their (arguable) lack of understanding of their situation was not a result of their mental impairment, but rather their religious beliefs.

Capacity and unwise decisions

A very important principle in the Mental Capacity Act is that:

> A patient is not to be treated as unable to make a decision merely because he makes an unwise decision. (Section 1(4))

Doctors must acknowledge that there is a real temptation to assume that because a patient is making a decision they believe to be foolish, the patient must therefore lack capacity. This is a temptation that should be resisted. However, the word 'merely' is important in this provision. If there is evidence that a patient is failing to understand the issues and they are making a foolish decision, then these two pieces of information together can be used to produce a finding of lack of capacity.

The limits of consent

It does not follow that any treatment given by a doctor is lawful as long as a patient consents. If a doctor provides utterly inappropriate treatment (e.g. prescribes unsuitable medication or performs an unnecessary operation), then that can be negligent, even though the patient consents. The patient has no right to demand any particular treatment and a doctor should only offer those treatments which a responsible body of medical opinion would think suitable. In *R v BM* [2018] EWCA Crim 560, a tattooist who removed a person's ear for 'cosmetic reasons' as part of body modification was convicted of a serious assault. He was not a trained medic and there was no medical reason for the procedure.

Ensuring patients are sufficiently informed

The legal significance of not properly obtaining consent

There are two possible legal consequences that can flow from the fact a patient is not sufficiently informed about the risks that attach to their treatment. If, as a result of the lack of information, the patient does not understand in broad terms the nature of the treatment, then they have not given effective consent and so any touching of them will be a criminal offence and/or a tort of battery. However, if the patient does understand in broad terms the nature of the treatment, a claim in the tort of negligence can still be brought if the patient was not told of the risks associated with the treatment.

Disclosure of material risks

The law requires that a doctor inform a patient of the 'material risks' associated with treatment. The leading authority is now *Montgomery v Lanarkshire Health Care* [2015] UKSC 11:

> The doctor is … under a duty to take reasonable care to ensure that the patient is aware of any material risks involved in any recommended treatment, and of any reasonable alternative or variant treatments. The test of materiality is whether, in the circumstances of the particular case, a reasonable person in the patient's position would be likely to attach significance to the risk, or the doctor is or should reasonably be aware that the particular patient would be likely to attach significance to it.

It should be noted that the doctor should consider not only whether a reasonable patient in the patient's position would think the information significant, but also whether this particular patient would see it as significant. In that case, the failure to disclose to the patient the risk of shoulder dystocia and related complications to her child if she proceeded with a vaginal delivery was found to be negligent.

When thinking about this duty it may be helpful to separate out two questions:

- What are the risks that any reasonable patient might attach significance to?
- What are the risks that this particular patient might attach significance to?

Answering the second question will require the doctor to find out from the patient what is important in their life, what they enjoy spending their time doing, and what they are hoping to be able to do after the operation. They can then determine if there are risks that are particularly relevant to the patient.

Although non-material risks do not need to be disclosed, if a patient asks about particular risks, they must, of course, be disclosed, whether minor or not. So, if a musician asks about risks which may affect their performance, they should be told of all such risks.

The 'therapeutic exception'

Lord Steyn in *Chester v Afshar* [2004] UKHL 41, para 16 has accepted that in 'wholly exceptional' cases it may be in the patient's best interests not to tell them of a material risk. That would be where, in the words of Lords Kerr and Reid in *Montgomery v Lanarkshire Health Care* [2015] UKSC 11 it 'would be seriously detrimental to the patient's health' to disclose the risk. An example might be where the disclosure of the risk would induce a serious panic attack. The therapeutic exception cannot be relied upon simply on the basis that if the risk were disclosed the patient would refuse to consent to the treatment.

The form of the disclosure

Not only must the doctor disclose the risk, they must also make sure the patient understands the risk. So, disclosing risks at great speed will not be adequate. Lords Kerr and Reid in *Montgomery v Lanarkshire Health Care* [2015] UKSC 11 explained: 'The doctor's duty is not … fulfilled by bombarding the patient with technical information which she cannot reasonably be expected to grasp.' Providing a written summary of the risks may be appropriate in some cases.

The difficulties of succeeding in a negligence claim based on non-disclosure of risk

A patient who seeks to bring a negligence action based on a failure to disclose a risk faces an uphill challenge. First, they need to prove that the material risk was not disclosed to them. Second, they need to show that they have suffered a loss. This is important because if a doctor fails to disclose a risk but then goes on to perform a successful operation, it will be hard to show that the patient was worse off as a result of the negligence. Therefore, it is very unlikely they will be awarded any damages. Third, if they can show a loss (e.g. the operation goes wrong and leaves them in a worse position than they were before), they need to show the failure to disclose the risk caused that loss. To do that they need to show they would not have consented to the operation if they had been told of the risk (or, perhaps, would have had the operation at a different time). Where the patient is seriously ill or in pain, that may be very difficult to prove (see also ➲ p. 156).

The treatment of patients who cannot consent

If an adult patient lacks capacity, then decisions can be made on their behalf under the Mental Capacity Act 2005. It should be recalled that the law presumes people to have capacity and so the Act should only be used if the patient is shown to lack capacity.

If a patient lacks capacity, then the following questions should be asked:

- Has the patient created an effective advance decision (sometimes called a living will)? If so, the decision must be respected if it is a refusal of treatment.
- Has the patient created an effective lasting power of attorney (LPA)? If so, the person named in the LPA ('the donee') has the authority to make the decision.
- Has the court appointed a deputy? In which case the deputy must make the decision.
- If there is no advance decision, LPA, or deputy then a decision can be made by a medical professional or family member based on what is in the patient's best interests.

Each of these kinds of cases will be explored in more detail in the following sections..

Advance decisions

When is an advance decision effective?

For someone (P) to make an advance decision, the following must be shown:

- P was over 18 when the advance decision was made.
- P had mental capacity when the advance decision was made.
- The decision specifies treatments is not to be given. A request to be given particular treatment is not binding on medical professionals, but can be taken into account in deciding whether to provide a treatment.
- P lacks capacity at the time a decision is to be made. An advance decision has no effect if P currently has capacity.
- If the advance decision rejects life-saving treatment it must be signed by P and witnessed by a third party. If the decision does not concern life-saving treatment then it need not be signed.

An advance decision can cease to be effective if any of the following apply:

- P has, with capacity, withdrawn the advance decision. A withdrawal can be done orally or in writing.
- After making an advance decision, P has created an LPA. It will then be assumed that P wants his or her LPA to be respected rather than the advance decision.
- If P has acted in a way clearly inconsistent with the decision, then it does not apply. In *HE v A Hospital NHS Trust* [2003] EWHC 1017 (Fam), while a Jehovah's Witness, a woman had signed an advance decision refusing blood transfusions, but later married a Muslim man and stopped attending her church. This was taken to be behaviour inconsistent with the advance decision and so a blood transfusion could be given to her.
- If 'there are reasonable grounds for believing that circumstances exist which P did not anticipate at the time of the advance decision, and which would have affected his decision had he anticipated them' (section 25(4) Mental Capacity Act 2005). This may be relevant if there have been medical advances in treatment which were not known about at the time the advance decision was made. Possibly, it might be used in a case where a family strongly objects to the advance decision being followed and the doctor believes that had P known the family would object, they would not have wanted the advance decision to apply.

The trickiest issue can be a medical professional having to decide whether the advance decision was meant to apply to a particular situation. This might arise particularly in cases where the advance decision had not been drafted with the benefit of medical advice. If, for example, the advance decision says that P should not receive treatment if they are 'a vegetable', it might be difficult to know precisely what that term meant. Some comfort may be found in section 26(2):

> A person does not incur liability for carrying out or continuing the treatment unless, at the time, he is satisfied that an advance decision exists which is valid and applicable to a treatment.

There is a similar provision giving protection from legal liability to a person who incorrectly believes they must follow an advance decision. It is worth noting this provision does not require the medical professional to have a reasonable belief. It is enough that they are complying with or disregarding what they genuinely believe to be an advance decision.

Ethical issues and advance decisions

There is a lively debate among ethicists over the use of advance decisions. Supporters of advance decisions claim that it is an important aspect of the principle of autonomy that a person can set down what should happen to them if they lose capacity. It can be argued that if a person has lost capacity, then someone has to make decisions on their behalf and it is better for that someone to be the individual themselves when they had capacity, than a medical professional, court, or family member. Ronald Dworkin has argued that people have 'critical interests': key values which form the basis of a person's values and that these continue even when a person has lost capacity. If, therefore, they regard it to be undignified to suffer severe dementia, they should be allowed to refuse such treatment if that condition befalls them.

On the other side of the argument, there are those who claim that a person who has lost capacity no longer has a connection with the person who wrote the advance decision. It is as if they have become a new person. The values and principles which used to matter to them no longer have relevance. Those who take this view tend to argue that the advance decision should carry little or no weight. Instead, the decision should be made based on what is in the best interests of the person they current are.

Some commentators have proposed a middle view, arguing that advance decisions should carry some weight, but so too should the individual's current interests. Supporters of such a view might suggest that an advance decision should be followed but not if it causes the current person significant or serious harm.

Lasting powers of attorney

If P wants a particular person to make decisions on their behalf if they lose capacity, then P can make an LPA. Commonly, a spouse, partner, or close friend is appointed the LPA. There are two kinds of LPAs: ones that deal with property and finance issues, and ones that deal with health and welfare issues only. The same person can be asked to do both roles. It is possible to appoint more than one LPA if someone wishes. If that happens, then that person is the one who makes the decision for P when P loses capacity. An LPA is only effective if executed by P when over the age of 18 and having capacity. The LPA must be registered at the Court of Protection to be effective. If the LPA is seeking to make a medical treatment, it is important to check they have been registered as an LPS to make health and welfare decisions (and not only financial decisions).

If an LPA is appointed, they are the ones who can make decisions over treatment. If they refuse to consent to treatment, this refusal must be respected and can only be overridden if a court order is obtained. If an LPA requests treatment, the medical professional is not obliged to provide it but may do so if they think that is appropriate. If the refusal of treatment will lead to death, then the LPA must specifically state that the attorney can make a decision to refuse life-sustaining treatment.

Deputy

If a person lacks capacity and there is a need to have decisions made on their behalf at a regular interval then a court can appoint a deputy. This is normally done in cases where there is a dispute between family members over who should be making the decisions on behalf of a relative. The court is not likely to appoint a deputy in order to resolve a single issue. If a deputy is appointed, they have the authority to make financial decisions, but any health issues should be referred to the Court of Protection.

Decisions that cannot be made on behalf of a person without capacity

Section 27 of the Mental Capacity Act lists decisions which cannot be made on behalf of a person lacking capacity. These are:
- consent to marriage or enter a civil partnership
- consent to have sexual relations
- consent to a decree of divorce or dissolution of a civil partnership
- consent to a child being adopted
- the discharge of parental responsibility decisions
- giving consent to the use of gametes in assisted reproductive treatment under the Human Fertilisation and Embryology Acts 1990 and 2008.

The Mental Capacity Act 2005 introduced the role of the independent mental capacity advocate (IMCA). IMCAs are a legal safeguard for people who lack the capacity to make specific important decisions, including making decisions about where they live and about serious medical treatment options. They are used particularly where someone lacks capacity but does not have family members who can represent their interests or assist them in making decisions.

The best interests assessments

If a medical professional is making a decision on behalf of a patient who lacks capacity, they should make that decision based on what is in the best interests of a person lacking capacity. The Code of Practice offers some helpful guidance:

> When working out what is in the best interests of the person who lacks capacity to make a decision or act for themselves, decision makers must take into account all relevant factors that it would be reasonable to consider, not just those that they think are important. They must not act or make a decision based on what they would want to do if they were the person who lacked capacity.

The medical professional should remember that if the person is likely to re-gain their capacity, then, if possible, a decision should be delayed until they have the capacity to make the decision. This is particularly relevant in cases of patients who have a fluctuating capacity.

The Mental Capacity Act 2005 lists a number of factors that can be con-sidered when deciding what is in the person (P)'s best interests:

P's current views

Even if P lacks capacity, P's current feelings and wishes should be taken into account and they should be encouraged to participate in the decision-making process. This is certainly not to say the views of a person lacking capacity must be followed. However, they are a factor to be taken into account. Where two courses of action are equally good and P strongly prefers one, that would tip the scales in favour of that option. In one case, it was suggested that the closer P is to having capacity, the more weight will attach to their views. Where P feels very strongly about the decision and is likely to resist a certain form of treatment then that will be a strong factor against finding it to be in their best interests.

P's past views

When deciding what is in P's interests, the decision maker can take into account P's past wishes and feelings and any written statement (whether it is a binding advance decision or not). They can also take into account 'the beliefs and values that would be likely to influence his decision if he had capacity' and 'any other factors that he would be likely to consider if he were able to do so'. This requires the decision maker to look at the issue in the way the patient would look at it. As Baroness Hale in *Aintree v James* [2013] UKSC 67 put it:

> [I]n considering the best interests of this particular patient at this particular time, decision-makers must look at his welfare in the widest sense, not just medical but social and psychological; they must consider the nature of the medical treatment in question, what it involves and its prospects of success; they must consider what the outcome of that treatment for the patient is likely to be; they must try and put themselves in the places of the individual patient and ask what his attitude to the treatment is or would be likely to be; and they must consult others who are looking after him or interested in his welfare, in particular for their view of what his attitude would be.

A good application of this approach was *Ahsan v University Hospitals Leicester* [2006] EWHC 2624 (QB) where it was held that a devout Muslim woman who had lost capacity would want to be cared for in a way compatible with her religious and cultural beliefs. The fact she was unaware of how she was being treated did not matter. If P had a close relationship with a spouse, partner, or friend it might be thought P would want their interests to be considered too.

The views of P's relatives and carers on P's best interests

The view of P's relatives or 'anyone engaged in caring for the person or interested in his welfare' on what is in P's best interests can be taken into account. Note that relatives do not have the automatic right to make decisions about P, unless they have an LPA or have been appointed a deputy. Their views are to be taken into account, but are not binding. It should be emphasized that the interests of the relatives themselves are not to be taken into account, only their views on what is in P's best interests. If the relatives and medical professionals cannot agree on what is in P's best interests, it may be necessary to seek a court declaration.

The use of restraint or force

Where a person lacks capacity and there is a decision in P's best interests which requires that P be detained or have force used against him, then there are extra rules which must be complied with. These are known as the Liberty Protection Safeguards (LPS). These were introduced in the Mental Capacity Amendment Act 2019 and replace the old Deprivation of Liberty Safeguards (DoLS).

The meaning of force or restraint

The definition of the use of force is relatively straightforward. The Code of Practice produced the following non-exhaustive list of factors which would indicate whether someone is deprived of their liberty:

- Restraint is used, including sedation, to admit a person to an institution where that person is resisting admission.
- Staff exercise complete and effective control over the care and movement of a person for a significant period.
- Staff exercise control over assessments, treatment, contacts, and residence.
- A decision has been taken by the institution that the person will not be released into the care of others, or permitted to live elsewhere, unless the staff in the institution consider it appropriate.
- A request by carers for a person to be discharged to their care is refused.
- The person is unable to maintain social contacts because of restrictions placed on their access to other people.
- The person loses autonomy because they are under continuous supervision and control.

Where someone is deprived of their liberty, this breaches their rights under article 5 of the ECHR and so must be justified under the LPS.

A person will not be deprived of their liberty if the interference is a 'commonly occurring restriction on movement'. Arden LJ in *R (Ferreira) v HM Coroner for Inner London South* [2017] explained:

> The Strasbourg Court in Austin has specifically excepted from Article 5(1) the category of interference described as 'commonly occurring restrictions on movement'. In my judgment, any deprivation of liberty resulting from the administration of life-saving treatment to a person falls within this category. It is as I see it 'commonly occurring' because it is a well-known consequence of a person's condition, when such treatment is required, that decisions may have to be made which interfere with or even remove the liberty she would have been able to exercise for herself before the condition emerged. Plainly the 'commonly occurring restrictions on movement', which include ordinary experiences such as 'travel by public transport or on the motorway, or attendance at a football match', can apply to a person of unsound mind as well as to a person of sound mind.

Who decides if the Liberty Protection Safeguards are satisfied?

The 'responsible body' must decide if the LPS are satisfied. In outline, that is as follows:

- If the care is taking place mainly in an NHS hospital, then the responsible body is the 'hospital manager'.

- If the care is taking place in a non-NHS hospital, then the responsible body is the 'responsible local authority' in England or the local health board in Wales.
- If the care is carried out mainly through the provision of NHS continuing healthcare, the responsible body is the relevant clinical commissioning group in England or local health board in Wales.
- In other cases, the responsible body is the 'responsible local authority' (usually the authority that is meeting the person's needs or in whose area the person is ordinarily resident).

The Liberty Protection Safeguards requirements

The responsible body can authorize arrangements if the 'authorization conditions' are met. These are that:
- P lacks capacity to consent to the arrangements
- P has a mental disorder within the meaning of section 1(2) of the Mental Health Act 1983
- the arrangements are necessary to prevent harm to P and proportionate in relation to the likelihood and seriousness of harm to P.

Before authorizing the arrangements, there must be consultation with the following people in order to determine P's wishes and feelings:
- P.
- Anyone named by P as someone to be consulted.
- Anyone engaged in caring for P or interested in P's welfare.
- Any donee of a LPA or an enduring power of attorney.
- Any deputy appointed by the Court of Protection.
- Any appropriate person and any independent mental capacity advocate.

Before it can authorize arrangements, the responsible body must also:
- be satisfied that any duty to appoint an appropriate person or independent mental capacity advocate has been complied with
- have arranged a pre-authorization review which has been completed.

The pre-authorization review

If the responsible body believes the LPS are satisfied, there still needs to be a review by an independent person who is not involved in P's day-to-day care or treatment. That must be by an approved mental capacity professional (AMCP) or other approved professional (although the guidance on this is not at the time of writing available).

The AMCP must:
- meet with the person and consult all those listed previously as requiring consultation (if it is appropriate and practicable to do so)
- review the information and determine whether the authorization conditions are met.

Only once the AMCP (or authorized professional) has determined that the authorization conditions are met can the responsible body authorize the deprivation of liberty.

The effect of an authorization

The authorization can take effect immediately or be put into effect for up to 28 days later. The technical impact of the authorization is that it provides those carrying out the deprivation of liberty with a legal defence to any legal liability.

An authorization can last up to 12 months and can be renewed every 12 months up to a period of 3 years. Longer-term renewals are possible if P has a long-term condition. The responsible body can determine at any time that an authorization should come to an end if the authorization conditions are no longer met (e.g. P has regained capacity). In order to approve a renewal, the responsibly body must determine that:

• the authorization conditions continue to be met
• it is unlikely that there will be any significant change in the person's condition during the renewal period which would affect whether those conditions are met.

It must also perform the same consultation exercise it used for making the original authorization.

The responsible body must conduct a review in any of the following circumstances:

• Before an authorization is varied, or if that is not practicable or appropriate, as soon as practicable afterwards.
• If a reasonable request is made by a person with an interest in the arrangements.
• If the person becomes subject to mental health arrangements or requirements.
• If (in any other case) there has been a significant change in the person's condition or circumstances.

If P objects to the use of the LPS they can apply to the Court of Protection.

Consent and children

Introduction

A child is treated as a person under the age of 18. Treating a child without consent or legal authorization can be a criminal offence or a tort.

Children aged 16 or 17

The Family Law Reform Act 1969, section 8, deals with children aged 16 or 17. They are able to consent to 'treatment' for medical conditions, including diagnosis and procedures ancillary to treatment. It is generally thought that the section does not apply to non-therapeutic cosmetic surgery or organ donation. For non-therapeutic procedures, a court declaration that the procedure is in the child's best interests would be required. In Scotland, the age of consent is 16 (Age of Legal Capacity (Scotland) Act 1991).

Children aged under 16: consent

Children under 16 years old can consent to medical treatment if they are 'Gillick competent'. This phrase (following the leading case of *Gillick v West Norfolk Area Health Authority* [1985] 3 All ER 402) refers to a child who has sufficient maturity and understanding to make the decision. To be 'Gillick competent' the child must have 'sufficient understanding and intelligence to enable him or her to understand fully what is proposed'. This includes not only the medical issues, but also the 'moral and family issues'. In deciding whether a child is 'Gillick competent', the focus should be on the procedure at hand. A child may have capacity to consent to straightforward medical issues, but not more complex ones.

If the child is not 'Gillick competent' then consent can be provided by adults with parental responsibility. Parental responsibility is granted to all mothers (the woman who gave birth to the child). A father will have parental responsibility if he is married to the mother; is registered as the father of the child on the child's birth certificate; has entered a parental responsibility agreement with the mother and registered it at a court; or has obtained a parental responsibility order from the court.

Children aged under 16: refusal

What if a child under the age of 16 refuses to consent? The courts have made it clear that if a child refuses to consent to treatment, a person with parental responsibility can still provide consent to the treatment if the doctor has decided that the treatment will promote the child's welfare. Of course, in deciding whether the treatment will promote the child's welfare, the fact the child is refusing to consent is an important factor. A doctor is only likely to believe that it will promote a child's welfare to force medical treatment upon them if the child is facing death or a serious harm without the treatment.

Court orders

If both the child and parents are refusing to consent to surgery, the hospital should obtain a court order to authorize consent. The court will make an order based on what is in the best interests of the child. A doctor should not proceed without the consent of the child or parent or court order, unless the defence of necessity applies.

The defence of necessity

If there is no time to obtain the consent of the competent child or the parent with parental responsibility or a court order, then the doctor can only proceed if there is an emergency situation and there is no opportunity to obtain consent.

Ethical issues

Many ethicists are strongly critical of the approach taken by the courts in relation to consent and children. They believe that once it is decided that a child has the intellectual and moral capacities of an adult, there is no good reason not to treat them as an adult. Therefore, a competent child who refuses to consent to treatment should be respected just as for an adult.

As it is, it seems the law shows respect for the decision of a child if they are consenting to treatment, but the decision can be overridden if the child is disagreeing with the medical professionals. Supporters of the approach taken by the courts will say it is designed to ensure that children receive the treatment they ought to get. If the parent refuses to consent to the treatment, the competent child should be able to provide the legal authorization.

Conscience and conscientious objection

What is conscience?

The word 'conscience' comes from the Latin 'with knowledge'. Conscience in modern usage has a specifically moral flavour. It is generally understood to refer to an innate feeling about what is right and wrong. A sense of discomfort or 'pricking' of the conscience may alert the individual to the fact that a moral boundary is being breached. Conscience is thus a sort of internal moral monitor.

Conflicts can arise between accepted ethical protocols, social structures, and individuals' consciences. One of the difficult aspects of morality is knowing when to act on one's conscience, and when to abide by other ethical frameworks and practices. For instance, one may feel that it's important to show loyalty or solidarity with colleagues. But if a colleague is endangering patients, one's conscience might be 'pricked'.

Conscientious objection in medical practice

There are debates as to whether and how much individuals' consciences ought to be accommodated in medicine and other areas. On the one hand, allowing for 'conscientious objection' means that we acknowledge that people have different values. However, because of the intrinsically individual and private nature of conscientious objection, one may fear that it could be abused, allowing people free rein to express prejudices or whimsical beliefs. Where the holder of such beliefs is in a position of power, as doctors are, the freedom to act on individual moral principles, rather than those accepted by the profession, or by society, may mean that some groups of patients are systematically disadvantaged.

The psychological power of conscience

Psychologically, we tend to feel that what our conscience tells us is *necessarily* right, without further question. It would be nice to think that our conscience really taps into an absolute, universal moral truth, and that everyone's conscience is telling them the same thing. But people have radically different and often contradictory moral reactions to practices such as abortion and euthanasia. And those on both sides of the debate frequently describe their position as being informed by their conscience. This seems to suggest that at least some people's consciences are in fact wrong.

The variability of conscience

Conscience may be wrong—or may at least be regarded as wrong by others, even though it may seem utterly compelling to the individual. Not only this, but individuals may change their views over time. Actions that were undertaken based on the dictates of conscience may over the years appear to be straightforwardly wrong, even to the person who performed them. Conscience is thus an *unstable* basis for moral decision-making.

This raises the question of how far, if at all, we should accommodate the consciences of individual doctors in medical practice. Suppose a doctor's conscience tells them that abortion is equivalent to murder. Should they be allowed to practise despite the fact that abortion is legal in England, Scotland, and Wales? Would such a doctor's patients be disadvantaged?

Many people accept the idea that doctors should not be legally obliged to carry out abortions if they have a conscientious objection to doing so. The law makes provision for this, and merely requires that such doctors ensure that patients are not disadvantaged, by referring them to other colleagues. However, this raises some tricky questions. If one really feels that abortion is murder, then referring the patient to someone who will perform it is facilitating a murder.

Conscience and abortion

There is specific provision in the Abortion Act 1967, section 4, which means that a person with a conscientious objection to abortion is not under a legal duty to participate in an abortion. However, that does not apply if the abortion is necessary to save the life or prevent permanent injury to the physical or mental health of a pregnant woman.

The provision only applies to participation in relation to the abortion itself and does not apply to care of a patient prior to an abortion or the aftercare of a patient. Nor does it apply to administrative and managerial tasks associated with an abortion (*Greater Glasgow Health Board v Doogan* [2014] UKSC 68). Where the conscientious objection applies, the medical professional should refer the patient to a professional who has no such objections.

Additional reading

Department of Health. Safeguarding Patients: The Government's Response to the Recommendations of the Shipman Inquiry's Fifth Report and to the Recommendations of the Ayling, Neale and Kerr/Haslam Inquiries. 2007. London: The Stationery Office. Available at: ℛ http://www.official-documents.gov.uk/document/cm70/7015/7015.pdf.

Issues in death and dying

End of life care *178*
Euthanasia *180*
Assisted suicide *182*
Human rights and assisted dying *184*
Withdrawing/withholding treatment *186*
Debates over euthanasia *190*
Organ transplantation *192*
Living donors *196*
Donors who lack capacity *198*
Selling organs *198*
Non-life-saving transplants *199*

End of life care

Introduction

Death is inevitable, but this is not always a comfortable truth for society, patients, or the medical profession. It is part of our duty as doctors to care for patients along their whole life's journey and we must maintain the same standards of care at the end, as at the beginning. We must act with integrity and honesty and not shy away from difficult issues. We must strive to ensure that *all* of the patient's needs are addressed, psychological and spiritual as well as physical, in order that they might die at peace and with dignity. The GMC has issued very helpful guidance about the care of those at the end of life in its document, 'Treatment and care towards the end of life: good practice in decision making'.

Patients with capacity

When making decisions about ongoing treatment and resuscitation with someone who has capacity, the doctor's duty is to explain to the patient their options in a clear and honest manner. The doctor may advise, but must not put undue pressure on a patient to pursue a particular course of action. If an adult has capacity, no one else may give consent on their behalf. A patient with capacity has an absolute right to refuse to consent to treatment, even if without it they will die.

A patient with capacity might make decisions about his care that seem unwise to the medical team, for example, he might refuse surgery for a curable cancer. If a decision seems bizarre, it is acceptable to explore sensitively the reasoning behind it; however, the patient retains the right to control what happens to his body, and his decisions must be respected and acted upon, even if they are not rational or understood. Although adults with capacity may refuse treatment, no patient may demand treatment that the doctor does not deem to be in his best interests.

Patients lacking capacity

Before losing capacity, a patient may entrust LPA to another who is then authorized to make decisions on his behalf when his capacity is diminished. The attorney must have been granted specifically the power to make medical decisions. The attorney must make decisions in the patient's best interests and not simply make substituted judgements.

Efforts should also be made to discover if the patient has made any advance decisions about their end of life care. These decisions may be recorded in legally drawn up documents or take the form of conversations recorded in the hospital notes. It is good practice to get the patient to countersign the transcript of any conversation where significant decisions are made during an admission.

As stated previously, advance requests *for* treatment are not legally binding, although they help gain an insight into the patient's wishes and so will be given weight when deciding how to proceed in their best interests. A valid advance *refusal* of treatment is legally binding and must be respected. The position on advance decisions was discussed previously in Chapter 17 (➜ p. 160).

When decisions about significant medical treatment are being made for a patient who lacks capacity and has no one to support or represent them, the responsible doctor should approach their employing organization about appointing an IMCA, a requirement of the Mental Capacity Act 2005. The IMCA will gather information about the patient and subsequently represent their interests, but cannot actually make decisions on their behalf.

The patient who 'doesn't want to know'

If a patient does not wish to know the facts surrounding their illness or condition, sensitive attempts should be made to find out why. The patient's worries should be addressed but if all attempts to help them engage in conversation fail, their wishes must be respected. No one else may give consent to treatment or investigation on their behalf while they retain capacity, even at the patient's request.

For consent to be legally valid, it must be 'informed', and so this leaves the medical team in a difficult position should they wish to proceed to investigation and treatment as, technically, they are committing assault because the patient's consent is not truly valid. This dilemma should be explained to the patient. Most doctors would agree that they would proceed, pragmatically. Without bullying or coercion, the patient's decision to remain ignorant should be revisited regularly. All discussion should be recorded in the notes.

Discussions with family members

Families often have complicated dynamics. If a patient has capacity, they must give their permission before information about them can be discussed with anyone else. In the case of those who lack capacity, it is reasonable to assume that they would want those closest to them to be kept informed of their condition.

Conflict resolution

Honest, sensitive, and open communication with patient and relatives is the key to reaching a consensus about treatment. Trust is built by doctors admitting to uncertainty when it exists, managing expectations with compassion, and delivering a consistent message. Unfortunately, disagreements may still occur. It is usually possible to resolve these by involving a senior colleague, obtaining a second opinion, further discussion with all invested parties, or making use of local mediation services. If the conflict is unresolvable, it may be necessary to approach the courts for an independent ruling.

A doctor may withdraw from caring for a patient if they object to the decisions made about their care, for example, a Jehovah's Witness refusing a life-saving blood transfusion, but they must not do so until they have passed the responsibility of care on to another doctor who has willingly accepted.

Euthanasia

The meaning of euthanasia

The word *euthanasia* is derived from the Greek words, *eu* meaning good and *thanatos* meaning death. The word is often misused to describe an act that would be more accurately termed as 'mercy killing'—when somebody performs a deliberate act aimed at shortening life, motivated by compassion and the desire to alleviate suffering.

Types of euthanasia

There are several types of 'euthanasia' discussed in the literature:
* *Active* euthanasia: a positive act is performed, designed to bring about the death of a person who is suffering (e.g. a lethal injection).
* *Passive* euthanasia: no definitive act is performed, but treatment is withheld or withdrawn from the suffering patient with the intention that this will hasten their death.
* Euthanasia is *voluntary* when the sufferer has requested that their life is ended.
* Euthanasia is *non-voluntary* when the patient is unable or incompetent to request their life to be ended. Instead, a proxy, who considers death to be in their best interests, makes the decision for them.
* Euthanasia is *involuntary* when a patient does not want their life to be ended, but their wishes are disregarded. This term is rather an oxymoron; murder might be more accurate.

The legal definition of death

In *Airedale NHS Trust v Bland* [1993] 1 All ER 821, Lords Browne-Wilkinson, Goff, and Keith accepted that brainstem death was the definition of death for the purposes of medicine and law. Tony Bland, although suffering from a persistent vegetative state (PVS), was not brainstem dead and so was still alive. This was confirmed in *Re A (A Child)* [2015] EWHC 443 (Fam), where Heydon J seemed to accept that the law would follow the accepted medical approach. However, he emphasized that doctors should take into account particular religious views that differed from the legal approach.

Ethical debates over the definition of death

Debates over the definition of death tend to reflect debates about the value of life. For those who believe that the value in life is found in thoughts, beliefs, and mental awareness, then it is not surprising that brainstem death seems to be the natural definition of death. When there is no brain activity, there is nothing of value left in life. However, others see the value in life as beyond the brain and they may prefer the ending of the beating of the heart as indicating that the body has ceased to function as a biological whole.

The law concerning killing

There is no statute in British law defining murder. Instead, the criminal justice system that deals with killing has evolved through common law. 'Killing' is a morally neutral term which is defined as 'causing the death of', whereas premeditated unlawful killing, or 'murder', is heavy with moral implication. Murder is the most serious form of homicide, and conviction carries a mandatory sentence of 'life' imprisonment.

No form of euthanasia is permissible in British law and active euthanasia, often dubbed 'mercy killing' by the popular press, simply constitutes murder in the eyes of the law.

> '[M]ercy' killing by active means is murder ... that the doctor's motives are kindly will for some ... transform the moral quality of his act, but this makes no difference in law.
>
> Lord Mustill in Airedale N.H.S. Trust v Bland [1993] A.C. 789, 803.

Many doctors have come forward to the police or media over the years and admitted to deliberately hastening the deaths of one or more of their patients, but none of them has been convicted. Those who have subsequently appeared in court have used the 'doctrine of double effect' as a successful defence.

The doctrine of double effect

This doctrine was confirmed as part of the law by Devlin J in 1957 in the case of *R v Adams* [6]. A double effect occurs when a drug, usually an opiate, is given with the aim of relieving suffering even with the knowledge that administration of that drug may shorten the patient's life. The intention behind the action is to relieve suffering and the shortening of life is an unintentional, and therefore morally acceptable, side effect. This argument will only succeed where the substance administered does have pain-relieving effects. Where its sole effect is to kill the patient, the argument is unlikely to succeed.

Assisted suicide

While committing suicide is no longer illegal, assisting or encouraging someone else's attempt is unlawful, and carries a maximum sentence of 14 years' imprisonment. This is not the case throughout Europe, and in the Netherlands and Switzerland, voluntary euthanasia is legal. This has led to the emergence of 'death tourism' with people travelling from the UK to the assisted-suicide clinic 'Dignitas' in Switzerland, to end their lives.

The legal position on assisted suicide in Britain has raised ethical problems: a person may take their own life only if they have the means to do so independently. If they have the mental capacity to choose to end their lives, but not the physical ability to act on their choice, what then? Then, anybody who helps them carry out their wishes faces criminal prosecution.

However, the Director of Public Prosecutions has issued a Code of Practice for prosecutors to use in deciding whether or not to prosecute someone who has assisted or encouraged the suicide of others. This includes a list of 16 factors which would indicate that prosecution was suitable:

1. '[T]he victim was under 18 years of age;
2. the victim did not have the capacity (as defined by the Mental Capacity Act 2005) to reach an informed decision to commit suicide;
3. the victim had not reached a voluntary, clear, settled and informed decision to commit suicide;
4. the victim had not clearly and unequivocally communicated his or her decision to commit suicide to the suspect;
5. the victim did not seek the encouragement or assistance of the suspect personally or on his or her own initiative;
6. the suspect was not wholly motivated by compassion; for example, the suspect was motivated by the prospect that he or she or a person closely connected to him or her stood to gain in some way from the death of the victim;
7. the suspect pressured the victim to commit suicide;
8. the suspect did not take reasonable steps to ensure that any other person had not pressured the victim to commit suicide;
9. the suspect had a history of violence or abuse against the victim;
10. the victim was physically able to undertake the act that constituted the assistance him or herself;
11. the suspect was unknown to the victim and encouraged or assisted the victim to commit or attempt to commit suicide by providing specific information via, for example, a website or publication;
12. the suspect gave encouragement or assistance to more than one victim who were not known to each other;
13. the suspect was paid by the victim or those close to the victim for his or her encouragement or assistance;
14. the suspect was acting in his or her capacity as a medical doctor, nurse, other healthcare professional, a professional carer [whether for payment or not], or as a person in authority, such as a prison officer, and the victim was in his or her care;
15. the suspect was aware that the victim intended to commit suicide in a public place where it was reasonable to think that members of the public may be present;

16. the suspect was acting in his or her capacity as a person involved in the management or as an employee (whether for payment or not) of an organisation or group, a purpose of which is to provide a physical environment (whether for payment or not) in which to allow another to commit suicide.'

And a list of six factors which would indicate a prosecution was unsuitable:

1. '[T]he victim had reached a voluntary, clear, settled and informed decision to commit suicide;
2. the suspect was wholly motivated by compassion;
3. the actions of the suspect, although sufficient to come within the definition of the offence, were of only minor encouragement or assistance;
4. the suspect had sought to dissuade the victim from taking the course of action which resulted in his or her suicide;
5. the actions of the suspect may be characterised as reluctant encouragement or assistance in the face of a determined wish on the part of the victim to commit suicide;
6. the suspect reported the victim's suicide to the police and fully assisted them in their enquiries into the circumstances of the suicide or the attempt and his or her part in providing encouragement or assistance.'

From 1 April 2009 up to 31 January 2019, there have been 148 cases referred to the Crown Prosecution Service by the police, but in only 20 were there prosecutions and in three, convictions. The convictions tend to be in cases where a vulnerable person has been manipulated into attempting to commit suicide.

The guidance applies to assisted suicide and not euthanasia. It would be very rare for someone who actually kills another (even at their request) not to face prosecution. Frances Inglis was sentenced to 9 years imprisonment in 2010 after administering a lethal injection to her comatose son. The judge accepted that she acted out of love, but since her son was unconscious and not able to indicate his wishes, it was impossible for the judge not to find her guilty of murder.

Human rights and assisted dying

Many see the current law as fundamentally wrong. Articles 2, 3, 8, 9, and 14 of the ECHR have been employed by those claiming the right to assistance in suicide. So far, these challenges have been unsuccessful. The ECtHR is clear that there is a right under article 8 to decide the time and manner of one's death, but that right can be interfered with, if necessary, to protect the rights of others. The current UK law has been accepted as an appropriate balancing of the rights to protect people's freedom to commit suicide and the protection of vulnerable people being manipulated or bullied into ending their lives. However, the European Court has made it clear that the balance stuck by English law is permitted, but not required. The European Court has also upheld the Swiss law which, with safeguards, permits assisted euthanasia.

The Supreme Court in *R (Nicklinson) v Ministry of Justice* [2014] UKSC 38 and the Court of Appeal in *R (Conway) v Ministry of Justice* [2018] EWCA Civ 1431 have indicated that at the moment, they think any decision about whether the law on assisted dying should be reformed is best left to Parliament, rather than being changed by the courts. However, they have left open the possibility that in the future they might change the law to comply with human rights requirements.

Withdrawing/withholding treatment

While active euthanasia is unlawful, it is accepted that doctors may withhold or withdraw life-sustaining therapy from a patient if receiving it is not in their best interests. If the patient has capacity, this decision is theirs and it would be unlawful for a doctor to give them life-sustaining treatment to which they have objected. If the patient lacks capacity to consent, a best interests assessment is made. This is discussed in the section 'End of life care' (→ p. 178).

Persistent vegetative state

With today's technology, it is possible to sustain life, even when all hope of recovery is gone. Once such special situation is PVS, where the patient loses all higher cortical functions but the brainstem functions persist, allowing the patient to breathe independently. If patients in this state are provided with clinically assisted nutrition and hydration (CANH) they may survive indefinitely.

Whether something as basic as feeding should be considered a treatment, was clarified in the case of Anthony Bland, a 17-year-old who suffered irreversible brain damage, resulting in a PVS, after being crushed in the Hillsborough tragedy. Doctors agreed that there was no hope of recovery and, with the agreement of his parents, they approached the courts for permission to remove his nasogastric feeding without incurring a charge of murder. The Law Lords reasoned that the removal of his nasogastric tube was an omission, not an act and agreed that feeding *did* constitute a treatment. Given that he had no chance of recovery, treatment was not in his best interests and so his nasogastric feeding was withdrawn.

Their decision had potentially serious legal ramifications; for example, would it follow that a demented patient who could no longer feed himself be legally left to starve? No. That is because although it is lawful to withdraw artificial hydration or nutrition this does not permit staff to withhold food and water. That said, it might well not be in a patient's best interests to make them eat or take water if force was required.

For several decades, doctors seeking to withdraw CANH have sought the permission of the court to do so. However, in *Re Y* [2018] UKSC 46, the Supreme Court confirmed that court permission was not required where there was consensus among the medical team and the family of the patient. In cases of disagreement, an application to court to resolve the dispute was appropriate.

Do not attempt resuscitation decisions

The same principles govern the decision-making process about whether to attempt cardiopulmonary resuscitation (CPR) as do all issues in end of life care: if the patient has capacity, their views should be considered and respected. If they do not, decisions made on their behalf must be in their best interests.

Deciding not to attempt resuscitation in the event of a cardiopulmonary arrest means just that; making a do not attempt resuscitation (DNAR) order must not change the nature or quality of other treatments the patient receives.

Decisions about whether to resuscitate must be made as early as is appropriate in patients presenting with acute illness or those known to have life-limiting conditions. It is inappropriate and degrading for a patient to undergo doomed resuscitation attempts because no one took the time to consider whether the attempt was appropriate.

DNAR decisions must be made on an individual basis after considering all relevant factors, such as the likelihood of successfully restarting the heart, the chances of the patient's surviving and making a meaningful recovery, the burden recovery may bring (e.g. will survival of the acute arrest simply extend the dying process?), the patient's own wishes if they have capacity, and the views of those close to the patient who lacks capacity.

When cardiopulmonary resuscitation will be unsuccessful or is inappropriate

In certain situations, such as if a patient is known to be dying of a terminal illness, or CPR is extremely unlikely to be successful and the patient has expressed no wish to discuss the subject, it may be inappropriate to burden them with conversations about a resuscitation attempt that would be clearly distressing. However, these conversations must not be omitted because they may be uncomfortable for the medical team, only for the sake of the patient. If in doubt, the subject should be broached sensitively.

When cardiopulmonary resuscitation is likely to be successful

Patients with capacity

If a patient has capacity, their views should be sought. They should be counselled about likely outcomes of any resuscitation attempt and the burden of care in the face of survival to allow them to make an informed choice.

Patients without capacity

Some patients may have an advance refusal of resuscitation. If it is valid and applicable, it must be respected.

If a patient has appointed a LPA to make his medical decisions, this legal proxy can make resuscitation decisions in his best interests.

In the absence of either of these, the doctor responsible for the patient must make the decision in the patient's best interests. When gathering information about the patient's views and beliefs from those close to him, it is important not to give them the impression that they are being asked to make the decision about whether to attempt resuscitation. The responsibility for this decision lies with the medical team.

Neither patients, nor those close to them, may demand treatment and so no doctor is obliged to provide CPR if they do not feel it to be in the patient's best interests. This is, however, an extremely emotive issue and it would be prudent to resolve any conflict of opinion using the steps described previously.

Patient refusal of CPR

A case might arise where a patient with capacity does not wish to be resuscitated even when the doctors believe attempts would be successful and produce a good outcome. In this situation, the reasons for refusal should be explored fully, and it should be established that the patient understands the

implications of their decision. The competent adult retains the right to refuse treatment of all kinds, and acting against their wishes makes the doctor
guilty of battery or assault.

Once a DNAR order has been made, it must not override clinical judgement in the face of a situation arising that is outside the terms of the order.
For example, if a patient's tracheostomy become dislodged and rendered
them hypoxic, this could be remedied easily by replacing it, and it might not
be appropriate to allow this iatrogenic event to end their life.

Debates over euthanasia

The debate about whether euthanasia is morally acceptable and whether it should be legalized in the UK has raged for many years. There are three main camps in the euthanasia debate:

- Those who believe in the *sanctity of life* for its own sake, who oppose all forms of euthanasia and assisted suicide.
- Those who believe in the *quality of life*, such that a life of suffering might not be considered of value.
- Those who believe in the *autonomy of the individual*, such that a life has only the value attached to it by the person living it.

More will be said about each of these camps.

Sanctity of life

Supporters of sanctity of life claim there is a value that is inherent in all life. That is, a value which does not depend on how a person is feeling about their life, but is a value independent of the person's experience. So even if a person were to say 'My life is miserable, I would be better off dead', supporters of sanctity of life might reply 'Even though you think you would be better off dead, your life is still valuable'.

There are differences over the source of this value. Many supporters for the concept of a sanctity of life approach come from a religious perspective and would claim that God values all life, regardless of a person's experiences. A secular version might say that society values each member, which is why generally if someone is suicidal, our society tries to dissuade someone from committing suicide.

Many supporters of sanctity of life seem to view it as an absolute value, so that even if a person's life is full of pain, the sanctity value trumps that. However (and particularly in the secular version), it seems possible to claim that although society values everyone's life, this can be trumped if a person is experiencing misery and there is nothing that can alleviate that.

Quality of life

In opposition to the sanctity of life view, is the view that the value in a person's life is determined entirely by the person themselves. This is captured by the title of the play: 'Whose life is it anyway?' Supporters of this approach might say that if a person no longer sees value in their life, then why should anyone else force them to have a life they do not want?

This view has considerable attraction, but is not unproblematic. Normally, if a person wants to commit suicide, medical professionals and friends will try and dissuade them. Although the person thinks their life is awful, perhaps are wrong and things are going to get better. It may be, therefore, that there needs to be an element of objective assessment in this view. In other words, when a person thinks their life is worthless and this may seem a reasonable view to take. The difficulty is then: who decides if it is indeed a reasonable view?

Autonomy

Some would argue that the key concern is respect for autonomy (➲ p. 32). We should let people decide for themselves if they wish to die. We normally respect people's choices as to how to live their lives. The idea that others should force someone to do something normally requires a strong justification. Certainly, the argument that the decision is 'immoral' or 'foolish' is not normally sufficient.

The difficulty with this view is how we know if a person is making a genuine choice to die. A much-discussed scenario is the 'love-sick teenager' who wants to die as the 'love of their life' has left them. Some may be confident that in a few weeks they will feel better and will remember how they felt like that in past and are glad no one listened to them. However, that is an easy case, perhaps; harder are others might not.

A further issue of debate is if assisted dying were permitted, whether people would be pressurized into seeking it even though they did not really want it. That may be pressure from relatives or societal pressure if it becomes an expectation that certain categories of people (e.g. the old or disabled people) ought to seek death.

Organ transplantation

Introduction

Organ transplantation has been controversial since its earliest days. It raises a number of ethical questions and legal challenges.

Transplantation of organs from the dead

Are organ 'donors' really dead? Historically, a body had to show signs of decomposition before it was deemed to be dead. In the nineteenth century, death was associated with the cessation of breath and heartbeat. In the twentieth century, it became possible to extend heart function and ventilation, and medical technology reached the stage where organs could be transplanted. But the first surgeon to perform a heart transplant in Japan in 1968 was charged with murder, and even in other countries, the question of whether transplant surgeons were in fact killing the donor remained problematic.

The concept of brainstem death came into use as a way of redefining death so that doctors would not feel they were killing the patients from whom organs were retrieved, and would not be at risk of prosecution. (For a more detailed discussion of death, see ⴹ p. 180.)

Legal requirements for transplant from dead donors

In the UK, transplants are governed by the Human Tissue Act 2004, although that has been significantly amended by the Organ Donation (Deemed Consent) Act 2019. The 2019 Act changed the law so that a person was deemed to consent to organ donation 'unless a person who stood in a qualifying relationship to the person concerned immediately before death provides information that would lead a reasonable person to conclude that the person concerned would not have consented'.

There are two categories of 'excepted adults' to whom the rule of 'deemed consent' does not apply:
• person who has not been ordinarily resident in England for the 12 months before their death.
• person who for a 'significant period before dying lacked capacity to understand the law' on deemed consent (section 1(5)).

There are no firm rules on when the presumption of deemed consent will be rebutted. It need not be written evidence but it must be enough to 'lead a reasonable person' to decide that P would not have consented to the donation. This wording seems to suggest that it is not enough to simply raise a doubt about whether P consented.

What counts as a qualifying relationship?
Qualifying relationships are the following:
• Spouse or civil partner or cohabitant (NB: not former spouse).
• Parent or child.
• Brother or sister.
• Grandparent or grandchild.
• Nephew or niece.
• Stepfather or step mother.
• Half-brother or half-sister.
• Friend of long standing.

Can donors decide who should receive their organs?

The Department of Health has indicated that conditional donation is not acceptable. This means that potential donors cannot stipulate that their heart/kidney/and so on must go to a person of a particular race or religion. However, paired organ donation is permitted where a person gives an organ to someone and in return, they (or their partner) are given an organ.

From an ethical perspective, it is an interesting question whether—if conditional donation would increase the numbers of organs available—it should be allowed.

Whose interests should be paramount?

Under the law, the wishes of the deceased can trump the interests of those who need the organs. Some ethicists believe that once a person dies, they can have no interests and so no weight should be attached to their views. Others argue that this would not be consistent with other areas of law, where posthumous interests are recognized, for example, respecting the terms of someone's will. However, the debate goes on as to whether it is justifiable to respect a person's refusal to donate organs which can be of no further health benefit to that individual.

Too few donors?

The new legislation was introduced in 2019 because every year, bodies are buried or cremated along with organs that could be used to preserve the lives of others. And in the UK, many people die every year while waiting for organ transplants (℞ https://www.nhsbt.nhs.uk/what-we-do/transplantation-services/organ-donation-and-transplantation). Most of us would accept an organ if we needed one, and around 90% of the British public say they support organ donation. But only 28% were actually on the donor register prior to 2019. Organ donation raises a number of ethico-legal questions: is 'deemed consent' an acceptable way of trying to increase the number of organs available? What role, if any, should relatives play in deciding whether organs will be removed? Should we all feel morally obliged to donate organs?

> **Potential ways of increasing the number of available organs**
> - Allow payments for organs.
> - Relax restrictions on circumstances in which one can donate.

Deemed consent: points in favour

The main arguments in favour of a presumed consent model are as follows:
- First, it is assumed that doing so would increase the numbers of organs available.
- Second, because most people say they support organ donation, but a much smaller proportion registered as donors, it could be argued that an opt-out system better reflects the wishes of the population.

Standards of consent

However, there are some ethical questions to be asked here. 'Presumed' consent is not as exacting a standard of consent as that required for other medical interventions, or for research. We could not simply assume that a patient had consented for any other form of surgery. Why should we do so in the case of organ donation?

In fact, very few of the UK's population—and therefore, very few of the 90% who say they support organ donation—know the details about what organ donation involves. This has been raised as a concern by some ethicists, who fear that there is a willingness to trade on the public's ignorance, which may seem rather deceptive.

Clearly, consent obtained within the current system is poor, by normal medical. But perhaps normal medical standards are not the most appropriate ones for tackling organ donation.

A further problem lies in the risk of creating a marginalized group. In any opt-out system, those who wish to opt out need to understand and operate within that system. Those who are highly educated and powerful in society are much more likely to be aware (a) of the system's existence and (b) of how to opt out. Those who are poorly educated or vulnerable may be more likely to have their organs removed without ever realizing that they had a choice in the matter.

With educational programmes, awareness could be increased, but it is still almost certain that some people would slip through the net. The question is, would this be ethically worse than a system in which some people who *do* want to donate also slip through the net?

It is worth asking whether presumed consent really increases the numbers of organs available? Most people do not die in circumstances that make it possible to donate their organs. Changing the law cannot alter this fact. There is conflicting data as to whether opt-out systems do in fact increase the numbers of organs available for transplant. This is a complex issue and there are a number of factors that come into play. And questions remain about the role of relatives. In the current system, when relatives object, organs are not usually removed, even if the patient had explicitly wished for this. Deemed consent, therefore, does not provide a mandate for medical staff to override relatives' wishes, and this remains a potential barrier to donation.

Elective ventilation: should patients be kept on life support solely to optimize their organs for transplantation?

It is clinically possible for brainstem-dead patients to be kept ventilated in order to preserve their organs in optimal condition for transplant. This is known as elective ventilation. It is controversial, since such patients would not be treated for their own benefit, but for that of others—a departure from one of the primary assumptions about the ethical justification for medical treatment. Nevertheless, it could be argued that if a patient had indicated their wish to become a donor, treatment aimed at facilitating this *would* be in their interests, even though those interests no longer centre around the patient's own life. This is a somewhat grey area in legal terms and is an issue that remains ethically controversial.

Non-heart-beating donors

In purely clinical terms, organs obtained from brain-dead donors are better than those obtained from non-heart-beating donors. The brain-dead donor who is still breathing will have organs that are oxygenated and healthy. Organs obtained from non-heart-beating donors on the other hand will have had their oxygen supply cut off. Organs quickly deteriorate in these circumstances. Because of this, when the criteria for brainstem death were introduced, it was generally assumed that there would be no call for non-heart-beating donation. However, with the deficit of available organs, non-heart-beating donation has increased in recent years.

Apart from the quality of the organs, another problem with non-heart-beating donation is the question of whether cessation of heartbeat is really irrevocable, that is, whether the patient could be resuscitated. As the case below shows, there are some disturbing possibilities if non-heart-beating donors turn out not to be dead after all.

Box 18.1 Case A

In 2008, *The Telegraph* reported on the case of a 45-year-old man who had suffered a heart attack in Paris. Medics attempted to resuscitate the man and the transplant team were also summoned. It was concluded that the man could not be saved, but cardiac massage was continued until the arrival of the transplant team—an hour and a half later. The man was then transferred to an operating theatre where surgeons prepared to remove his organs. However, when they started operating, the patient began to breathe independently. Surgery was hastily brought to a halt. The patient survived, and after a difficult few weeks, was walking and talking.

🖑 http://www.telegraph.co.uk/news/newstopics/howaboutthat/2106809/Dead-man-wakes-as-transplant-surgeons-prepare-to-remove-his-organs.html.

Living donors

Most organs come from people who have been involved in traffic accidents or suffered from a stroke or cerebral haemorrhage. Even if more people join the donor register, improvements in traffic safety and medical advances in the treatment of stroke or haemorrhage mean that there is still likely to be a shortfall. Increasingly, where it is clinically feasible, organs and tissues are being obtained from living donors. This raises some different ethical and legal considerations.

Legal requirements for transplantation from living donors

It is a criminal offence to remove or use material from a living donor unless permitted under the terms of the Human Tissue Act 2004. The Human Tissue Authority (HTA) has produced detailed guidance on when donations from living donors are permitted.

Regenerative tissue (e.g. blood or bone marrow)

Where a living donor wishes to donate regenerative tissue, the primary legal question is whether or not consent has been provided.

Donated regenerative tissue cannot be used if it has been subject to commercial dealing, that is, if it has been bought or sold.

Non-regenerative tissue (e.g. kidneys)

Again, there must be effective consent to the removal of any tissue. The donor must understand the procedure and the risks involved, and the procedure must not involve material which has been subject to 'commercial dealing'.

The donation must comply with the Code of Practice on live donation produced by the HTA. The main elements of these are as follows:

- The donor must be informed of all the risks, including the possibility that the recipient may not benefit from the organ (a favourable clinical outcome cannot be guaranteed).
- The donor must meet with a clinician and independent assessor to discuss the procedure and they must be satisfied that there is adequate consent.
- If the donor is not genetically or emotionally related to the recipient approval is required from an HTA panel, who will require evidence from a psychiatrist on the reason for the donation.

Risk of harm to the donor

It is unlawful to remove an organ from a living donor if this would cause death or serious injury. For this reason, donation of a heart from a living patient would be illegal (even with the fully informed consent of the donor), but donation of a single kidney or lobe of a lung would not.

- John Stuart Mill famously asserted that the only justification for restricting someone's choices is to prevent harm to *others*. This is a fundamental part of what we understand by respect for autonomy, and is reflected in the ethico-legal framework that governs the practice of medicine in the UK. It is for this reason that an adult of sound mind has an absolute right to refuse treatment, even if this refusal will inevitably result in that person's death.

- It could be argued that to be consistent with this principle, we *should* allow anyone of sound mind to donate his/her organs—even if this would cause the death of the donor. It could be argued, therefore, that the law infringes rather than enhances the autonomy of potential donors in this respect.

Donors who lack capacity

If the donor is a child, then donation will be permitted only in exception-ally rare cases. Any donation must be approved by a panel from the HTA. A child who is Gillick competent (➔ p. 172) will be able to consent. A parent with parental responsibility may be able to consent if the donation would be in the child's best interests.

If the potential donor is an adult who lacks capacity, the donation must be in their best interests. This is likely to be hard to demonstrate. Any donation in these circumstances would need approval of the court and the approval of an HTA panel.

Selling organs

It has been suggested that allowing people to buy and sell organs com-mercially would overcome the current shortages. This raises a number of questions. The most obvious concern is whether it would actually achieve the desired effect. We cannot know in advance whether this really would increase the availability of organs to the required degree. To know for cer-tain, we would have to allow the practice and carefully observe the out-come. But some ethicists believe that this would be intrinsically wrong, on the grounds that the commodification of body parts is an infringement of human dignity. It has also been suggested that even if an open market in human tissues increased the number of organs available, this would benefit only the rich and powerful, while vulnerable, impoverished, or marginal-ized members of society would be exploited. A counterargument to this is that a properly regulated market in organs/tissues might actually empower people who have few other assets or opportunities.

Non-life-saving transplants

In recent years, a number of transplantations have taken place which aim not at restoring an organ, or the functioning of an organ, but improving the patient's quality of life. So-called face transplants are one example of this. However, the transplantation of limbs or digits is also on the increase.

It might be asked why face or limb transplants should merit extra attention. A key ethical question here is that of risk. Where a person receives a heart or liver transplant, it is usually 'life-saving'. That is, the patient would die without treatment. In the case of kidney transplants, the patient may be spared a lifetime of dialysis. It is generally expected that such transplants will improve the patient's health, and increase their lifespan.

Face or limb transplants however, will not necessarily have these effects. Indeed, they impose all the risks of transplantation, (including the need to take anti-rejection drugs, and the risks of surgery) but their benefits seem to be largely social, rather than clinical. A patient with severe facial injuries may feel better able to function in society with a more 'normal' appearance. Likewise, a person who has lost a hand may prefer a 'real' hand to a prosthesis, even though the functionality of a prosthesis is often superior.

This means that the risks involved cannot be balanced directly against clinical benefits in the way that other treatments or procedures can. If one takes the view that patient autonomy is the predominant ethical concern, the question of risk may not be such a problem. Provided that the patient makes an informed choice, it is his or her decision as to how the various risks and benefits weigh up against each other. However, doctors may feel uncomfortable about this.

Further ethical concerns may arise in view of the fact that if society were more accommodating, patients might be less eager to subject themselves to the risks of surgery. Wouldn't it be better if instead of undergoing surgery, patients with severe deformities, or missing limbs, felt less stigmatized by their differences?

It is undeniable that social preoccupations affect people's medical decisions in many ways. However, withholding treatment from patients on the off-chance that society will change its attitudes seems somewhat harsh. It is important to challenge the way we respond to problems in society, but as long as those problems remain, it is likely that some patients will endure pain and risk, in an effort to look as normal as possible.

Additional reading

General Medical Council. Treatment and care towards the end of life: good practice in decision making. 2010. Available at: ℘ http://www.gmc-uk.org/guidance/ethical_guidance/end_of_life_care.asp.

Potts M, Byrne PA, Nilges RG. Beyond Brain Death: The Case Against Brain Based Criteria for Human Death. Dordrecht: Kluwer; 2000.

Useful websites

Human Tissue Authority: ℘ https://www.hta.gov.uk/.

NHS Blood and Transplant: ℘ "https://www.organdonation.nhs.uk/" https://www.organdonation.nhs.uk/.

Doctors and the General Medical Council (GMC)

Introduction to the GMC *202*
The GMC's ethical guidance *204*
Investigating concerns about doctors *206*
Where to seek help with a clinical legal or ethical question *210*

Introduction to the GMC

What is the GMC?

The GMC is the regulatory body for UK doctors. It is only lawful to practise medicine in the UK if the doctor is on the medical register and licensed. The GMC decides whose names are on that register and who is licensed to practise.

The GMC sets, publishes, and polices ethical standards for doctors.

Types of registration

- *Provisional*: allows a doctor to be in an approved UK Foundation Year 1 programme.
- *Full*: allows a doctor to work in unsupervised medical practice or an approved Foundation Year 2 programme.
- *Specialist*: most UK consultants will have full specialist registration. Not all locum consultants will.
- *GP*: all GPs (including locums) working in UK health services, other than GPs in training, must be both on the GMC's GP Register and on a GP Performers List.

Professional and Linguistic Assessments Board

Doctors who qualify in medicine at a UK medical school will be admitted to the provisional list. But doctors who qualify overseas must satisfy the Professional and Linguistic Assessments Board of their linguistic and clinical ability before being licensed to practise in the UK. This involves taking a series of tests: see ℛ https://www.gmc-uk.org/registration-and-licensing/join-the-register/plab.

Revalidation

Every 5 years, every doctor needs to be revalidated: see ℛ https://www.gmc-uk.org/registration-and-licensing/managing-your-registration/revalidation. This involves showing that the doctor has kept up to date and is fit to practise. The revalidation process will generally be based on annual appraisals (which involve reflection on one's own practice) and any clinical governance information. For most doctors, this revalidation will be based on the recommendation of a 'responsible officer'—a senior doctor in the relevant organization. If there is no 'responsible officer', another senior doctor (a 'suitable person') may take on the responsible officer's role. If there is no responsible officer or suitable person, the doctor must make their own return to the GMC, giving evidence of the annual appraisals and showing that there are no concerns. In such cases, the GMC may require the doctor to undertake a written test. The revalidation is required to be licensed to practise. If you do not revalidate, you can remain on the register but not be licensed to practise.

The GMC's ethical guidance

The GMC's most important general statement about the duties of a doctor is 'Good Medical Practice'. It is regularly updated, and available at: ℘ https://www.gmc-uk.org/ethical-guidance/ethical-guidance-for-doctors/good-medical-practice.

'Good Medical Practice' states that doctors must:
- make the care of their patient their first concern
- be competent and keep their professional knowledge and skills up to date
- take prompt action if they think patient safety is being compromised
- establish and maintain good partnerships with their patients and colleagues
- maintain trust in them and the profession by being open, honest, and acting with integrity.

The general guidance in 'Good Medical Practice' is supplemented by detailed ethical advice, all of which is available at ℘ https://www.gmc-uk.org/ethical-guidance.

The areas covered by this guidance include:
- confidentiality
- consent and shared decision-making
- candour and raising concerns
- leadership and management
- prescribing
- children and young people
- end of life care at the end of life
- maintaining professionalism
- cosmetic interventions
- research.

Most of these areas are covered by specific chapters in this book. Two that are not are the 'duty of candour' and whistle-blowing.

The duty of candour

The preamble to the GMC's duty of candour guidance (℘ https://www.gmc-uk.org/ethical-guidance/ethical-guidance-for-doctors/candour---openness-and-honesty-when-things-go-wrong/the-professional-duty-of-candour) states:

Every healthcare professional must be open and honest with patients when something that goes wrong with their treatment or care causes, or has the potential to cause, harm or distress. This means that healthcare professionals must:
- tell the patient (or, where appropriate, the patient's advocate, carer or family) when something has gone wrong
- apologise to the patient (or, where appropriate, the patient's advocate, carer or family)
- offer an appropriate remedy or support to put matters right (if possible)
- explain fully to the patient (or, where appropriate, the patient's advocate, carer or family) the short and long term effects of what has happened.

Healthcare professionals must also be open and honest with their colleagues, employers and relevant organisations, and take part in reviews and investigations when requested. They must also be open and honest with their regulators, raising concerns where appropriate. They must support and encourage each other to be open and honest, and not stop someone from raising concerns.

Whistle-blowing

Where a doctor believes that patient safety, dignity, or comfort is being compromised, there is a duty on that doctor to take prompt action. This might involve a duty to notify the GMC if the local hierarchy cannot be relied upon to act: see ◌ https://www.gmc-uk.org/ethical-guidance/ethical-guidance-for-doctors/raising-and-acting-on-concerns. The law has various mechanisms for protecting against victimization and dismissal of doctors who raise concerns.

Investigating concerns about doctors

Anyone can raise with the GMC a concern about a doctor, and doctors can raise a concern about themselves.

Only about 20% of the concerns raised with the GMC go on to the investigation stage.

What is investigated?

An investigation will begin if the concern (if found proved) would need some sort of sanction. Any breach of any of the ethical guidance could lead to a sanction, but the GMC is concerned with anything which might affect the doctor's fitness to practise or affect the public's confidence in the medical profession. Thus, as well as misconduct, the GMC may investigate (for instance) allegations of very poor clinical performance, criminal convictions/cautions, physical or mental health concerns affecting a doctor's ability to practise, and inadequate ability to speak English.

What to do if you are being investigated

- Get in touch immediately with your defence organization.
- Respond promptly and fully to requests by the investigator.
- Get emotional support: investigations can be stressful.

What will the investigation involve?

Whatever the GMC thinks is necessary. But it will write to the doctor's employers asking for any relevant information, and if it thinks that it is necessary to take immediate action to suspend the doctor pending the outcome of the investigation, it will refer the case to the Medical Practitioners Tribunal Service (MPTS) for the MPTS to consider an interim suspension: see ℜ https://www.mpts-uk.org/hearings-and-decisions/hearing-types-and-how-they-work/interim-orders-tribunals.

There will be such a referral if the case relates to a criminal conviction or caution (other than one relating to minor offences such as parking offences), or if there has been a determination against the doctor by another regulatory body. See ℜ https://www.gmc-uk.org/concerns/information-for-doctors-under-investigation/how-we-investigate-concerns/opening-an-investigation.

How long will the investigation take?

It depends on what needs to be done. The GMC website estimates that it can take 2 months to obtain witness statements, 2 months to obtain expert reports, 3 months to assess a doctor's health, 3 months to assess a doctor's knowledge of English, and 6 months to assess a doctor's performance. See ℜ https://www.gmc-uk.org/concerns/information-for-doctors-under-investigation/how-we-investigate-concerns/our-investigation-process.

Voluntary erasure

A doctor can make an application for voluntary erasure from the medical register: see ℜ https://www.gmc-uk.org/registration-and-licensing/managing-your-registration/changing-your-status-on-the-register/giving-up-your-registration-and-licence-to-practise. However, that will not succeed if an investigation is about to start or is being undertaken. A statement of good standing is required to be voluntarily removed from the register.

Making a decision

When the necessary information is available, it is considered by a medical and a lay assessor, and they jointly decide what should happen next. The options are:

- to conclude the case with no further action
- to issue a warning
- to agree undertakings with the doctor
- to refer the case to the MPTS.

The criteria used are found here: ℘ https://www.gmc-uk.org/concerns/information-for-doctors-under-investigation/how-we-make-decisions.

Referral to the MPTS

This will occur if it is decided that there is a realistic prospect that the factual allegations against the doctor *and* a realistic prospect that, if those facts are found proved, they would mean that the doctor's fitness to practise is impaired.

Impaired fitness to practise might occur in a variety of circumstances. The GMC guidance highlights the following:

- The doctor's performance has harmed patients or put patients at risk of harm.
- The doctor has shown deliberate or reckless disregard of their clinical responsibility towards patients.
- The doctor's health is compromising patient safety.
- The doctor has abused patient trust or violated patient autonomy or another fundamental right.
- The doctor has behaved dishonestly, fraudulently, or in a way designed to mislead or harm others.
- The doctor's behaviour is such that public confidence in doctors generally might be undermined if the GMC took no action.

The MPTS (℘ https://www.mpts-uk.org/) is independent of the GMC. It is composed of medical and lay members, and if the chair is not legally qualified, there is a legal adviser who advises the tribunal on the relevant law (but is not involved in the decision-making).

The procedure is governed by the General Medical Council Fitness to Practise Rules 2004. Guidance about what to expect at a hearing are available here: ℘ https://www.mpts-uk.org/doctors-and-representatives/resource-for-doctors-medical-practitioners-tribunals.

It is common for doctors to be represented at MPTS hearings by a barrister or a solicitor, but they may represent themselves. The GMC is always legally represented, and the GMC's legal representative conducts the case.

The tribunal decides:

- if the facts alleged by the GMC have been found proved
- if the doctor's fitness to practise is impaired as a result of the facts found proved
- if any action should be taken.

Fitness to practise is assessed as at the date of assessment, looking forward, but of course informed by the past. Thus, if the allegations relate solely to a clinical failure, and the doctor has, since that failure, remediated so that there are no continuing concerns, there is unlikely to be a finding of impaired fitness to practise. Some matters are not capable of remediation—particularly those which (if not met with a sanction) affect public confidence in the profession.

If the doctor's fitness to practise is impaired, the tribunal can:

- take no action
- accept undertakings offered by the doctor if the GMC agrees
- place conditions on the doctor's registration for up to 3 years
- suspend the doctor's registration for up to 12 months
- erase the doctor's name from the register ('striking off').

Where fitness to practise is not impaired, a warning can be given.

Undertakings are monitored by the GMC.

Where a doctor is suspended or made subject to conditions, the case will be reviewed by the MPTS to see if the doctor's fitness to practise is still impaired and what, if any, restrictions are still needed.

If a doctor is erased from the register, after 5 years they can apply for their name to be restored. The application is considered by the MPTS.

The decisions of the MPTS are published on its website.

A decision by the MPTS to erase, suspend, or impose conditions on registration can be appealed by the doctor. The GMC may also appeal an MPTS decision. If the Professional Standards Authority thinks that an MPTS decision is insufficient to protect the public, it may refer the case to the High Court: see ℜ https://www.professionalstandards.org.uk/.

Where to seek help with a clinical legal or ethical question

Faced with a clinical legal or ethical dilemma, most of us start with our peers. As with any other clinical question, clinical law and ethics are absorbed during training and then practice so it is worth asking your friends. If you draw a blank, seek advice from an experienced clinician. The ward or practice sister may have encountered your present dilemma. Failing that, seek out the person who is responsible for the patient.

If the question remains unanswered, there are a variety of resources, but the order in which you consult them will depend on the nature and urgency of the request.

A clinician who has been seeing patients regularly over 20 years will have encountered most clinical dilemmas, including the one you are facing. Your organization may have access to a clinical ethics committee, and you may be able to pose your question during a clinical ethics committee meeting or to an individual member in the interim. Most hospitals and general practices have lead clinicians or managers for litigation, and your question may be familiar to them because of their line of work.

There will be a firm of solicitors standing behind the trust or practice group. They will provide advice to protect the interests of the organization; this may or may not be helpful to the patient—interests often coincide. Clinicians subscribing to a defence organization can certainly ask for advice; but again, that will be focused primarily on promoting the member's interests. By following the advice you are given, it is very likely you will avoid criticism.

The GMC provides a wealth of advice and guidance in relation to generic patients who present with clinical ethical or legal dilemmas. But they never give advice in relation to the patient in front of you. Royal Colleges and innumerable speciality organizations vary widely in their provision. Few will provide advice in relation to a particular patient in a practicable timescale. Some clinical legal departments have been developed, providing specific advice locally in response to the dilemmas that patients pose, and it is to be hoped that these will proliferate. Since it can be seen that the provision of answers to clinical questions founded on the law (rather than on the other 'basic sciences' employed in medicine) are sparse.

Additional reading

Wheeler R. Clinical law updates. University Hospital Southampton NHS Foundation Trust. 2021. Available at: http://www.uhs.nhs.uk/HealthProfessionals/Clinical-law-updates/Clinicallawupdates.aspx.

Medical research

Introduction to medical research *212*
Nuremburg Code and Declaration of Helsinki *214*
Forms of research *216*

Introduction to medical research

The practice of research on humans poses myriad ethical challenges. It inescapably involves a tension between urge of the researcher to solve a scientific problem, the interests of society at large, and the interests of the individual research subjects.

In ethical terms, there can be a clash between a utilitarian calculation which suggests that sacrificing the interests of one individual is an acceptable way of securing benefits for many patients, and a deontological approach which regards human lives as being intrinsically valuable, so that they cannot be factored into this kind of cost/benefit analysis. Another way to put this is that the utilitarian believes 'the ends justify the means', while the deontologist holds that 'it is wrong to treat a human being as a mere means to an end'.

Most ethical codes regulating research on humans seek to prioritize the protection of the rights of participants. Thus, it is the deontological approach that is enforced.

Broadly speaking, research on human subjects is divided into therapeutic research and non-therapeutic research.

Therapeutic research

Therapeutic research involves the use of drugs or procedures that are administered to patients who are suffering from the specific condition that the drug/procedure is intended to treat. What makes it different from ordinary treatment is that the intervention is still in the testing phase. This means that the expectation is that patients might experience some therapeutic benefit. However, since the intervention is still under investigation, the exact nature of the risks, side effects, and efficacy may not be known.

Often, patients involved in this kind of research may have very serious diseases, possibly life-threatening. In one sense, therefore, they may have little to lose. Participating in research may offer the only possibility of an improvement in their condition.

Non-therapeutic research

Non-therapeutic research involves testing a procedure or drug on healthy individuals in order to determine its effects. Participants in this kind of research are not expected to gain any benefits from their involvement. Indeed, they may suffer harm as a result of their participation.

Scientific validity

It is widely agreed that experimentation on human beings must be scientifically valid in order to be ethically acceptable. If a study is ill conceived or poorly executed, it may put participants at risk without yielding any scientifically useful information. Poor research produces poor results; such research is unethical in that subjects are exposed to risks to produce invalid or bogus results with no probative value.

Therefore, the likelihood that any benefits outweigh the risks, is skewed.

Because of the importance of scientific validity, research involving human participants should be reviewed by experts in the field, to ensure that it conforms to accepted scientific principles and has a thorough knowledge base. Analysis of data produced should be in line with the best statistical approach possible for the data set and data should not be excluded from analysis to improve the results.

Nuremburg Code and Declaration of Helsinki

After the Second World War, the world was horrified by revelations of the experiments performed by Nazi doctors, in which human beings were used as expendable research subjects. Many people were killed in the course of the various research activities undertaken by the Nazis. Among those who survived, many suffered lifelong health problems as a result of the appalling abuse that they had been subjected to.

One of the striking aspects of the Nuremberg trials was the attempt made by some of those accused to defend themselves by highlighting the absence of international guidelines governing the conduct of research. Ultimately, the Nuremburg Code was published; in future, no perpetrator of atrocities would ever be able to make such a claim again. The Nuremberg Code was the first set of international guidelines on research on humans, and it consisted of ten principles:

1. Voluntary consent of the subject is essential.
2. The experiment should produce fruitful results for the good of society, unprocurable by other means.
3. The experiment should be designed and based on an understanding of the natural history of the disease and/or animal experimentation such that the anticipated results justify the experiment.
4. The experiment should avoid unnecessary physical and mental suffering.
5. No experiment should be conducted where there is an a priori reason to believe death or disabling injury will occur.
6. The degree of risk should not exceed the importance of the problem to be solved.
7. The subject must be protected against even remote possibilities of injury/death.
8. Only scientifically qualified persons should perform the experiment.
9. During the course of the experiment the subject should be at liberty to terminate it at any time.
10. The scientist in charge must be prepared to terminate the experiment if he believes there is a likelihood of injury, disability, or death.

These ten principles were adopted by the World Medical Association, founded in 1947, and were revised and published as the Declaration of Helsinki in 1964 and which was last updated in 2013. The latest version can be found here: ℘ https://www.wma.net/policies-post/wma-declaration-of-helsinki-ethical-principles-for-medical-research-involving-human-subjects/.

The key principles in the declaration are the importance of protecting patients from harm, ensuring there is valid consent and protecting confidentiality.

Protection from harm

The Declaration makes clear that:

> While the primary purpose of medical research is to generate new knowledge, this goal can never take precedence over the rights and interests of individual research subjects.

In order to interpret the requirement to protect research participants from harm, it is necessary to consider what is meant by the term and to establish what degree of *risk* is acceptable (➔ p. 212). It is widely agreed that the risks involved in research should be 'minimal'. But how exactly should this be quantified? The Royal College of Physicians has in its 2007 guideline attempted to quantify this minimal risk as where the chances of serious injury or death are remote and can be ignored, minimal risk involves a risk of death of less than 1/1,000,000.

Consent

In order for research to take place, consent must be obtained. The Declaration of Helsinki outlines the following requirements:

> In medical research involving human subjects capable of giving informed consent, each potential subject must be adequately informed of the aims, methods, sources of funding, any possible conflicts of interest, institutional affiliations of the researcher, the anticipated benefits and potential risks of the study and the discomfort it may entail, post-study provisions and any other relevant aspects of the study. The potential subject must be informed of the right to refuse to participate in the study or to withdraw consent to participate at any time without reprisal. Special attention should be given to the specific information needs of individual potential subjects as well as to the methods used to deliver the information.

Researchers must also be alert to the possibility of undue influence between patients and their physicians. The doctor–patient relationship is a subtle one but it is clear that the asymmetry of power may lead some patients to feel that they are under pressure to be subjects for research or that their treatment would suffer if they did not take part. It should always be made clear that this is not the case. Where the subject is in such a dependent relationship, the Declaration of Helsinki (paragraph 27) states that consent must be obtained by an independent physician.

Consent and the unconscious patient

However, some research cannot be carried out except on patients who are unconscious, or who have lost capacity. For example, testing interventions on patients who are admitted following severe head trauma. In these cases, it will not be possible to obtain legally binding consent. Studies that involve these participants are likely to come under very sharp scrutiny from ethics committees, in order to ensure that risks are minimal, and that there really are no alternatives to the recruitment of non-consenting patients. Where patients *are* recruited without consent, their next of kin must be consulted as soon as this is feasible. And the patient's own consent must be obtained as soon as he or she does regain consciousness/capacity.

Confidentiality

It is generally considered essential that subjects in research can be assured that their personal data may only be accessed by those involved with the trial and that they have specifically consented to their data being used for the research protocol. Principle 24 of the Declaration of Helsinki states:

> Every precaution must be taken to protect the privacy of research subjects and the confidentiality of their personal information.

Forms of research

There are a range of types of research. Some raise particular ethical issues.

Randomized clinical trials

A problem that arises in clinical trials is the supposition that by entering a patient into a trial a researcher may be knowingly offering a treatment that is not felt to be in their best interests but in the interests of scientific research and future patients. This is thought by some to be solved by insisting that there is genuine uncertainty as to what is best, a state of clinical equipoise.

Equipoise

Clinical equipoise is believed to exist where there is genuine uncertainty in the expert medical community as to whether a treatment/intervention is beneficial. This allows for subjects to be allocated to different arms of a clinical trial. If an investigator has genuine and valid reasons to believe that treatment A is better than treatment B then the clinician would be obligated to give treatment A to the subject. Subjects involved in randomized controlled clinical trials would need to know that such a state of equipoise exists. Equipoise allows researchers to continue investigations until the appropriate level of evidence has been found.

This concept of equipoise has been disputed by some who have argued that the obligations of researchers to subjects are not the same as the obligations of physicians in the context of routine clinical care. Others have also argued that in the context of new drugs reaching phase III studies they are more likely to be effective than not, especially when industry sponsored.

However, it is a widely accepted normative principle in the context of the ethical justification for randomization in clinical trials. It is true though that equipoise is not a necessary nor sufficient condition for a trial to be justified. Some design bias in trials may rule out equipoise.

Subjects with terminal disease

The situation in terminally ill patients and patients with cancer is more complex. Research in these situations often involves 'last-ditch' attempts to maintain life by the use of drugs or techniques which may have little evidential backing. In this situation, the distinction between experimentation and research may become muddied as treatments are given on an individualized speculative basis outside of a formal research protocol. Paragraph 37 of the Helsinki protocol supports the use of experimental treatments where the principal purpose is saving life or alleviating suffering.

Research on children

Research on children is problematic for many people, involving as it does the use of subjects for research who cannot legally give consent. However, there are diseases that are specific to childhood and it is recognized that children, in pharmaco-physiological terms, are not just small adults. Using drugs, which have only been tested on adults, in this setting might be considered to be a priori an unethical act. In some respects, then, the ethical demands mandate proper research on children.

Under the Medicines for Human Use (Clinical Trials) Regulations 2004, a minor may not be involved in a trial without the consent of a parent or a person with parental responsibility and the Declaration of Helsinki (paragraph 16) instructs investigators to obtain the assent of the minor in a trial in addition to the consent of the appropriate adult.

The Medical Research Council (2004) has published guidelines relating to research on children, which can be accessed on their website (℞ https://www.mrc.ac.uk/documents/pdf/medical-research-involving-children).

Research and adults lacking capacity

It possible to conduct research on those who lack mental capacity, but only under very restricted circumstances, set out in the Mental Capacity Act 2005, sections 30–35. Detailed guidance on when this may be permitted and the paperwork that needs to be completed can be found at ℞ http://www.hra.nhs.uk/resources/before-you-apply/consent-and-participation/adults-unable-to-consent-for-themselves/.

Broadly speaking, the ethics encompassing the use of incompetent adults is a balance of the utilitarian principle of maximizing benefit for society in general and the concept of the rights of the individual person and their 'best interests'. If the former dominates the ethical balance, then non-therapeutic research would be allowed on incompetent adults if the benefits outweighed the potential harm. However, how much harm would be acceptable, for a consequentialist argument can justify extreme harm? If the best interests of the patient are the prime determining factors, then no research would be acceptable on incompetent patients if they do not stand to benefit.

Research in the developing world

Concerns regarding the conduct of clinical trials were first raised in the late 1990s where trials into the effects of oral zidovudine on vertical transmission of HIV were taking place in Africa. The ethical problem raised was of the control group not being given an effective treatment as mandated by the Declaration of Helsinki, leading to accusations of double standards and exploitation. The counterargument was that as the default treatment in the countries concerned was nothing, subjects could not be seen to be having worse than standard treatment.

This issue has not gone away—concerns have been raised as recently as 2012 that up to 80% of subjects in some trials have not been informed about the nature of the study. However, it needs to be borne in mind that while many of the developing countries' health needs can be met by improved water, sanitation, and nutrition, 58% of the deaths from infectious diseases occur in the poorest 20% of countries. Research into malaria, HIV/AIDS, and other infectious diseases is thus essential.

Medical education

Introduction to medical education *220*
Consent in medical training *221*
Confidentiality in medical training *222*
Practising on the dead? *224*

Introduction to medical education

It is axiomatic that in order for a society to continue to have healthcare, the oncoming generations of doctors need to be trained in their profession and specialty. While much of the knowledge base required can be gained from texts, teaching aids, and demonstrations, it remains the case that medical students and doctors in training need to cultivate their clinical skills on patients.

There is an inherent ethical tension in this, as the patients may not themselves benefit. Indeed, in procedural training there is a particular risk of harm. The old adage of 'see one, do one, teach one' used to be commonly accepted, indicating both the pressures that can weigh on doctors to acquire and transmit skills quickly and effectively and the blithe assurance that this is an adequate approach to the challenges involved in teaching and learning medicine.

To modern practitioners and students, the adage now seems not just outdated, but irresponsibly glib. Learning, performing, and teaching a specific surgical intervention, for example, are all very different processes. Those who are good at one element may not excel in another. In recent years, the importance of good teaching has been more widely recognized.

The role of patients in medical training has also come under scrutiny. There is a higher expectation that patients should be informed about the presence or participation of students in their care. Patients have, in theory at least, the right to give or withhold their consent to this. Again, this represents a departure from the expectations and assumptions of the past.

Consent in medical training

It is essential that medical students or trainee or student doctors gain the consent of patients when they are interacting with and examining them. Their obligations in this respect are just as stringent as those of a qualified doctor. Even when the patient is incompetent and care is being given on the best interests principle, it is advisable, as in any other circumstance, for students to identify who they are and what their position is, as a matter of common courtesy. (Even if they are not convinced that the patient notices or cares about this, it is better to err on the side of courtesy than to risk appearing to ignore or belittle the patient.)

It is important from the perspective of truth telling that patients understand whom they are dealing with. Medical students or student doctors, as they are sometimes called, and trainees in any specialty should explain their position in the hierarchy when interacting with patients, both as a matter of good manners but also in terms of being truthful. Consent obtained for a procedure where the patient has *not* been informed of the involvement of students, is not ethically sound. It fails to respect patient autonomy.

Of course, obtaining consent in advance may not be possible in certain circumstances such as in the operating theatre or intensive care unit where students and postgraduate students may be taught. Nevertheless, wherever possible, students and trainees should identify themselves to the patient and/or relative and explain their position.

Patients should be informed that they have a right to refuse the involvement of students in their care, and that if they should choose to exercise this right, it will not affect the standard of care. The consent obtained should be meaningful, specific, and explicit, rather than a blanket consent.

- Consent must be obtained for presentation of cases to groups whether the patient is present or not.
- Consent must be obtained and documented for any examination under anaesthetic for educational purposes.

Confidentiality in medical training

Qualified doctors have an obligation to respect the confidentiality of their patients. But how does the obligation of confidentiality apply to medical students?

Medical students and trainee doctors are also bound by obligations of confidentiality. They are expected to keep the personal details of any particular patient confidential, and not to discuss their personal or medical information with others.

However, this clearly raises some difficulties. In the course of education, students, graduate and undergraduate, and educators have to discuss patients. This is a necessary part of the educational process. While theoretical teaching and observation can go some way towards medical education, students must at some point interact with real patients. As soon as they do so, questions of confidentiality will arise. This is complicated, in the student situation, by the fact that students are obliged to discuss their patients with their peers as well as their teachers.

Confidentiality in the student environment thus entails a kind of containment. Qualified doctors' obligations of confidentiality do not preclude their discussion of cases in the broader multidisciplinary team. Likewise, students' obligations encompass case discussion with supervisors, teachers, and peers, where this is a necessary part of their learning.

Beyond this 'envelope', patient details and information should remain confidential and should not be discussed beyond the teaching unit concerned.

Being clear about confidentiality

It may be tempting for medical students and trainee doctors to reassure patients that 'everything you say is confidential'. However, patients do not necessarily interpret this in the same way as the students themselves. Because of this, it is not sufficient simply to assure patients of 'confidentiality'. Instead, students and trainee doctors should explain to patients as clearly and simply as possible, the ways in which their information will be used. In particular, they should emphasize that patients' details may be discussed as part of their teaching with supervisors and peers.

> NB: unless patients have accurate information about the ways in which confidentiality applies, their consent for student involvement in their treatment will not be ethically valid.

Practising on the dead?

There is an inherent tension in teaching medical students procedures with the involvement of real patients. Students are caught between wanting to learn procedures but knowing that their lack of expertise may lead them to risk harming patients. It is clear that students do have to learn somehow. Yet in order to be able to be beneficent, students run the risk of maleficence!

There are various ways of attempting to navigate this ethical problem. One example is the increasing use of high-fidelity simulators in medical training. This allows students to gain skills before interacting with patients.

Yet even with the use of such tools, there must at some point come a moment when a student or trainee attempts a procedure for the first time on a real patient. How should this transition be achieved in the most ethically acceptable manner?

In some parts of the world, medical students are expected to practise endotracheal intubation on newly deceased patients. Some years ago, there was a wave of public concern in response to media reports that medical students in some hospitals in the US were practising cannula insertion on 'dead and nearly dead patients'.

These reports, as well as drawing condemnation from the public, elicited some defensive comments from physicians who had practised or endorsed this themselves. Several physicians pointed out that, although these practices may seem distasteful, they are ultimately necessary for students' learning. And in the longer term, they are beneficial for patients.

One question here is whether it matters at all how we treat the dead. Can a dead person be harmed? If not, should it be acceptable to 'use' people in this way? There is disagreement over the answer to this question from the ethical perspective. Legally, the position is more straightforward. There are strict legal restrictions on what can be done to dead bodies. Moreover, as noted previously, some of these procedures were carried out on 'nearly' dead patients.

In UK law, only medical interventions 'in the best interests' of the patient can be undertaken on a person who lacks capacity. So even if the patient has irrevocably lost consciousness, and will inevitably die very soon, any medical procedure or treatment would have to meet this requirement.

A further point to consider here is that if we regarded the bodies of dead or nearly dead people as being commodities to be used for the benefit of others, this would have far wider implications. If so, it would suggest bodies could, or perhaps *should*, be used for medical research purposes, regardless of the person's known wishes.

Dignity

Another concept that people sometimes appeal to in these circumstances is that of 'dignity'. Some people would be horrified at the idea that their dead or dying body might be used as a practice tool for medical students. The difficulty with this is that 'dignity' is such a subjective concept. Some people might welcome the idea that their body could be beneficial for others after their death, and regard this as being consistent with their idea of dignity. Others might view the prospect with horror, and believe strongly in the idea that dead or dying bodies should be treated with reverence, and not subjected to medically unnecessary intervention.

NB: dignity is a subjective concept. Only if we consult the patient can we know what they regard as being dignified.

Ultimately, there is only one way of being sure that such practices are ethically acceptable. And that is to gain the consent of the patient *before* they die, or lose consciousness. It is worth asking why, in hospitals where these practices have been commonplace, no one thought of attempting to take this approach. One answer is that it is uncomfortable to have this kind of discussion with a patient. Yet doctors have uncomfortable discussions with patients all the time. And it may seem highly unethical that in order to protect *themselves* from discomfort, doctors choose to use people's bodies in ways that they have not consented to.

Perhaps the best way around the need to learn such procedures should be the use of embalmed cadavers where prior consent has been obtained.

Ethico-legal issues by medical specialism

22 Ethico-legal issues by medical specialism A–M *229*

23 Ethico-legal issues by medical specialism N–V *261*

Ethico-legal issues
by medical specialism A–M

Introduction 230
Anaesthetics: child refusing treatment 232
Cardiac surgery: candour 234
Dentistry: Gillick competence 236
Dermatology: a right to treatment? 237
Diabetology: maintaining clinical records 238
Elderly care: refusal of treatment 240
Emergency department: knife crime 242
Emergency department: restraint/self-defence 243
Endocrinology: wishes/feelings 244
ENT: consent/necessity 245
Family planning: Gillick competence 246
Gastroenterology: Mental Health Act 247
General practice: cultural circumcision 248
General surgery: need for clinicians to keep up to date 250
Genetics: confidentiality 252
Gynaecology: abortion 253
HIV: confidentiality 254
Intensive care: DNACPR 255
Interventional radiology: relative risks 256
Maxillofacial: candour 258

Introduction

Clinicians rarely encounter solitary 'ethico-legal' dilemmas. As an example, issues of capacity and consent are intertwined with questions relating to what treatment should or should not be proposed; whether compulsion is indicated; or whether hazardous treatment (or its avoidance) might be lawful.

The scenarios offered here are perforce artificial, since most focus on a singular clinical legal or ethical point. Naturally, most aspects of clinical legal and ethical practice impinge on most of the multifarious specialities that comprise twenty-first century clinical practice.

The reader is encouraged to read every vignette bearing their own speciality in mind, since as the GMC and the Nursing and Midwifery Council correctly remind us, clinical law and ethics touch all facets of clinical care.

Anaesthetics: child refusing treatment

Relevant legal cases

- *Chester v Afshar* [2004].
- *Gillick v West Norfolk & Wisbeck Area Health Authority* [1986].

> James, a 15-year-old boy, entered the anaesthetic room prior to the re-moval of an ingrowing toenail. He had travelled by train 90 miles with his parents for the surgery under general anaesthesia, entailing his parents both losing a day's pay. He provided consent for his surgery in the out-patient department 4 weeks ago, and this was reaffirmed on the pro-posed day of the surgery, earlier in the day ward. No premedication had been used.
>
> James then declared that he was unwilling to proceed, despite repeated attempts at persuasion and consolation. His mother, accompanying him, suggested that he should be forcibly restrained. James weighed 105 kg, and it would not be a simple matter to restrain him.

Ethical considerations

It may be in James' medical best interests to undergo the procedure. If he does not, his parents will have wasted a lot of time and money to get him to hospital. However, if the procedure is forced on him, it may cause him harm, both psychologically, and possibly physically, if he attempts to flee or fight, and has to be restrained. This, given the relatively low urgency of his medical situation, weighs against forcible treatment. James' age might be a consideration in arguing that his consent is not required, since he is a minor. However, the problems involved in coercive treatment do not disappear just because the patient is a minor.

Legal situation

Clearly, this procedure would not have been recommended if it were not deemed to be medically necessary. As James is under the age of 16, con-sent can be given by his parents (if they have parental responsibility). His father will have parental responsibility if married to the mother, if registered as the father on James's birth certificate, or if he has an order from the court. If the doctor decides the treatment is not in James's best interest, the treatment should not be undertaken, even though his parents want him to have it. James' willingness to undergo the procedure may be significant in determining what his best interests are.

If James had Gillick competence then although he can consent to proced-ures, the current case law states he would have no right to refuse. Where a child refuses, a parent with parental responsibility can consent and give legal authorization for the procedure. While it is common for the refusals of Gillick competent children to be overruled in life-or-death cases, this is rare in practice if the procedure is elective.

Recommendation

Where neither life nor limb is at stake, the refusal of a competent child should be respected. It would be neither proportionate nor necessary to anaesthetize him against his will, since without surgery the discomfort and inconvenience of his toenail will remain, but nothing worse. If he is sent back to the ward further to consider his position, doubtless his parents will have a view, given the time and expense that a fruitless day out will have cost them. They may yet cajole him to submit, later in the day; or may end up taking him home without surgery, his ears ringing, where after a few months more misery associated with the toenail (and his parents' irritation), he will probably acquiesce to surgery. Another possibility is that James could be offered a sedative or premedication to calm him down so that his fear of surgery is reduced. Alternatively, discussion with James might elicit some of his fear. If it is the general anaesthetic that is the primary source of his anxiety, the operation could be carried out under local anaesthetic.

Cardiac surgery: candour

Relevant legal cases
* *Chatterton v Gerson* [1981].
* *Montgomery v Lanarkshire Health Board* [2015].

> An otherwise healthy 63-year-old man required coronary surgery to treat
> five-vessel disease. During the operation, a swab was placed temporarily
> behind the heart to make the surgery easier. At the end of this routine
> procedure, drains were placed, the chest was closed, and he was trans-
> ferred to the cardiac intensive care unit for postoperative care. After an
> uneventful night, a routine X-ray next morning revealed radio-opaque
> threads within the cardiac shadow; these were diagnosed as being indica-
> tive of a retained swab. Later that day, the patient, went back to theatre
> to have the swab removed. As the chest was reopened, his blood pres-
> sure fell, and after cardiorespiratory resuscitation neurological signs of a
> stroke were elicited. Three weeks later, he had a dense left hemiplegia.
>   An internal inquiry concluded that the patient had pre-existing (but hith-
> erto undiagnosed) cerebrovascular disease onto which the perioperative
> hypotension was superimposed, causing the stroke. However, this was
> not a unanimous finding, with a substantial minority in the inquiry panel
> believing that the stroke was haemorrhagic, unrelated to the hypotensive
> episode. The hospital risk department now seek advice as to whether a
> duty of candour has been engaged.

Ethical considerations
At one time, disclosure of medical mistakes was thought to be a complex
issue since there may be little benefit to the patient in knowing of the error.
Indeed, the patient may be distressed by this. However, there is now general support for a duty of candour. One of the ethical reasons in support of
a duty of candour is to maintain patients' trust in doctors and hospitals. This
trust may be undermined if information is kept secret, and in practice it is
very hard to ensure that patients or others will not find out information that
has been kept from them. The discovery of deliberate deception is arguably
much more damaging than an open acknowledgement of failing.

Legal situation
The risk should be disclosed. There is a duty to disclose the harm. A medical professional, in any case, should never lie to a patient or mislead a
patient about their treatment. If that is done with intent to prevent legal
proceedings that could even amount to the offence of fraud.

The patient's consent for the removal of the swab should have been
obtained, if he had capacity. At that point, the purpose of the operation
should have been disclosed.

Recommendation

Despite current confusion between statutory and professional regulatory thresholds, it is inescapable that the retained swab caused, at the very least, reoperation. Accordingly, clinicians and the hospital must be candid with the patient and his relatives that the swab was retained in error, and that this led to an otherwise avoidable (re)operation. An apology would be appropriate. What is less clear is the causal link between the reoperation and the stroke. Until uncertainties such as this are resolved as far as they can be, candour must be tempered by acknowledgement to the patient or relatives that the difference in opinions on causation persist. Uncertainties should not be portrayed as certainties.

Dentistry: Gillick competence

Relevant legal cases

- *Gillick v West Norfolk & Wisbeck Area Health Authority* [1986].
- *In the Matter of Charles Gard* [2017].
- *Re W (A Minor) (Medical Treatment: Court's Jurisdiction)* [1992].

> A 14-year-old needed dental extraction, due to two carious teeth. She presented for the procedure with her aunt, who did not have parental responsibility for her niece.

Ethical considerations

A key ethical question here is whether the child herself is able and willing to consent to the extraction. At 14 years old, it is very likely that a child will have the ability to understand the risks and benefits of a tooth extraction, and hence to make a decision as to whether they are willing to undergo the treatment. Because of this, the aunt's lack of parental responsibility may be irrelevant here. However, if the child (a) refuses treatment or (b) lacks the competence to make a decision, things will be more complex.

Legal situation

Minors do not have a default right to consent to or refuse medical treatment. These decisions will be made by their legal guardians. However, a child may be deemed to be 'Gillick competent'. To do so, they must demonstrate that in relation to the issue involved, in this case dental extraction, they can understand the benefits, risks, and complications of (and alternatives to) extraction, retain that information, and come to a decision, which they can then communicate, free of coercion.

Recommendation

If the child is Gillick competent (which seems likely in the absence of any reason to suppose otherwise), she can provide consent. In practice, if the child is accompanied by his/her parents or guardians, the clinician is likely to involve them in the discussion even though they may not have a formal role to play in giving consent. If the child is *not* Gillick competent, the dentist will need the consent of a person with parental responsibility or, if that is impossible, an order from the court authorizing the treatment. In an emergency situation (e.g. if the child's life was in danger or she was in unbearable pain) and there was not time to obtain a court order, the dentist could proceed with the procedure and rely on the defence of necessity. Similarly, if the child is Gillick competent, but refuses dental treatment (in the absence of consent from a person with parental responsibility), a court order authorizing the treatment will be required.

Dermatology: a right to treatment?

Relevant legal cases

- *R (Burke) v General Medical Council* [2005].

A 20-year-old woman with moderately severe late-onset acne on her face had tried the obvious topical and oral preparations without success. She powerfully asserted that her facial rash was 'utterly ruining my life'. The patient demanded Roaccutane®, a preparation of isotretinoin which her friends had told her works well in resistant acne, but that she had not yet been prescribed. Her doctor had explained that this drug is a powerful teratogenic, and that she should have monthly pregnancy tests during treatment period, prior to the monthly prescriptions. The doctor also advised the patient that Roaccutane® can have serious psychiatric side effects in some cases. She was not dissuaded by either of these concerns, and was not prepared to agree to the pregnancy tests. She demanded the drug despite the doctor's worries.

Ethical considerations

The simplest way of respecting the *autonomy* of this patient would be to provide treatment and allow the patient herself to determine whether the risks are acceptable. However, a doctor need not prescribe a drug not believed to be in the patient's best interests. But there is also an issue of *justice* here. There is nothing in the vignette to suggest that the patient is more at risk of the psychiatric side effects than anyone else. This makes it harder to demonstrate that the treatment can be withheld 'in her best interests' if it would be provided to a male patient who made the same request. Effectively, withholding treatment prioritizes the interests of a potential person over the current request of an actual one!

Legal considerations

The law will never require a medical professional to give treatment against their wishes. A doctor must decide what treatment (or set of alternative treatments) are appropriate for this patient. The patient can select which of the offered treatment she wishes to accept. She cannot be forced to undergo a pregnancy test and so her doctor must decide whether, even without the pregnancy tests, it is an acceptable treatment to offer her.

Recommendation

A sensible course of action would be to discuss with the patient why she is reluctant to undergo pregnancy testing. It may be that she would change her mind. If not, a second opinion could be sought.

Diabetology: maintaining clinical records

Relevant legal cases

The Hospital v JJ (by his litigation friend, the Official Solicitor) [2019] EWCOP 41.

A 57-year-old man with insulin-dependent diabetes was admitted with a urinary infection at around 11.00 am, while the hospital was on 'black alert', due to an almost overwhelming influx of sick patients. Septic and hyperglycaemic, he temporarily lacked capacity. It was not clear whether he had taken his customary morning dose of insulin. In view of his particular metabolic derangement, it was decided to give him a stat dose of insulin, and this was administered while he was in the emergency department (ED) at 11.20 am. The administration was recorded on the hospital's newly installed electronic prescribing system. The patient was moved to the acute medical unit, arriving at midday. His prescription chart was scrutinized on arrival, and the clinicians noted that the decision to administer stat insulin had not been carried out in the ED; the electronic record showing no evidence of the drug being given. The staff concluded that ED staff had been too busy to give the insulin, and (inadvertently) gave the patient a second dose, around 35 minutes after the first. The patient suffered no lasting ill effects, but the subsequent investigation into the serious matter of giving the same dose of insulin twice revealed a hitherto unknown 'cold spot' in the hospital's Wi-Fi network, explaining why a recorded dose given in the ED could not be seen as given by those using computers in the acute medical unit.

Ethical considerations

While the patient in this case was not harmed, there may still be an ethical question about whether he should be informed of the mistake. In one sense, this might seem needlessly harmful: the patient might feel distressed, angry, or anxious. At the same time, it is important that mistakes are acknowledged and learnt from. Disclosure can be an important part of this. In this particular case, it seems that no individual was personally at fault, rather, the failure arose through unforeseen problems in the system. This highlights the need both for careful testing of such systems, and for speedy and effective responses to problems when they arise. Informing the patient is not a necessary aspect of this, but may help in cementing the process of dealing openly with mistakes as they arise.

Legal issues

As fortunately the patient suffered no ill effects, no legal action is likely.

Recommendation

The GMC's 'Good Medical Practice', under the domain of knowledge, skills, and performance, makes it clear that doctors' clinical records should include any drugs that are prescribed to the patient. In this case, the doctor was entitled to believe that the electronic prescription had been successfully saved in the system, and that subsequent insulin dispensing would be recorded on each occasion the nurses administered a dose. There was no suggestion that the newly installed electronic prescribing system could be unreliable due to faulty 'coverage'. The clinicians involved all took reasonable steps to ensure that the patient had the correct dose of insulin at the correct time, and no blame was attached to them for this unexpected clinical outcome.

Elderly care: refusal of treatment

Relevant legal cases

- *Re B (Adult: Refusal Medical Treatment)* [2002].
- *St George's Healthcare NHS Trust v S* [1998].

An 82-year-old woman had been permanently incapacitated by the stroke that led to her hospital admission. It had been impossible for her to make decisions relating to her treatment for the past 4 months. She could swallow safely, but could only eat very slowly. She needed to be fed by her carer, and several hours were required to feed her sufficient food to sustain her. She resolutely removed every nasogastric tube that was passed, within hours of its placement, and nasogastric feeding had proved to be impractical.

The clinicians looking after her all agreed that a percutaneous endo-scopic gastrostomy (PEG) tube would be in her best interests, and their experience in managing these tubes assured them that the patient would be unable to pull this out. The lady's daughter was strongly opposed to gastrostomy insertion, but chose not to give her reasons for this oppos-ition. With a gastrostomy in place, the patient would be able to go to a nursing home; her benefits would be used to pay for this placement, and the tenancy on her rented house (where her daughter and granddaughter also lived) would lapse.

Ethical considerations

The patient's best interests seem to be the primary ethical concern here. The PEG tube is deemed best because she cannot tolerate a nasogastric tube. However, we are told that she can eat safely, but that it is time-consuming for her carers. This being the case, it's not clear that the PEG tube is obviously the best solution from a medical perspective. There may be questions about resource allocation too. The patient is managing accept-ably in her current situation, but the clinicians are reluctant to allow her to continue taking up so much of the carer's time. To complicate matters, there is the question of whether the relatives are motivated by their con-cern for the patient, or by self-interest.

A further question of justice arises in regard to the relatives' benefit status. Are they being treated with extra suspicion because of their eco-nomic vulnerability? Or is the question mark over their motivations a justi-fiable concern that would apply to any relative making a similar objection?

Legal situation

Under the Mental Capacity Act 2005, decisions about patients who lack capacity must be made based on assessment about what is in the best interests of that patient. Although the views of family members should be sought and can be taken into account, they do not determine the out-come of the assessment. If there is fierce disagreement, a court order can be sought to confirm that the procedure is in the best interests of patient (section 15(c), Mental Capacity Act 2005). However, there is no need for a court order to be obtained in this case, but if you were unsure what was in the best interests of the patient a court declaration could be sought.

Recommendation

The medical staff need to be consider carefully whether a PEG tube really is in the patient's best interests. They should try to do this objectively, without being influenced by their suspicions about the next of kin's motives. If they are satisfied that this is the case, they should explain their reasoning to the daughter, and proceed with the treatment. If they are unsure, they should seek a court declaration as to the best interests of the patient.

Emergency department: knife crime

Relevant legal cases

- *ABC v St George's Healthcare NHS Foundation Trust* [2017].

A 21-year-old woman presented with a knife wound to the ED. She had been walking home with her groceries when a hooded man demanded her purse and phone. She had swung a bag at his head, missed, and was slashed in the arm. He ran away, declaring himself a member of a banned terrorist group.

The victim lived with her two younger sisters on an estate notorious for revenge crime. She insisted, for her own safety, that the police should not be informed of the attack. Her wound was sutured, and she left the hospital before she could be given her follow-up appointment. The nurse practitioner believed that her admission must be reported to the police, but was uncertain whether this was correct.

Ethical considerations

It is important that patient trust in medical staff is protected. This makes things difficult when patients ask for secrecy or confidentiality in situations where healthcare staff may have conflicting duties. Where such conflicts arise, it is better to discuss them with the patient rather than act without their knowledge. Because of this, it is ethically sensible for healthcare professionals to be aware of what situations do call for a breach of patient confidentiality.

Legal situation

The starting point is that medical information is protected by the duty of confidentiality and must not be disclosed. However, a breach of confidence is permitted, but not required, where there has been a serious crime. This seems to be on the borderline of being serious crime or not. The crime here is not one of terrorism so there is no obligation to report the crime.

Recommendation

In this situation, the patient has already left and it's not clear whether her identity or contact details are available. This means that any information given to the police will be passed on without her knowledge. The GMC asserts an explicit obligation to report a knife attack but provides no obligation to disclose P's identity; and prevents disclosure if she refuses to discuss with police. This has the effect of alerting the police to a knife wielder-at-large while protecting P.

Emergency department: restraint/self-defence

Relevant legal cases

- *R v Gladstone Williams* [1984].

> Staff in the ED were concerned about a patient who was a regular attender. A pattern had emerged when following treatment for minor ailments: he was abusive and threatening to staff as he left the department. On the last occasion, a junior nurse feared that he might hit her. The ED staff sought advice as what they should do if this behaviour should continue or deteriorate.

Ethical considerations

Vulnerable patients might be the very patients who pose a risk to others. Tensions may be exacerbated by the understandable psychological distress of medical staff who fear attack simply because they are trying to do their job. This creates an ethical dilemma between the effort to benefit the patient, and the importance of protecting healthcare staff. There is a question here as to whether the patient should be regarded as a potential criminal (e.g. if he assaults staff) or as someone who is unable to control his behaviour, in which case he may need psychiatric treatment. Nevertheless, on the basis of the information given in the scenario, this patient has not attacked anyone. This might militate against undertaking coercive measures such as banning the patient, or restraining him in future. However, it would be advisable to ensure that there are staff on hand to step in if the patient were to become violent.

Legal situation

'Banning' persistently unruly patients from ED may seem an attractive prospect, but it is highly unlikely that a court would impose a meaningful ban that would also prevent a citizen from seeking assistance if he was seriously ill. If anyone believes an attack on someone is imminent, a reasonable amount of force can be used in defence.

Recommendation

A formal written warning from the medical director may temper the patient's behaviour. A referral to liaison psychiatry may also be helpful. Irrespective of the patient's capacity, staff have a right to defend themselves. They may use force which is reasonable in the circumstances if it is necessary to protect themselves, patients, and staff. They may also seek the help of security, or the police.

Endocrinology: wishes/feelings

Relevant legal cases

- *Wye Valley NHS Trust v Mr B* [2015].
- *Aintree University Hospitals NHS Foundation Trust v James* [2013].

A doctor was treating an elderly insulin-dependent diabetic patient, with severe vascular disease. His left foot had been ischaemic for some months, and was starting to develop gangrenous toes. Superadded infection had caused his fragile diabetes to become increasingly difficult to manage, and he had been referred to the vascular surgeons to consider a below-knee amputation. The patient lacked capacity to consent to the amputation, but he nevertheless had strong views in respect of his leg, consistently refusing the surgery. Discussions with his family revealed that the topic had been discussed frequently in the last 18 months. Despite his incapacity during this period (and lack of any advance decision to refuse treatment, or statement), he had always asserted that he wished to die with two feet attached, and regularly cited his own father's distress that he had survived after his leg had been blown off by a mortar round: 'He'd rather have stayed put and died on that battlefield.'

Both endocrine and vascular teams consider amputation to be in this man's best interests.

Ethical considerations

This is a case in which the previous and current interests of the patient may conflict. Although in the past, the patient had firm views as to amputation, he now lacks capacity. Amputation is in his medical best interests, but the situation is complicated by the patient's continuing objection. Even though he now lacks capacity to refuse treatment, his unwillingness to undergo the procedure may in itself affect its likelihood to benefit him. Some patients who lose capacity may also lose the strong beliefs and preferences they previously had. This is not the case for this patient, who seems to retain his convictions.

Legal situation

The Mental Capacity Act 2005 requires decisions to be made in the patient's best interests. However, in deciding what is in a patient's best interests, it is important to make an individual assessment taking into account their views and feelings, and the values they lived their life by. This does not mean that the views of a person who has lost capacity have to be followed, but they must be given respect.

Recommendation

The wishes and feelings of a patient, even if only informally presented, must be given very serious consideration. If dissonance within the clinical team, or between clinicians and relatives, remains after this consideration, the Court of Protection should be approached when serious medical treatment is proposed that is ostensibly contrary to the patient's wishes. The purpose of the approach is to seek a declaration as to where the incapacitated patient's best interests lie.

ENT: consent/necessity

Relevant legal cases

- *Chatterton v Gerson* [1981].
- *Re F (Mental Patient Sterilisation)* [1990].
- *Mohr v Williams* 104 NW 12 (SC Minn 1905).

> A 36-year-old man had a protuberant ear, and agreed with his surgeon that this anomaly should be corrected. Neither patient nor surgeon expressed an opinion with respect to the right pinna. Following reasonable disclosure, he consented to left pinnaplasty. During the surgery, under general anaesthesia, after successfully correcting the affected side, the surgeon became aware of a new asymmetry, since the right ear was now obviously far more protuberant than the (operated) left side. Alarmed at this result, the surgeon now wondered if he should operate on the right side, under the same anaesthetic.

Ethical considerations

The surgeon is motivated by beneficence: it seems very likely that the patient would want the surgery to result in a symmetrical appearance, and by operating now, it would avoid the need for further anaesthesia. However, the difficulty is that without having obtained consent, it is not entirely clear whether the procedure is in keeping with the patient's autonomy. We cannot be sure that the patient would accept the need for the additional procedure. As the procedure is not life-saving or otherwise medically indicated, the ethical balance swings in favour of bringing the patient round in order to discuss what additional procedures, if any, he wants to undergo.

Legal situation

The surgeon requires valid consent for any medical procedure, unless it is a medical emergency and without treatment the patient will suffer death or need life-saving treatment (*Mohr v Williams* 104 NW 12 (SC Minn 1905)). That exception does not apply in this case and it cannot be said that the consent to the left pinnaplasty is also consent to the right ear. It will be unlawful to operate on the right ear.

Recommendation

The surgeon should wake the patient up, and when he regains capacity, and has had a few days to consider the situation, he can decide whether he wants surgery on the right side. The surgeon cannot know whether the patient will be pleased with the current results, and should await the patient's verdict. This is not a situation where the patient's life or serious irremediable harm will occur in the absence of immediate further treatment, so the principle of *necessity* does not apply. A wise surgeon would take note of this situation, and ensure that the possibility of further surgery is discussed with the patient beforehand.

Family planning: Gillick competence

Relevant legal cases

- *Gillick v West Norfolk & Wisbeck Area Health Authority* [1986].
- *Re W (A Minor) (Medical Treatment: Court's Jurisdiction)* [1992].
- *Re X (A Child)* [2014] EWHC 1871 (Fam).

> A 14-year-old girl had sought contraceptive advice in a contraception clinic. When advised to discuss her concerns with her parents, she insisted that they must not be told that she had attended the clinic, or that she had been given advice. Clinic staff were unsure as to what their duties were in regard to the girl's parents.

Ethical considerations

Protecting patient confidentiality is an important ethical requirement in medicine. However, because this girl is so young—below the legal age of consent—the clinician may feel uneasy about whether to advise her, or try to inform her parents that she is having, or planning to have sex. There are risks that this girl may be exposed to if she embarks on a sexual relationship. Yet a breach of trust may drive the patient further into secrecy, and may increase the risk that she will have unsafe sex. Also, given that the doctor here has only offered advice rather than any intervention, any justification for breach of confidence is rather weak.

Legal situation

The Gillick decision makes clear that if a young person is Gillick competent, she is entitled to the protection of confidentiality.

Recommendation

If the patient *is* Gillick competent, their entitlement to confidentiality is as binding as that of any other patient. Nevertheless, as Lord Fraser exhorted clinicians in the Gillick case, all available opportunities must be taken during clinical encounters relating to reproductive decision-making to warn children of the dangers related to sex, the advisability of sharing their information with their parents, and the risks they take in not doing so.

Gastroenterology: Mental Health Act

Relevant legal cases
- *R v East London and the City Mental Health NHS Trust ex parte von Brandenburg* [2003].

A 24-year-old woman had been admitted from ED after taking a large paracetamol overdose. At this stage, the patient had capacity and had strongly asserted that she wanted no treatment, but the duty psychiatrist had reviewed her and concluded that she was both mentally ill and that she fulfilled the criteria to be detained under the Mental Health Act 1983, which she duly was. While in ED, her levels had been checked, and emergency treatment to reduce very high levels of the drug was administered without her consent.

Subsequently, while the patient was still sectioned under the Mental Health Act 1983, 72 hours after her injury, there were clear signs of severe hepatorenal damage. It became urgent to provide support for her hepatic function, and renal replacement therapy, both of which she again refused to accept. The nursing staff were concerned about the legality of imposing these treatments against the patient's wishes.

Ethical considerations
Treating a patient without consent is always an ethically fraught undertaking. In cases of mental illness, capacity assessments can be very challenging. Mental illness does not necessarily render someone incapable of consenting to, or refusing treatment. In situations of life-or-death refusals, the boundary between an irrational but capacitous refusal, and a refusal stemming from lack of capacity associated with mental illness can be almost impossible to discern. In this case, the patient has been consistent in her ongoing refusals of treatment. In addition, the proposed treatment requires a high level of cooperation from the patient; ongoing enforced treatment may be traumatic and even harmful for the patient.

Legal situation
Treatment under the Mental Health Act 1983 can only be given for a mental disorder. However, this includes physical illness that is ancillary to a mental disorder. Here, the emergency treatment of her paracetamol overdose (which she took due to the psychiatric illness she had been sectioned for) was given on the basis of treatment of physical illness ancillary to her depression. It can, therefore, be authorized under the Mental Health Act.

Recommendation
Here, the key issue is capacity. If the patient does have capacity, her refusal of treatment must be respected despite the fact that she has a mental illness and even if her refusal will foreseeably cause her death. For a decision of such gravity, it is worth seeking second opinions on a capacity assessment, as well as input from a psychiatrist.

General practice: cultural circumcision

Relevant legal cases

- *Re L and B (Children: Specific Issues: Temporary Leave to Remove from the Jurisdiction: Circumcision)* [2016].

A GP was asked to refer a 3-year-old boy to a surgeon in a private hospital for a cultural circumcision. The child had attended the doctor's clinic with his father, who remarked that the child's mother was unwell and was not able to attend the appointment.

Ethical considerations

There are ethical controversies surrounding the practice of cultural circumcision, which is usually carried out on young children who are unable to give consent. Despite this, such circumcisions are legal in many countries, including the UK. Perhaps because of the somewhat contentious nature of circumcision, it is expected that both parents should give consent for the procedure rather than only one as in most other paediatric medical interventions.

Legal situation

Generally, for routine surgery consent of one parent is sufficient. However, in the case of cultural circumcisions, it is wise to have the consent of both parents. If the parents disagree, the issue should be taken to a court to resolve.

Recommendation

The GP should inform the father that both parents' consent is required for this particular procedure. Without the mother's consent, the referral cannot be made. It might also be noted there is a body of opinion that male circumcision is not a medically necessary procedure and it would be preferable to allow the child, when old enough, to decide whether they wish to be circumcised.

General surgery: need for clinicians to keep up to date

Relevant legal cases

- *Lillywhite v UCL* [2005].
- *Bolam v Friern Hospital Management Committee* [1957].

An 8-year-old obese boy presented with a clinical picture of appendicitis that warranted treatment; the history revealed a 6-day illness. The consultant surgeon reviewed him at 9.00 am on a Monday, within 4 hours of his arrival in hospital, and advised the boy's parents that an open appendicectomy was required. In seeking their consent, she disclosed her plan to make a Lanz incision in the right iliac fossa, and extract the inflamed appendix. She made it clear that the incision might have to be extended considerably if copious pus and complex adhesions were encountered, which was foreseeable in these circumstances. She also disclosed the theoretical possibility of using a laparoscopic approach, but explained that she did not believe this was the best procedure for this child. During the operation, an extensive appendix mass was encountered. The surgeon set out to remove this, and in doing so made several holes in the small bowel, 15 cm of which needed to be resected, and the resulting anastomoses protected by a loop ileostomy.

During a multiprofessional discussion a few days later, her colleagues raised the question as to why she had operated at all. It was pointed out that within the last 10 years, conservative management of appendix masses, using intravenous antibiotics and supportive care, had radically reduced the requirement for early surgery in children. The surgeon accepted that she was unaware of this development. Was her overall management reasonable?

Ethical considerations

Surgeons have a duty to keep abreast of the literature, to ensure they adapt and advance their practice in accordance with what has been learnt. A failure to do this may be the result of negligence, laziness, or arrogance. If so, it would seem that the surgeon has acted immorally. Yet surgeons also have many other claims on their time. Balancing the need to keep up to date with the immediate demands of patients may be a tricky business. In this particular case, we are told that the benefits of conservative management had become apparent over 10 years. The length of time may make us more inclined to view the surgeon as having failed in her moral duty. This failing is compounded by the fact that she caused injury to her patient, not just by virtue of performing a more invasive procedure than was necessary, but by further harming the patient during surgery.

Legal issues

If the case goes to court as a negligence case it will be asked whether the surgeon was acting in line with a responsible body of medical opinion based on the state of knowledge at the time of the procedure. The court will ensure they will not be judged by the state of knowledge at the time of the trial. A court will expect professionals to keep abreast of developments, but not of articles in obscure journals or matters which it would not be reasonable for them to know about.

Recommendation

It is instructive to compare the surgeon's rejection of the laparoscopic operation with her non-disclosure of conservative management of the appendix mass. She disclosed and then dismissed laparoscopy on the basis of her clinical judgement. Whether or not you agree with her choice, she was entirely reasonable in adopting the principle of dealing with a complicated appendicitis as an open operation. In this context, there was more than one reasonable option for treatment. By contrast, she had failed to keep up with modern practice, since she was oblivious to the possibility of conservative management. If she had known about it, and disclosed it as a possibility to the parents, they would have been entitled to prefer the non-operative approach, even if that leads to a second opinion. As it was, they were denied that choice. That is not to say that operative treatment was unreasonable. Simply that where a choice exists, patients or parents should be made aware of it, giving them an opportunity to seek the alternative disclosed. Once more, the 'knowledge' domain of the GMC's 'Good Medical Practice' exhorts us to keep our professional knowledge up to date.

Genetics: confidentiality

Relevant legal cases

- *ABC v St George's Healthcare NHS Trust* [2015].

A 39-year-old woman presented to neurologists with abnormal movements and a change in her personality, although she retained her capacity. After investigation, the clinical diagnosis of Huntington's disease was made. The patient had two daughters, the older being 20 years old and engaged to be married. Following genetic confirmation, the patient refused to disclose her diagnosis to her daughters. At a multidisciplinary meeting, the ethical issue of non-disclosure was raised, particularly since the foreseeable risk of inheriting the Huntington's gene and inadvertently passing it on to her future children was relevant to the oldest daughter.

Ethical considerations

The default ethical position is usually to maintain patient confidentiality. Here, the patient has received a devastating diagnosis, but still retains capacity. Arguably, she has a moral responsibility to inform her daughters that they may be at risk, but whether the medical professionals have the right or the obligation to do so, or to force her to do so is less clear. Overriding the patient's wishes in this scenario may cause lasting damage to her and to her family. And the patient's refusal to disclose the diagnoses may be something that she changes her mind about as time passes and she comes to terms with her situation. Nevertheless, this dilemma is difficult for medical staff, who may envisage the daughter finding out, perhaps too late to use diagnostic testing for her own children. Respect for confidentiality necessarily comes at a cost to others who may wish to know information relating to their family or loved ones.

Legal situation

Generally, a patient with capacity can defend their private information, notwithstanding the risk this may confer to their family. In *ABC v St George's Healthcare NHS Trust* [2015], a case with similar facts to this, the Court of Appeal accepted that a doctor could inform the relatives of a man diagnosed with Huntington's disease, indeed, that they might be under a legal duty to so.

Recommendation

Respect for patient confidentiality requires that doctors do not override patients' wishes about disclosure, even though they may strongly disagree with the patient's decision. However, the clinician is perfectly entitled to do their best to persuade patients to share their information and if sensitively approached, it may be that the patient will eventually make the decision to disclose.

Gynaecology: abortion

Relevant legal cases

- *Health Board V Doogan* [2014].

> A 24-year-old woman presented at 11 weeks of gestation for a termination of pregnancy. A vaginal pessary of prostaglandin needed to be prescribed, but the doctor's cultural beliefs precluded her from providing this prescription.

Ethical considerations

There is a conflict between the interests of the patient and the beliefs of the doctor here. Respect for the patient's autonomy dictates that she should receive the requested intervention. Beneficence also suggests that this is the appropriate course of action, since termination of pregnancy within the first trimester is medically safer than undergoing pregnancy and childbirth. However, the treatment is intended to end the life of the fetus. This remains an ethically contested area in UK society. While the doctor has the legal right to refuse involvement with abortion, they have an obligation to refer the patient to someone else.

This disadvantages the patient who may experience delays before being able to access treatment. For the doctor who truly believes that abortion is murder, referring a patient to someone else may still amount to complicity in murder.

Legal perspective

The Abortion Act 1967 permits a doctor, on grounds of conscience, to avoid involvement with abortion; but the GMC imposes the obligation, in the circumstances, to refer the patient to another doctor.

Recommendation

The doctor must refer the patient to a colleague. Any doctor who feels that to make such a referral is unacceptable to his/her conscience cannot really practise medicine within a framework that permits abortion.

HIV: confidentiality

Relevant legal cases

- *ABC v St George's Healthcare NHS Foundation Trust* [2017].

> A 36-year-old man had a new diagnosis of HIV/AIDS. He had had many sexual partners, estimated as hundreds over the last 18 months. He refused to warn past or prospective partners of his potential risk to them, although insisted his sexual practice was safe. A colleague in genitourinary medicine questioned whether irrespective of the patient's wishes, his HIV status should be disclosed.

Ethical considerations

The patient's interest in maintaining confidentiality may be in conflict with the interests of the man's sexual partners. However, it is not a certainty that there is any such risk. Moreover, one might argue that this is a matter of personal responsibility for each adult to decide whether or not to practise safe sex, not the responsibility of healthcare professionals to police people's personal lives.

Legal situation

Confidentiality must be preserved unless there is a very strong reason not to. The risk of someone acquiring HIV might be. The case would be strongest where the patient had one regular sexual partner where the risk of acquiring HIV from the patient would be higher and a limited breach of confidentiality (just to the partner) could take place. Even then, breach would be permitted, but not required. In this case where there are multiple partners, it is not clear that any one of them is at especially high risk and the risk could only be avoided by breaching confidentiality to a large number of people.

Recommendation

The proposal of mass disclosure to all this man's partners is impractical, and for this reason rather than primarily due to concerns over confidentiality, such steps have not been taken. In cases where there is one or a small number of identifiable partner(s) to whom a patient may pose an infective risk, it may be justifiable to disclose the risk if the patient will not do so; but this is not invariably the case, and advice—either from a senior clinician, or from a clinical ethics committee—should be sought in these circumstances.

Intensive care: DNACPR

Relevant legal cases

- *Tracey v Cambridge University Hospital NHS Foundation Trust* [2014].
- *Winspear v City Hospitals Sunderland NHS Foundation Trust* [2015].

> A 51-year-old lady had while capacitous an immense interest and engagement with her treatment decisions for an inoperable lung cancer. Very soon after her diagnosis, she suffered a traumatic fracture of her neck, and after a sudden deterioration, paralysis, and ventilation was required, precluding her capacity to decide whether she wanted to be resuscitated in the event of cardiorespiratory arrest. In the early hours of the morning, the registrar looking after her appended a do not attempt cardiopulmonary resuscitation (DNACPR) order to her notes, but did not consult her relatives before doing so. He had not discussed this decision with his patient before she lost her capacity.

Ethical considerations

DNACPR decisions can be difficult, since patients do not have the right to demand CPR, and discussions about end of life situations can be sensitive. However, as with all medical decisions, patients have the right to be informed about aspects of their care. In the case of DNACPR, if CPR is withheld in the patient's best interests, or on the grounds of futility it will be necessary to discuss with the patient or their relatives in order to have a full picture of what is in their best interests or what they might hope to achieve through undergoing CPR. An opportunity to learn the patient's views was lost in this case. Patients will inevitably have personal information that may be, unbeknownst to their doctors, highly relevant to a DNACPR decision. Perhaps their life insurance policy, earmarked for their children, will mature in the next 36 hours? Or a family wedding is imminent? Clinicians may worry about upsetting patients with DNACPR discussions, but it is worth noting that many medical discussions have the potential to be upsetting, and this does not mean they can be omitted. Sensitive communication is the key to minimizing any distress caused. They may also wish to challenge the decision through a second opinion.

Legal situation

A DNACPR notice should not be appended to a patient's notes without a discussion with the patient (if they have capacity) or their relatives (if they lack capacity).

Recommendation

Patients or their relatives must be consulted over DNACPR decisions where it is practicable to do so, unless the consultation will cause the patient *harm*, rather than merely distress. Nevertheless, once consultation has been achieved, the decision itself rests with the doctor.

Interventional radiology: relative risks

Relevant legal cases

- *Birch v UCL* [2008].
- *Montgomery v Lanarkshire Health Board* [2015].

> A man in his 50s with a history of headaches was suspected of having an intracranial vascular anomaly. He was offered two options of initial management: cerebral angiography via arterial catheterization, or magnetic resonance angiography, avoiding catheterization. He was told that the catheter technique would provide clearer images of the anatomy, leading to a more certain diagnosis. He was encouraged to choose this approach by the head of department. However, the operating surgeon was unsure as to whether there was a need to disclose other information.

Ethical considerations

There is an ethical requirement to ensure patients are fully informed about procedures, including their likelihood of success, risks and side effects, and the risks and benefits of any alternatives, including doing nothing. Even when doctors have strong feelings about the most appropriate intervention, it is their responsibility to explain this and justify it to the patient, rather than relying on providing selective information in order to nudge the patient towards the 'right' decision.

Legal situation

The Supreme Court decision of *Montgomery v Lanarkshire Health Board* [2015] makes it clear that all material risks should be disclosed to a patient. That is, all risks that a reasonable patient or this particular patient would attach significance to. There is a 'therapeutic exception', which will rarely apply, in cases where the distress to the patient caused by informing them of the risks outweighs the benefit of doing so.

Recommendation

Any information that would influence a reasonable patient in their decision should be disclosed. In this instance, where there are two alternatives envisaged, the relative risks of stroke associated with both procedures must be disclosed, among other information. Since the numeric risk of stroke in catheterization is recognized, and magnetic resonance angiography would be safer in this respect than catheterization, this difference between the two procedures would influence reasonable decision-making.

Maxillofacial: candour

Relevant legal cases
• *Montgomery v Lanarkshire Health Board* [2015].

> A 53-year-old Muslim man was involved in a road traffic collision, sustaining serious facial and mandibular injuries. During a subsequent elective flap transfer procedure, it became evident that a fascial defect at the site of the donor tissue needed to be repaired, and the surgeon elected to use a pig-based material. The significance of using such tissue in a Muslim patient did not occur to the surgical team at the time of its insertion. However, after the issue was recognized, a decision needed to be made as to whether the patient should be informed.

Ethical considerations

The problem here relates to the likelihood of harming the patient either psychologically, just through knowing about the pork-derived material, or even physically, if he insists on having it removed. However, respect for the patient's autonomy requires that he should be informed of issues that are likely to be important to him. It's possible that he may be a non-practising Muslim, in which case the use of pork derivatives may not be a problem. But this cannot be known until he is informed. Some might argue that there are many ingredients in medicines and patients cannot be informed about every conceivable aspect of a treatment or product. There are also questions about who should be informed. A vegetarian might also object to the use of pork derivatives, as might a Jew. There is a balance here between patients' obligations in terms of informing themselves as to which treatments and procedures might be objectionable, and the doctors' obligations in ensuring that where they have reason to think that a particular product might be problematic, they should ensure the patient is aware. In this situation, the recognition of the potential problem has come too late in the day to have the discussion in advance.

Legal situation

The GMC (and the other professional regulators in the UK) are unanimous in asserting that 'if something goes wrong', the patient should be informed. However, legally, the use of pig tissue will only count as a 'notifiable safety incident' if it causes prolonged psychological distress. If there is no risk of that, the disclosure may not be legally required. That said, if a doctor lies to a patient in order to avoid legal proceedings, that could amount to the criminal offence of fraud. Further, even if not legally required, it might be thought good professional practice to inform the patient. Indeed, failure to do so may well be viewed as misconduct by a professional body.

Recommendation

Once the clinicians have identified that porcine material was used, there is an obligation to notify the patient about this. The patient may choose to do nothing about it, or he may wish to take steps to remedy the situation, but if the clinicians fail to disclose the information, the patient may feel that he has been deceived, if he ever finds out. In this kind of situation, it would be advisable to put measures in place to ensure that all patients are informed about materials containing pork-derivatives in advance of any elective surgery.

Additional reading

General Medical Council. Domain 1: knowledge skills and performance. In: Good medical practice. 2013. Available at: ℞ https://www.gmc-uk.org/ethical-guidance/ethical-guidance-for-doctors/good-medical-practice/domain-1---knowledge-skills-and-performance.

Chapter 23

Ethico-legal issues
by medical specialism N–V

Neonatal surgery: Jehovah's Witnesses 262
Neonatology: consent 263
Neurology: the clash of rights between a child and parents 264
Neurosurgery: information governance 265
Neurosurgery: innovation 266
Neurosurgery: preservation of evidence 268
Obstetrics: needle phobia 269
Ophthalmology: statutory disclosures 270
Paediatric cardiology: unlicensed equipment 271
Plastics: disclosure 272
Renal: capacitous adult refusing treatment 274
Respiratory: unwise decisions 275
Rheumatology: doctrine of double effect 276
Speech: capacity 277
Trauma and orthopaedics: necessity 278
Urology: liberty 279
Vascular surgery: disclosure 280

Neonatal surgery: Jehovah's Witnesses

Relevant legal cases

- *Re J (A Minor) (Medical Treatment)* [1992].
- *Gillick v West Norfolk & Wisbech Area Health Authority* [1986].

> A premature baby, 28 weeks and 1.4 kg with necrotizing enterocolitis, developed a gut perforation, and required surgery within the next 6 hours. It was a Friday evening. Her parents were Jehovah's Witnesses. They wanted their baby to live, but steadfastly refused to consent to her being given a blood transfusion. Intraoperative blood loss and the necessity for blood transfusion were both clinically inevitable. The anaesthetist would not start the case without blood and platelets being available.

Ethical considerations

The intervention appears to be very clearly in the best interests of the patient. However, religious convictions may be regarded as outweighing health or even life itself. This is why refusals of blood can be very frustrating for medical professionals whose urge to save life is thwarted. In the case of parents making decisions for children, however, the situation is complicated by the fact that the child is not in a position to make their own decision.

Legal situation

As the parents are refusing to consent, the ideal option is to obtain a court order authorizing the procedure. It is very likely the court will make the order. Court orders in such cases can be obtained very rapidly, but if the child's life is in danger without immediate intervention a doctor can proceed with the operation and seek to rely on the doctrine of necessity.

Recommendation

If the parents are implacably opposed to transfusion, there is sufficient time to make a telephone application to the Court of Protection for a Specific Issue Order under section 8 of the Children Act 1989, authorizing a lawful blood transfusion. Most parents in this situation are grateful for this legal provision, inserted into the statute after consultation with the Jehovah's Witnesses. The telephone number for emergency applications to the Court of Protection is 020 7421 8824.

Neonatology: consent

Relevant legal cases

- *Re S (Child as Parent: Adoption: Consent)* [2017].
- *Gillick v West Norfolk & Wisbech Area Health Authority* [1986].

A 13-year-old girl delivered a term baby, who was unwell. Conforming with good practice, the neonatologist wished to obtain consent to perform a lumbar puncture on the baby but was uncertain as to whether the 13-year-old mother could provide this.

Ethical considerations

A mother would normally expect to be the one to give consent for a medical procedure. Here, the mother herself is a minor, however, which may call into question her ability to make decisions for herself, let alone another person. There may be a risk that her decisions would be unwise, or even harmful for the baby. However, in this scenario, there is no suggestion that the mother would refuse the procedure for her child. Additionally, the question of justice may be important here: it might seem unjustly discriminatory to deny this mother the right to make decisions on behalf of her baby, on the grounds of her age alone. After all, even though she is very young, she *is* also the mother of a child.

Legal situation

A woman who is delivered of a baby automatically has parental responsibility for the baby, irrespective of her own age. In the case of very young mothers, following antenatal planning the local authority will often ensure that either they or a family member, often maternal grandmother, will share parental responsibility with the young mother.

Recommendation

As long as the mother can establish her Gillick competence to provide consent for her baby's lumbar puncture, she has the right to do so.

Neurology: the clash of rights between a child and parents

Relevant legal cases

- *Gillick v West Norfolk & Wisbeck Area Health Authority* [1986].
- *In the Matter of Charles Gard* [2017] EWCA Civ 410.
- *Re X (A Child)* [2020] EWHC (Admin) 1958.

A newborn baby suffered an exorable neurological deterioration, initially of unknown origin, which later became linked with mitochondrial disease. Despite exhaustive investigations, no treatment could be found to halt the progression of the illness and by 3 months of age the child was dependent on invasive ventilation and enteral nutrition though a gastrostomy. As the weeks were passing, he was tolerating smaller and smaller daily volumes of tube feeds due to apparent gut obstruction. His increasing transit time was thought to reflect reducing enteric muscle activity. The clinicians looking after him were unanimous that continued treatment was no longer in his best interest. This contrasted sharply with the views of his parents, who wished to exercise their parental rights and insist on his transfer to a clinic in Austria, which was offering a treatment for his mitochondrial disease, albeit one that was not supported by any published or verifiable evidence.

Ethical considerations

Cases such as these raise not only legal and clinical questions, but deeper philosophical disputes. Parents may prioritize risky or unproven treatments, where clinicians view the case as being futile. For parents, the need to know they have done everything possible can be imperative, even if it has little chance of success. Moreover, they may feel that any extra time they can have with their child is worthwhile. This discrepancy often leads to a breakdown of trust and communication. Careful and sensitive discussions may mitigate these problems, but once trust is lost, it is very hard to rebuild. If this has happened, a consultation with a clinical ethics committee can help to ensure that parents' views are formally recognized and considered. Sometimes a clinical ethics committee's judgement may be accepted where a mere clinical refusal of treatment is not.

Legal issues

Decisions must be made based on what is in the child's best interests. Parents have no right to demand treatment for their children. If necessary, a court declaration could be sought confirming it would be lawful to follow the clinical view.

Recommendation

Recent legal judgments have made clear that the child's best interests must prevail. Where the rights of a child are in conflict with his parents' expressed rights to a private and family life, as in this case, the child's right must be the paramount consideration. To resolve such a deeply engrained difference of strongly held beliefs between parents and clinicians, recourse to the court may be inevitable.

Neurosurgery: information governance

Relevant legal cases

- *Christian Institute v Lord Advocate* [2016].

> At the depot of a bicycle hire company contracted to the hospital for staff use, a ward discharge summary is found on the ground. It contained patient identifiable data, including clinical and demographic information. Does such data loss matter?

Ethical considerations

Any breach of patient confidentiality represents a failing of moral duty on the part of those who are responsible. In practice, human beings are fallible, and mistakes may happen. A conscientious health professional will be aware of this and make efforts to ensure that they do not transport sensitive data in situations where they may be unable to keep track of it effectively. Where a breach occurs, it is important that those concerned own up to it, and try to identify ways of avoiding such errors in future. As with other instances in which mistakes or errors occur in medicine, there may be grounds for thinking that the patients should be informed of the breach.

Legal matters

If there is a concern that there has been a breach of confidentiality (e.g. that the paper has been read by unauthorized people), the duty of candour would require a disclosure to the patient. The hospital would want to do all it could to limit the extent to which there was disclosure of the information.

If the document has been read by unauthorized people it is unlikely the hospital or medical professional will be subject to a legal case, unless it can be shown that an economic loss has been caused. The patient may seek an injunction to prevent people disclosing the information further.

The Information Commissioner's Office regularly imposes fines on NHS trusts for data losses and this can generate significant reputational damage. These can be imposed even if no patient suffered harm as a result.

Recommendation

Ironically, patients are sometimes more concerned over the loss of their demographic (rather than clinical) data. Such a breach of data protection law must be reported to the Information Commissioner's Office and a detailed local investigation will ensue. The transition to electronic data records will to an extent reduce the frequency of incidents relating to loss of paper documents, but the wholesale inadvertent transfer of confidential electronic files to the wrong recipient remains an unresolved problem in clinical life.

Neurosurgery: innovation

Relevant legal cases

- *Simms v Simms* [2004].
- *R (Burke) v General Medical Council* [2005].

> Thirty-five years ago, a surgeon inadvertently let go of the ventricular component of a ventriculoperitoneal shunt, and with horror watched it drop back inside the patient's head. The indication for surgery was to remove the infected shunt, so this was a serious matter, not least because with the nidus of infection lying within the brain, the patient could not be cured without removing the fragment. Neurosurgical ventriculoscopy was unheard of (at least in the jurisdiction the surgeon was working) so it was indeed an innovative act when he took a small cystoscope and a pair of grabbers and extracted the shunt.
>
> There will be occasional instances when the urgency of the situation justifies untested innovation; absent the innovative act, the patient will die or suffer irreparable harm. As an example, a doctor once succeeded in placing a surgical cricothyroidotomy with the sharp end of a coat hanger while in mid-air, at 25,000 feet. Without it, the patient would have died. But the same action in a normally equipped ED would have been unthinkable. This provides us with useful guidance; 'rare circumstances' where time is of the essence, life or limb is immediately about to be lost, and the intervention would be impossible without an innovative step will be an extraordinary event. But should such circumstances arise, innovate.

Ethical considerations

There is a hazy boundary between acceptable variations of clinical practice and innovation. This is particularly true of surgery. Here, it can be useful to think about the motivations behind such innovation. In the case described previously, there was a justification based on the urgency of the situation. In other situations, the surgeon may be motivated primarily by a wish to try out a new idea or method. Where there is no justification based on urgent need, innovation is more properly to be regarded as a matter of research. There exists a well-established procedure for the ethical review of research, which should always be the first consideration for a surgeon who wants to try an unproven approach unless, as here, the innovation is the only way of avoiding catastrophic results for the patient. In this particular case, it seems that an accident had generated this urgent situation—something which in itself may cause some ethical concern. From a moral perspective, it seems advisable that the patient should be informed afterwards, both about the innovative procedure and about the sequence of events that gave rise to it.

Legal matters

The major legal issue that could arise is a claim for negligence. A doctor will not be negligent if they are following a respected body of medical opinion. But therein lies the risk of innovation. If a doctor can show there were good grounds for the innovation, and particularly if it was needed to deal with a novel or life-threatening case, the courts are very likely to be sympathetic.

Recommendation

The introduction of untried or untested interventions into clinical practice is presumed to be a very bad idea, for obvious reasons. As a matter of principle, the risks and benefits of any intervention must be rigorously evaluated and then only adopted if the accumulated evidence supports the change of practice.

In the more usual clinical environment, neither time nor the clinical situation justify hasty innovation. If you feel that your innovation would improve the clinical outcome or have some other benefit, by all means investigate, evaluate, and make a proposal based on evidence. In most institutions, a multiprofessional committee scrutinizes potential innovations, and it should be involved in every step of the implementation of innovative interventions. On a larger scale, innovations costing the NHS significant money are scrutinized by NICE, who will take a view on cost benefit.

When you are unable to determine whether your innovation, (perhaps extraordinarily close to common practice with only the subtlest of variations) requires the same rigour of evaluation as those exhibiting a more obvious step-change, seek advice; but don't guess, and never innovate in isolation.

Neurosurgery: preservation of evidence

Relevant legal cases
* *Aintree University Hospitals NHS Foundation Trust v James* [2013].

A 22-year-old man was admitted from the ED with a head injury after being kicked and trampled upon. He was intubated and ventilated, incapacitated. A healthcare assistant pointed to a clear footprint on the left side of his head. It was evident that he might die of his neurological injury.

The police requested a photograph of the footprint, in order to identify the assailant, noting (correctly) that it would soon fade, or be washed away. The consultant in charge noted that the patient was unable to provide consent for clinical photography and might be reluctant to identify his assailant, fearing revenge.

Ethical considerations
The conflict here is between respect for the patient's autonomy to consent or refuse to be photographed, and a broader public interest in gaining evidence to apprehend criminals. The patient's lack of capacity means that he cannot give consent. Ordinarily, if a patient can't consent, doctors should act in his best interests. However, here the proposed course of action is not directly connected with the patient's best interests, but with the requirements of justice. This might be seen to override the need for consent, especially since the taking of the photo will not directly harm the patient's health.

Legal situation
As the patient currently lacks capacity, the photograph could be taken if that was thought in the best interests of the patient, which it might be given that the patient may want to press charges. However, the MCA can only be used if it is not reasonable to wait until the patient has capacity to make the decision. If it would be feasible to wait until the patient has capacity, that should be done. The police have no authority to require a photograph to be taken. If a photograph is taken, a court could authorize its disclosure under the Police and Criminal Evidence Act 1984 or the Terrorism Act 2000.

Recommendation
As the footprint is likely to deteriorate, if the photograph is taken at all, it will have to be without the patient's consent. However, the photograph could then be kept until the patient is able to give a view on it. This approach would balance the public interest in obtaining evidence to convict a criminal, with the patient's interest in deciding whether to allow the photograph to be used.

Obstetrics: needle phobia

Relevant legal cases
- Re MB (Medical Treatment) [1997] 2 FLR 426.

A 24-year-old woman, carrying her first pregnancy, required a Caesarean section due to the lie of her baby. Electively admitted for this at 39 weeks, she disclosed for the first time her morbid fear of injections, reporting that this had precluded her from having any dental treatment. Knowing that Caesarean section involves injections, she was afraid that as she is moved into the anaesthetic room she will refuse consent due to her terror of needles, and her baby will die.

Ethical considerations
It is important for patients to trust that their decisions will be respected, including decisions to refuse treatment. However, needle phobias may result in a patient refusing treatment that they wish on some levels to accept. It is important not to assume that a phobia or a seemingly irrational decision is in itself evidence of a loss of capacity.

Legal situation
Pregnant women have the right to refuse treatment even if it will result in the death of their fetus. However, if they are deemed to lack capacity, treatment can be carried out in their best interests. The patient should be asked in advance, when her capacity is assured, to provide consent for necessary and proportionate sedation, restraint, and any other restrictive techniques that may need to be employed to ensure her safety and that of her baby. This consent will explicitly anticipate her incapacity when faced with a needle.

Recommendation
Needle phobia can render a patient temporarily incapacitated. If this is a known problem, it should be discussed well in advance of the procedure, and alternatives to needles may be considered. The patient should be informed that if she loses capacity, because of her phobia, doctors will treat her in her best interests, if necessary using forms of restraint. If the patient does panic or refuse treatment, and doctors treating her believe that it is due to the needle phobia, they must ensure that a capacity assessment is carried out and fully documented.

Ophthalmology: statutory disclosures

Relevant legal cases

• *H (A Healthworker) v Associated Newspapers Ltd* [2002].

> An 80-year-old man, a new patient to the treating doctor, presented for
> treatment of his failing eyesight. Initial examination revealed that his sight
> was too poor to allow him lawfully to drive. At the end of the consult-
> ation, he utterly rejected this notion, stating he would get into his car and
> drive 25 miles home. He insisted that the doctor must not disclose his
> visual impairment to any authority.

Ethical considerations

It is important to respect patient confidentiality so that trust between
doctor and patient can be maintained. However, this is not an absolute
requirement. Confidentiality can be breached in some situations. Where
a breach is necessary (and here the possibility that the patient may pose a
danger to others is significant), it is vital to discuss this with the patient, and
to inform them if any breach of their confidentiality is planned.

Legal situation

There is a legal requirement to inform the Driver and Vehicle Licensing
Agency (DVLA) of impairments that render patients unsafe to drive. The
doctor cannot use force to prevent the patient driving away, but could alert
the police.

Recommendation

The doctors should try as far as possible to explain to the patient why it
is important that he should stop driving. The doctor should encourage the
patient to inform the DVLA. If it becomes evident that this does not occur,
the doctor should inform the patient that she will inform the DVLA, but will
give the patient a reasonable time to do so himself beforehand.

Paediatric cardiology: unlicensed equipment

Relevant legal cases
- *Simms v Simms* [2004].
- *R (Burke) v General Medical Council* [2005].

A professor of paediatric cardiology approached the local ethics committee because he wished to use an unlicensed implantable defibrillator in a 5-year-old. The device's adult version is commonplace and holds all necessary regulatory qualifications, but the scaled-down version has no such approval.

Ethical considerations

Untested or unlicensed equipment and medical interventions are not uncommon in the treatment of children, largely because the recruitment of children into clinical trials is ethically complex. Most medical products are designed for use in adults, and doctors have to make adjustments to accommodate them for use in children. This inevitably results in a degree of uncertainty and possibly of additional risks for children. However, the alternative would be to expose children to risks in clinical trials. There seems no perfect ethical solution here.

Legal situation

As long as the professor can show that his proposed use would be accepted as a sound medical treatment by a respected body of medical opinion (the Bolam test), he will not be liable in tort. The professor should ensure the parents of the child are informed that the proposed treatment is unlicensed when obtaining their consent.

Recommendation

Many drugs and devices are unlicensed for children. Provided the person with parental responsibility is made fully aware of the limitations, risks, benefits, alternatives, and uncertainties that prevail in these clinical circumstances and that the use of the device conforms with reasonable cardiac practice, and is in the child's best interests, there is no objection to the use of the device.

Plastics: disclosure

Relevant legal cases

• *Montgomery v Lanarkshire Health Board* [2015].

A 20-year-old woman was referred with a tattoo over the posterior triangle of her neck, the result of an old injury caused by being stabbed with a pencil. The graphite tip of the pencil, broken off and retained subcutaneously, had caused the tattooing. She wished to have the mark removed.

The surgeon who was going to perform the excisional surgery disclosed the risks of bleeding, infection, and a prominent scar, but failed to disclose either that damage to the accessory nerve could result, or that this damage could have an effect on the muscles that nerved supplied. On the basis of the disclosure, the patient provided consent for surgery.

Regrettably, the excisional biopsy inadvertently included the trunk of the accessory nerve, affecting the muscles of the shoulder girdle. Unbeknown to the surgeon, the patient was a keen and successful archer, a member of the Olympic squad. She was now unable draw her bow or aim an arrow. If she had known of the potential risk to her sporting career posed by the removal of her tattoo, she says she would have avoided surgery, and used camouflage makeup instead.

Ethical considerations

In order to give fully informed consent, patients need to know about the risks of the treatments being offered, and to have a chance to compare these with other potential treatments, and with the possibility of doing nothing. In this case, because the procedure was elective, and was being undertaken for primarily cosmetic purposes, it is very feasible that the patient would have chosen to avoid the risk of nerve injury. However, because this risk was not disclosed, she was unable to make this judgement. Clinicians sometimes feel they cannot disclose every conceivable risk related to a particular procedure, and this is true; however, respect for autonomy requires an engagement with the patient to find out which risks are likely to be most significant for them.

Legal situation

Following the decision of the Supreme Court in *Montgomery v Lanarkshire Health Board*, the surgeon should disclose all substantial risks. Those are defined as risks that a reasonable person or the particular patient would attach significance to. In this case, the surgeon should have taken reasonable steps to find out about the patient's lifestyle so she could have informed the patient of risks that would be significant to her.

Recommendation

Foreseeable complications of surgery should be disclosed; an operation within the posterior triangle may put the accessory nerve at risk. A discussion with the patient in advance of the procedure would have elicited her involvement in archery, and enabled a discussion to take place about the risks of nerve injury balanced against the visual improvement to be gained from surgery. In this scenario, the surgery had already gone ahead, meaning that there was little chance of remedying the situation, and also that the clinician might be at risk of being sued in negligence. For future procedures, a better level of discussion and disclosure should be sought in advance of the procedure, and this should take into account the patient's profession and activities, and the ways that the procedure might affect them.

Renal: capacitous adult refusing treatment

Relevant legal cases
- *Aintree University Hospitals NHS Foundation Trust v James* [2013].

A 18-year-old woman suffered an acute kidney injury after taking a para-cetamol overdose. Her hepatic injury was resolving. The renal opinion as to whether she would need long-term renal replacement therapy was divided, but the majority view was that she would become independent of dialysis within 6 months. The patient had a highly developed view of her own image and lifestyle, and she was adamant that she would rather die than suffer long-term treatment. Several independent assessors have concluded that she has the capacity to make these decisions.

Ethical considerations
The conflict here is between autonomy—respect for the patient's wish to refuse dialysis, and beneficence—the doctors' concern for her welfare. There is an added question raised by the fact that she has taken an overdose which might suggest that she has been suffering from depression or another mental illness. However, since she is deemed to have capacity, the overdose itself cannot be taken to indicate that she is incapable of making a decision relating to dialysis.

Legal situation
Patients with mental capacity may make unwise, irrational, or random de-cisions; irrespective of their visceral disagreement, clinicians must abide by these. If there is disagreement over whether the patient has mental capacity a legal declaration from the Court of Protection could be sought.

Recommendation
It would be advisable to explore sensitively the patient's reluctance to re-ceive dialysis. The consequences of failing to do so should be clearly ex-plained. Counselling and psychiatric support should be offered if they are needed. Where staff strongly disagree with her refusal of treatment, it may help to discuss the case with the hospital's clinical ethics committee. The patient may also benefit from this, in feeling that her wishes are being con-sidered. Ultimately, however, if the patient has capacity for this decision and persists in her refusal, those treating her are obliged to respect that refusal.

Respiratory: unwise decisions

Relevant legal cases

- *Wye Valley NHS Trust v Mr B* [2015].
- *Aintree University Hospitals NHS Foundation Trust v James* [2013].

A 65-year-old long-term smoker was in end-stage respiratory failure, being managed on oxygen. She lived at home, and smoked cigarettes while using her oxygen concentrator. She refused to stop smoking—it was her only pastime. Smoking is contraindicated for oxygen-dependent patients but remains relatively common (℘ http://www.ncbi.nlm.nih.gov/pmc/articles/PMC3188038/). However, for oxygen-dependent smokers, there is a risk that the cigarette may ignite the oxygen. In this patient's case, cylinders of oxygen were being stored in the house, so that if the oxygen concentrator failed, she would still have an oxygen supply. Her house was in the middle of a five-house terrace of two-storey buildings.

This situation had been unchanged for 18 months, but a new community care manager had been appointed, and became aware of the arrangement. He ascertained that the patient could not and would not smoke outside. A decision had to be made, he asserted. She must either give up smoking, or agree to have her oxygen removed since she was putting herself and other residents of the building at risk. The patient said she could not face life without cigarettes and for herself, she was happy to accept the risk.

Ethical considerations

There are several areas of conflict here. Respect for the patient's autonomy entails that she should be allowed to continue smoking, and beneficence requires that she should not be deprived of the oxygen she needs. This puts her at risk, and this is her own choice. Two factors complicate this: firstly—is the patient being unfairly penalized because she's a smoker? Around a fifth of oxygen-related fires occur in non-smokers, so preventing this patient from smoking doesn't entirely remove the risk. However, the risk that the patient is contemplating also affects those living around her.

Legal situation

As she has mental capacity, this patient has the right to choose to continue to smoke and forego the oxygen, even if this will shorten her life. Her decision must be respected, however foolish others might believe it to be.

Recommendation

This is a situation in which exploration of all the possibilities would be sensible. Perhaps the patient could be offered accommodation in a place that allows her to get outside more easily in order to smoke, while not having to forego her oxygen. Another possibility might be to enable her to remove her nasal cannulae while she has a cigarette. Alternatively, the backup oxygen cylinders could be removed from the house so that if there were a fire it would be more contained. The draconian option that she has been presented with seems quite extreme. This is a situation in which careful analysis of the risks and facts would be useful. If the risks pertained only to this particular patient, as a competent adult, she would be entitled to choose this risk. However, the risk to her neighbours is an important factor.

Rheumatology: doctrine of double effect

Relevant legal cases

- *Re A (conjoined twins)* [2001].

A 64-year-old woman had been suffering for many years with rheumatoid arthritis, of increasing severity, and florid extra-articular disease. Her illness had recently been complicated by lymphoma, and she was receiving palliative care. It had been suggested that since her pain was resistant to all conventional remedies, injection of analgesia (with side effects of respiratory depression) was the only realistic method of relieving her pain even though this might mean that she would die sooner than she would have done otherwise.

The patient and her relatives were pleading with the medical staff to bring about an end to her misery by shortening her life.

Ethical considerations

Some doctors and many members of the public believe that deliberately ending a patient's life is ethically acceptable in cases such as this. Although in some countries deliberately ending a patient's life is legally permitted, in the UK, anyone who does so faces being prosecuted for murder. Patients and their relatives may not always realize this, and may put pressure on doctors. Those who disagree with the UK's legal stance on this, whether doctors or patients, should lobby parliament for a change to the legislation. There is a distinction between attempting to alleviate someone's suffering and deliberately seeking to end her life. This is known as the 'doctrine of double effect'. It means that providing treatment to ease symptoms may be acceptable even if it also shortens the person's life. However, shortening of life must not be the *aim* of the treatment.

Legal situation

Taking any clinical step with intention to end life is unlawful in the UK. However, life-shortening interventions are permissible if the aim is to improve the patient's symptoms. If more medication is given than is necessary to relieve pain, there is a risk it might be determined that the intention was to shorten life. However, the patient should not be denied the medication they need to relieve pain, for fear of a murder conviction.

Recommendation

Every step should be taken to ensure that the patient's symptoms are being adequately treated. Medical staff should clarify to the patient and her relatives that any deliberate attempt to shorten the patient's life is unlawful. Any treatment options that might alleviate her symptoms should be carefully discussed, including their risks and side effects. In difficult cases, where the patient or relatives are unhappy with the situation, it may be useful to consult the clinical ethics committee.

Speech: capacity

Relevant legal cases

- *St George's NHS Trust v S* [1992].

> An 89-year-old lady had a stroke, leaving her with an unsafe swallow, but her capacity for decision-making was retained. She had had a gastrostomy tube placed, to allow her to have enteral feeds. Despite speech and language therapy staff and nurses repeatedly warning her that drinking was likely to result in aspiration of fluids into her lungs, the patient was adamant that she wished to take that risk, and got pleasure from drinking. The speech and language therapy staff remained anxious, and were uncertain of what they could do, legally and ethically.

Ethical considerations

It looks here as if the patient's autonomy is in conflict with her best interests. However, a closer analysis calls this into question. The patient feels that she benefits from the pleasure she gets from drinking, and that the risks involved are outweighed by this pleasure. The medical staff understandably do not want to see the patient harmed by aspiration once they have gone to the bother of enabling enteral feeding. In effect, they are prioritizing a different understanding of beneficence to the view that the patient takes.

Legal situation

A mental capacity assessment should be performed. As long as she is aware of the relevant information and uses that to make a decision, she has mental capacity. If she has mental capacity her decision must be respected, even though her decision might be regarded as foolish. It is important in this case to ensure she is fully aware of the risks and the consequences of continuing to drink.

Recommendation

It is reasonable for staff to attempt to persuade the patient to forego drinking, but not for them to prevent her from doing so. Their attempts at persuasion should focus on the risks involved, so that the patient is fully aware of them when deciding whether to continue drinking against medical advice. The patient might want to make an advance directive.

Trauma and orthopaedics: necessity

Relevant legal cases
- *Wye Valley NHS Trust v Mr B* [2015].
- *Aintree University Hospitals NHS Foundation Trust v James* [2013].

> A 27-year-old man was brought into the ED having fallen off his motor-
> cycle at 60 mph. He had a compound fracture of his right thigh which was
> angulated, and despite emergency manoeuvres in the ED, there were no
> pulses below the groin on the right side. The trauma and orthopaedics
> registrar telephoned, since he had decided that the patient needed sur-
> gery to explore the femoral artery, which he suspected had been severed
> by the bony fragments. The patient lost consciousness on arrival, and was
> now being ventilated due to an associated head injury. The registrar felt
> uncomfortable about operating without the patient's consent, and was
> uncertain as to the best course of action.

Ethical considerations

There is an apparent conflict here between respect for autonomy and beneficence. However, his consent for the procedure cannot be obtained since
he is unconscious. In non-urgent cases, it would seem best to wait for the
patient to regain capacity so that he can decide whether to undergo surgery.
However, the patient is at risk of losing a limb if the exploratory surgery is
delayed and therefore the balance weighs in favour of intervention.

Legal situation

As the patient is unable to give or refuse consent and a decision needs to
be made imminently to protect the patient from serious harm, you can
perform the surgery. Doing so will be in the best interests of the patient,
who currently lacks capacity, and so will be authorized under the Mental
Capacity Act 2005.

Recommendation

The best course of action here is to operate despite the fact that it is not
possible to obtain consent. Failing to operate may result in permanent irremediable harm; above-knee amputation may be required unless emergency
surgery is performed. However, the degree of intervention should include
only what is absolutely necessary to save the leg until the patient is con-
scious and able to consent.

Urology: liberty

Relevant legal cases

- *HL v United Kingdom* [2002] ECHR 417.
- *P v Cheshire West and Chester Council* [2014] UKSC 19.

> A 69-year-old man was admitted following a history of deterioration in his urinary stream. The clinical diagnosis was consistent with advanced prostatic cancer, and it was anticipated that the patient would be in hospital for a minimum of 2 weeks. Six years ago, the patient had had a severe stroke, and since then had been unable to communicate. His treatment decisions had since then been taken in his best interests, but in the absence of close family or friends, an IMCA had been used to assist clinicians in ascertaining where his best interests lay. He appeared to have no inclination to leave the ward; on the contrary, he appeared settled, comfortable, and content. But the senior nurses were concerned that he is being deprived of his liberty.

Ethical considerations

Deprivation of liberty is a serious ethical concern especially where the patient's wishes to leave are being ignored or overridden. In cases where the patient's wishes are not immediately evident, as in this situation, it is necessary to try to understand their body language and other signs. Realistically, in this particular scenario, the patient is unlikely to be able to live independently again, so wherever he is accommodated, his options will be restricted. However, given that we are told that the patient appears happy where he is, there is no obvious reason to think that his current situation is problematic.

Legal situation

A deprivation of liberty occurs if 'The person is under *continuous supervision and control* and is *not free to leave*, and the person *lacks capacity to consent* to these arrangements'. Once the point is reached whereby the incapacitated patient no longer requires to be in hospital for life-sustaining treatment, if he nonetheless must remain in hospital, perhaps awaiting a residential placement, he is then deprived of his liberty. This will need to be authorized by the hospital under the LPS regime.

Recommendation

From the current perspective, the patient needs to have his deprivation of liberty authorized, as he has no prospect of regaining capacity, and the duration of his stay is uncertain.

Vascular surgery: disclosure

Relevant legal cases

- *Montgomery v Lanarkshire Health Board* [2015] UKSC 11.

> A 49-year-old man with multiple risk factors for atherosclerosis needed a
> carotid endarterectomy. The consultant surgeon seeking consent for this
> procedure chose not to disclose the risk of stroke, since in her personal
> experience of operating on similar cases, the risk was less than 0.1%. Her
> practice was to disclose risks that occur only more frequently than 0.1%.

Ethical considerations

The patient has an interest in knowing the risks related to any intervention
he receives. However, there is a question about how great a risk must be
in order for it to be worth mentioning. Any procedure may have an almost
infinite number of associated risks whose likelihood of occurring is very
small. A doctor has to choose the most relevant risks to discuss with the
patient. However, they may not know what *is* most relevant to the patient
without undergoing some exploratory discussion, and this is an essential
part of the process.

Legal situation

Following the decision in *Montgomery v Lanarkshire Health Board*, a surgeon must disclose all substantial risks. In that case, the failure to disclose
a 9–10% risk of a very serious complication was negligent. It is not for the
surgeon to decide whether a risk is substantial, rather the test is whether
a reasonable patient, or this particular patient, would attach significance to
the risk. A risk of 0.1% is low, but the consequences of that risk are very
serious and so a court may well treat that as a substantial risk. This and
many other judgments over the last 30 years have explicitly prohibited clinicians from using a numeric 'threshold' to rule out the disclosure of rare
risks. Irrespective of the rarity of a foreseeable complication of treatment,
if the risk of that complication was relevant to the circumstances of the
particular patient, it should be disclosed.

Recommendation

This might be seen as a borderline case as to whether the risk would be
seen as substantial. However, the safest course of action is always to disclose a risk, unless you are completely confident it would be found to be
not substantial.

Part 5

Statutory provisions

24 Abortion Act 1967 *283*

25 Female Genital Mutilation Act 2003 *287*

26 Gender Recognition Act 2004 *289*

27 Human Fertilisation and Embryology Act 1990 *291*

28 Human Rights Act 1998 (European Convention on Human Rights) *299*

29 Human Tissue Act 2004 *307*

30 Mental Capacity Act 2005 *323*

31 Mental Health Act 1983 *339*

32 Suicide Act 1961 *349*

33 Surrogacy Arrangements Act 1985 *351*

Abortion Act 1967

The regulation of abortion *284*
Conscientious objection to abortion *285*

The regulation of abortion

The starting point of the law is that an abortion is a criminal offence. The follow section sets out when it is lawful.

Abortion Act 1967

Section 1

(1) Subject to the provisions of this section, a person shall not be guilty of an offence under the law relating to abortion when a pregnancy is terminated by a registered medical practitioner if two registered medical practitioners are of the opinion, formed in good faith—

    (a) that the pregnancy has not exceeded its twenty-fourth week and that the continuance of the pregnancy would involve risk, greater than if the pregnancy were terminated, of injury to the physical or mental health of the pregnant woman or any existing children of her family; or

    (b) that the termination is necessary to prevent grave permanent injury to the physical or mental health of the pregnant woman; or

    (c) that the continuance of the pregnancy would involve risk to the life of the pregnant woman, greater than if the pregnancy were terminated; or

    (d) that there is a substantial risk that if the child were born it would suffer from such physical or mental abnormalities as to be seriously handicapped.

(2) In determining whether the continuance of a pregnancy would involve such risk of injury to health as is mentioned in paragraph (a) or (b) of subsection (1) of this section, account may be taken of the pregnant woman's actual or reasonably foreseeable environment.

(3) Except as provided by subsection (4) of this section, any treatment for the termination of pregnancy must be carried out in a hospital vested in the Secretary of State for the purposes of his functions under the National Health Service Act 2006 or the National Health Service (Scotland) Act 1978 or in a hospital vested in a National Health Service trust or an NHS foundation trust or in a place approved for the purposes of this section by the Secretary of State.

(3A) The power under subsection (3) of this section to approve a place includes power, in relation to treatment consisting primarily in the use of such medicines as may be specified in the approval and carried out in such manner as may be so specified, to approve a class of places.

(4) Subsection (3) of this section, and so much of subsection (1) as relates to the opinion of two registered medical practitioners, shall not apply to the termination of a pregnancy by a registered medical practitioner in a case where he is of the opinion, formed in good faith, that the termination is immediately necessary to save the life or to prevent grave permanent injury to the physical or mental health of the pregnant woman.

Conscientious objection to abortion

This section deals with cases where a professional has a conscientious objection to dealing in abortion.

Abortion Act 1967

Section 4

(1) Subject to subsection (2) of this section, no person shall be under any duty, whether by contract or by any statutory or other legal requirement, to participate in any treatment authorised by this Act to which he has a conscientious objection:

Provided that in any legal proceedings the burden of proof of conscientious objection shall rest on the person claiming to rely on it.

(2) Nothing in subsection (1) of this section shall affect any duty to participate in treatment which is necessary to save the life or to prevent grave permanent injury to the physical or mental health of a pregnant woman.

(3) In any proceedings before a court in Scotland, a statement on oath by any person to the effect that he has a conscientious objection to participating in any treatment authorised by this Act shall be sufficient evidence for the purpose of discharging the burden of proof imposed upon him by subsection (1) of this section.

Female Genital Mutilation Act 2003

The offence of female genital mutilation *288*

The offence of female genital mutilation

This describes the offence of FGM.

Female Genital Mutilation Act 2003, section 1

(1) A person is guilty of an offence if he excises, infibulates or otherwise mutilates the whole or any part of a girl's labia majora, labia minora or clitoris.

(2) But no offence is committed by an approved person who performs—
   (a) a surgical operation on a girl which is necessary for her physical or mental health, or
   (b) a surgical operation on a girl who is in any stage of labour, or has just given birth, for purposes connected with the labour or birth.

(3) The following are approved persons—
   (a) in relation to an operation falling within subsection (2)(a), a registered medical practitioner,
   (b) in relation to an operation falling within subsection (2)(b), a registered medical practitioner, a registered midwife or a person undergoing a course of training with a view to becoming such a practitioner or midwife.

(4) There is also no offence committed by a person who—
   (a) performs a surgical operation falling within subsection (2)(a) or (b) outside the United Kingdom, and
   (b) in relation to such an operation exercises functions corresponding to those of an approved person.

(5) For the purpose of determining whether an operation is necessary for the mental health of a girl it is immaterial whether she or any other person believes that the operation is required as a matter of custom or ritual.

Gender Recognition Act 2004

Gender recognition *290*

Gender recognition

This provision sets out the general scheme for recognition of gender.

Gender Recognition Act 2004

Section 1

(1) A person of either gender who is aged at least 18 may make an
application for a gender recognition certificate on the basis of—
(a) living in the other gender, or
(b) having changed gender under the law of a country or territory
outside the United Kingdom.

(2) In this Act 'the acquired gender', in relation to a person by whom an
application under subsection (1) is or has been made, means—
(a) in the case of an application under paragraph (a) of that
subsection, the gender in which the person is living, or
(b) in the case of an application under paragraph (b) of that
subsection, the gender to which the person has changed under
the law of the country or territory concerned.

(3) An application under subsection (1) is to be determined by a Gender
Recognition Panel.

Section 2

(1) In the case of an application under section 1(1)(a), the Panel must
grant the application if satisfied that the applicant—
(a) has or has had gender dysphoria,
(b) has lived in the acquired gender throughout the period of two
years ending with the date on which the application is made,
(c) intends to continue to live in the acquired gender until death, and
(d) complies with the requirements imposed by and under section 3.

(2) In the case of an application under section 1(1)(b), the Panel must
grant the application if satisfied—
(a) that the country or territory under the law of which the applicant
has changed gender is an approved country or territory, and
(b) that the applicant complies with the requirements imposed by
and under section 3.

(3) The Panel must reject an application under section 1(1) if not
required by subsection (1) or (2) to grant it.

Human Fertilisation and Embryology Act 1990

Activities involving embryos *292*
Prohibition on germline cells *292*
Prohibitions on storage and use of gametes *293*
Definition of mother *293*
Definition of father *294*

Activities involving embryos

This provision sets out the regulations under the Human Fertilisation and Embryology Act 1990 concerning human embryos.

Human Fertilisation and Embryology Act 1990

Section 3

(1) No person shall bring about the creation of an embryo except in pursuance of a licence.

(1A) No person shall keep or use an embryo except—
   (a) in pursuance of a licence, or
   (b) in the case of—
      (i) the keeping, without storage, of an embryo intended for human application, or
      (ii) the processing, without storage, of such an embryo, in pursuance of a third party agreement.

(1B) No person shall procure or distribute an embryo intended for human application except in pursuance of a licence or a third party agreement.

(2) No person shall place in a woman—
   (a) an embryo other than a permitted embryo (as defined by section 3ZA), or
   (b) any gametes other than permitted eggs or permitted sperm (as so defined).

(3) A licence cannot authorise—
   (a) keeping or using an embryo after the appearance of the primitive streak,
   (b) placing an embryo in any animal or
   (c) keeping or using an embryo in any circumstances in which regulations prohibit its keeping or use.

(4) For the purposes of subsection (3)(a) above, the primitive streak is to be taken to have appeared in an embryo not later than the end of the period of 14 days beginning with the day on which the process of creating the embryo began, not counting any time during which the embryo is stored.

Prohibition on germline cells

This provision regulates germline cells.

Human Fertilisation and Embryology Act 1990

Section 3A

(1) No person shall, for the purpose of providing fertility services for any woman, use female germ cells taken or derived from an embryo or a foetus or use embryos created by using such cells.

(2) In this section—
   'female germ cells' means cells of the female germ line and includes such cells at any stage of maturity and accordingly includes eggs; and
   'fertility services' means medical, surgical or obstetric services provided for the purpose of assisting women to carry children.

Prohibitions on storage and use of gametes

This provision deals with the regulation around the storage and use of gametes.

Human Fertilisation and Embryology Act 1990

Section 4
(1) No person shall—
  (a) store any gametes, or
  (b) in the course of providing treatment services for any woman, use—
    (i) any sperm, other than partner-donated sperm which has been neither processed nor stored,
    (ii) the woman's eggs after processing or storage, or
    (iii) the eggs of any other woman, except in pursuance of a licence.
(1A) No person shall procure, test, process or distribute any gametes intended for human application except in pursuance of a licence or a third party agreement.
(2) A licence cannot authorise storing or using gametes in any circumstances in which regulations prohibit their storage or use.
(3) No person shall place sperm and eggs in a woman in any circumstances specified in regulations except in pursuance of a licence.

Definition of mother

This provision defines who is a mother in cases of assisted conception.

Human Fertilisation and Embryology Act 1990

Section 27
(1) The woman who is carrying or has carried a child as a result of the placing in her of an embryo or of sperm and eggs, and no other woman, is to be treated as the mother of the child.
(2) Subsection (1) above does not apply to any child to the extent that the child is treated by virtue of adoption as not being the woman's child.
(3) Subsection (1) above applies whether the woman was in the United Kingdom or elsewhere at the time of the placing in her of the embryo or the sperm and eggs.

Definition of father

This provision defines who is a father in cases of assisted conception.

Human Fertilisation and Embryology Act 1990

Section 28

(1) Subject to subsections (5A) to (5I) below, this section applies in the case of a child who is being or has been carried by a woman as the result of the placing in her of an embryo or of sperm and eggs or her artificial insemination.

(2) If—

    (a) at the time of the placing in her of the embryo or the sperm and eggs or of her insemination, the woman was a party to a marriage, and

    (b) the creation of the embryo carried by her was not brought about with the sperm of the other party to the marriage, then, subject to subsection (5) below, the other party to the marriage shall be treated as the father of the child unless it is shown that he did not consent to the placing in her of the embryo or the sperm and eggs or to her insemination (as the case may be).

(3) If no man is treated, by virtue of subsection (2) above, as the father of the child but—

    (a) the embryo or the sperm and eggs were placed in the woman, or she was artificially inseminated, in the course of treatment services provided for her and a man together by a person to whom a licence applies, and

    (b) the creation of the embryo carried by her was not brought about with the sperm of that man, then, subject to subsection (5) below, that man shall be treated as the father of the child.

(4) Where a person is treated as the father of the child by virtue of subsection (2) or (3) above, no other person is to be treated as the father of the child.

(5) Subsections (2) and (3) above do not apply—

    (a) in relation to England and Wales and Northern Ireland, to any child who, by virtue of the rules of common law, is treated as the legitimate child of the parties to a marriage,

    (b) in relation to Scotland, to any child who, by virtue of any enactment or other rule of law, is treated as the child of the parties to a marriage, or

    (c) to any child to the extent that the child is treated by virtue of adoption as not being the man's child.

(5A) If—

    (a) a child has been carried by a woman as the result of the placing in her of an embryo or of sperm and eggs or her artificial insemination,

    (b) the creation of the embryo carried by her was brought about by using the sperm of a man after his death, or the creation of the embryo was brought about using the sperm of a man before his death but the embryo was placed in the woman after his death,

    (c) the woman was a party to a marriage with the man immediately before his death,

- (d) the man consented in writing (and did not withdraw the consent)—
  - (i) to the use of his sperm after his death which brought about the creation of the embryo carried by the woman or (as the case maybe) to the placing in the woman after his death of the embryo which was brought about using his sperm before his death, and
  - (ii) to being treated for the purpose mentioned in subsection (5I) below as the father of any resulting child,
- (e) the woman has elected in writing not later than the end of the period of 42 days from the day on which the child was born for the man to be treated for the purpose mentioned in subsection (5I) below as the father of the child, and
- (f) no-one else is to be treated as the father of the child by virtue of subsection (2) or (3) above or by virtue of adoption or the child being treated as mentioned in paragraph (a) or (b) of subsection (5) above, then the man shall be treated for the purpose mentioned in subsection (5I) below as the father of the child.

(5B) If—
- (a) a child has been carried by a woman as the result of the placing in her of an embryo or of sperm and eggs or her artificial insemination,
- (b) the creation of the embryo carried by her was brought about by using the sperm of a man after his death, or the creation of the embryo was brought about using the sperm of a man before his death but the embryo was placed in the woman after his death,
- (c) the woman was not a party to a marriage with the man immediately before his death but treatment services were being provided for the woman and the man together before his death either by a person to whom a licence applies or outside the United Kingdom,
- (d) the man consented in writing (and did not withdraw the consent)—
  - (i) to the use of his sperm after his death which brought about the creation of the embryo carried by the woman or (as the case maybe) to the placing in the woman after his death of the embryo which was brought about using his sperm before his death, and
  - (ii) to being treated for the purpose mentioned in subsection (5I) below as the father of any resulting child,
- (e) the woman has elected in writing not later than the end of the period of 42 days from the day on which the child was born for the man to be treated for the purpose mentioned in subsection (5I) below as the father of the child, and
- (f) no-one else is to be treated as the father of the child by virtue of subsection (2) or (3) above or by virtue of adoption or the child being treated as mentioned in paragraph (a) or (b) of subsection (5) above, then the man shall be treated for the purpose mentioned in subsection (5I) below as the father of the child.

(5C) If—

- (a) a child has been carried by a woman as the result of the placing in her of an embryo,
- (b) the embryo was created at a time when the woman was a party to a marriage,
- (c) the creation of the embryo was not brought about with the sperm of the other party to the marriage,
- (d) the other party to the marriage died before the placing of the embryo in the woman,
- (e) the other party to the marriage consented in writing (and did not withdraw the consent)—
  - (i) to the placing of the embryo in the woman after his death, and
  - (ii) to being treated for the purpose mentioned in subsection (5I) below as the father of any resulting child,
- (f) the woman has elected in writing not later than the end of the period of 42 days from the day on which the child was born for the other party to the marriage to be treated for the purpose mentioned in subsection (5I) below as the father of the child, and
- (g) no-one else is to be treated as the father of the child by virtue of subsection (2) or (3) above or by virtue of adoption or the child being treated as mentioned in paragraph (a) or (b) of subsection (5) above, then the other party to the marriage shall be treated for the purpose mentioned in subsection (5I) below as the father of the child.

(5D) If—

- (a) a child has been carried by a woman as the result of the placing in her of an embryo,
- (b) the embryo was not created at a time when the woman was a party to a marriage but was created in the course of treatment services provided for the woman and a man together either by a person to whom a licence applies or outside the United Kingdom,
- (c) the creation of the embryo was not brought about with the sperm of that man,
- (d) the man died before the placing of the embryo in the woman,
- (e) the man consented in writing (and did not withdraw the consent)—
  - (i) to the placing of the embryo in the woman after his death, and
  - (ii) to being treated for the purpose mentioned in subsection (5I) below as the father of any resulting child,
- (f) the woman has elected in writing not later than the end of the period of 42 days from the day on which the child was born for the man to be treated for the purpose mentioned in subsection (5I) below as the father of the child, and
- (g) no-one else is to be treated as the father of the child by virtue of subsection (2) or (3) above or by virtue of adoption or the child being treated as mentioned in paragraph (a) or (b) of subsection (5) above, then the man shall be treated for the purpose mentioned in subsection (5I) below as the father of the child.

(5E) In the application of subsections (5A) to (5D) above to Scotland, for any reference to a period of 42 days there shall be substituted a reference to a period of 21 days.

(5F) The requirement under subsection (5A), (5B), (5C) or (5D) above as to the making of an election (which requires an election to be made either on or before the day on which the child was born or within the period of 42 or, as the case may be, 21 days from that day) shall nevertheless be treated as satisfied if the required election is made after the end of that period but with the consent of the Registrar General under subsection (5G) below.

(5G) The Registrar General may at any time consent to the making of an election after the end of the period mentioned in subsection (5F) above if, on an application made to him in accordance with such requirements as he may specify, he is satisfied that there is a compelling reason for giving his consent to the making of such an election.

(5H) In subsections (5F) and (5G) above 'the Registrar General' means the Registrar General for England and Wales, the Registrar General of Births, Deaths and Marriages for Scotland or (as the case maybe) the Registrar General for Northern Ireland.

(5I) The purpose referred to in subsections (5A) to (5D) above is the purpose of enabling the man's particulars to be entered as the particulars of the child's father in (as the case may be) a register of live-births or still-births kept under the Births and Deaths Registration Act 1953 or the Births and Deaths Registration (Northern Ireland) Order 1976 or a register of births or still-births kept under the Registration of Births, Deaths and Marriages (Scotland) Act 1965.

(6) Where—
   (a) the sperm of a man who had given such consent as is required by paragraph 5 of Schedule 3 to this Act was used for a purpose for which such consent was required, or
   (b) the sperm of a man, or any embryo the creation of which was brought about with his sperm, was used after his death, he is not, subject to subsections (5A) and (5B) above, to be treated as the father of the child.

(7) The references in subsection (2) above and subsections (5A) to (5D) above to the parties to a marriage at the time there referred to—
   (a) are to the parties to a marriage subsisting at that time, unless a judicial separation was then in force, but
   (b) include the parties to a void marriage if either or both of them reasonably believed at that time that the marriage was valid; and for the purposes of this subsection it shall be presumed, unless the contrary is shown, that one of them reasonably believed at that time that the marriage was valid.

(8) This section applies whether the woman was in the United Kingdom or elsewhere at the time of the placing in her of the embryo or the sperm and eggs or her artificial insemination.

(9) In subsection (7)(a) above, 'judicial separation' includes a legal separation obtained in a country outside the British Islands and recognised in the United Kingdom.

Human Rights Act 1998 (European Convention on Human Rights)

The right to life *300*
The right to protection from torture *300*
Prohibition of slavery and forced labour *300*
The right to liberty and security *301*
The right to a fair trial *302*
The right not to suffer punishment without legal
    authorization *302*
The right to respect for private and family life *303*
The right to freedom of thought, conscience, and religion *303*
The right to freedom of expression *304*
The right to freedom of assembly and association *304*
The right to marry *305*
The right to protection from discrimination *305*

The right to life

This article articulates the right to life, protected through the Human Rights Act 1998.

European Convention on Human Rights

Article 2

1. Everyone's right to life shall be protected by law. No one shall be deprived of his life intentionally save in the execution of a sentence of a court following his conviction of a crime for which this penalty is provided by law.
2. Deprivation of life shall not be regarded as inflicted in contravention of this Article when it results from the use of force which is no more than absolutely necessary:
   (a) in defence of any person from unlawful violence;
   (b) in order to effect a lawful arrest or to prevent the escape of a person lawfully detained;
   (c) in action lawfully taken for the purpose of quelling a riot or insurrection.

The right to protection from torture

This article articulates the right to protection from torture or inhuman or degrading treatment, protected through the Human Rights Act 1998.

European Convention on Human Rights

Article 3

No one shall be subjected to torture or to inhuman or degrading treatment or punishment.

Prohibition of slavery and forced labour

This article articulates the right to protection from slavery and forced labour, protected through the Human Rights Act 1998.

European Convention on Human Rights

Article 4

1. No one shall be held in slavery or servitude.
2. No one shall be required to perform forced or compulsory labour.
3. For the purpose of this Article the term 'forced or compulsory labour' shall not include:
   (a) any work required to be done in the ordinary course of detention imposed according to the provisions of Article 5 of this Convention or during conditional release from such detention;
   (b) any service of a military character or, in case of conscientious objectors in countries where they are recognised, service exacted instead of compulsory military service;
   (c) any service exacted in case of an emergency or calamity threatening the life or well-being of the community;
   (d) any work or service which forms part of normal civic obligations.

The right to liberty and security

This article articulates the right to liberty and security, protected through the Human Rights Act 1998.

European Convention on Human Rights

Article 5

1. Everyone has the right to liberty and security of person. No one shall be deprived of his liberty save in the following cases and in accordance with a procedure prescribed by law:
   - (a) the lawful detention of a person after conviction by a competent court;
   - (b) the lawful arrest or detention of a person for non-compliance with the lawful order of a court or in order to secure the fulfilment of any obligation prescribed by law;
   - (c) the lawful arrest or detention of a person effected for the purpose of bringing him before the competent legal authority on reasonable suspicion of having committed an offence or when it is reasonably considered necessary to prevent his committing an offence or fleeing after having done so;
   - (d) the detention of a minor by lawful order for the purpose of educational supervision or his lawful detention for the purpose of bringing him before the competent legal authority;
   - (e) the lawful detention of persons for the prevention of the spreading of infectious diseases, of persons of unsound mind, alcoholics or drug addicts or vagrants;
   - (f) the lawful arrest or detention of a person to prevent his effecting an unauthorised entry into the country or of a person against whom action is being taken with a view to deportation or extradition.
2. Everyone who is arrested shall be informed promptly, in a language which he understands, of the reasons for his arrest and of any charge against him.
3. Everyone arrested or detained in accordance with the provisions of paragraph 1 (c) of this Article shall be brought promptly before a judge or other officer authorised by law to exercise judicial power and shall be entitled to trial within a reasonable time or to release pending trial. Release may be conditioned by guarantees to appear for trial.
4. Everyone who is deprived of his liberty by arrest or detention shall be entitled to take proceedings by which the lawfulness of his detention shall be decided speedily by a court and his release ordered if the detention is not lawful.
5. Everyone who has been the victim of arrest or detention in contravention of the provisions of this Article shall have an enforceable right to compensation.

The right to a fair trial

This article articulates the right to a fair trial, protected through the Human Rights Act 1998.

European Convention on Human Rights

Article 6

1. In the determination of his civil rights and obligations or of any criminal charge against him, everyone is entitled to a fair and public hearing within a reasonable time by an independent and impartial tribunal established by law. Judgment shall be pronounced publicly but the press and public may be excluded from all or part of the trial in the interests of morals, public order or national security in a democratic society, where the interests of juveniles or the protection of the private life of the parties so require, or to the extent strictly necessary in the opinion of the court in special circumstances where publicity would prejudice the interests of justice.

2. Everyone charged with a criminal offence shall be presumed innocent until proved guilty according to law.

3. Everyone charged with a criminal offence has the following minimum rights:
   (a) to be informed promptly, in a language which he understands and in detail, of the nature and cause of the accusation against him;
   (b) to have adequate time and facilities for the preparation of his defence;
   (c) to defend himself in person or through legal assistance of his own choosing or, if he has not sufficient means to pay for legal assistance, to be given it free when the interests of justice so require;
   (d) to examine or have examined witnesses against him and to obtain the attendance and examination of witnesses on his behalf under the same conditions as witnesses against him;
   (e) to have the free assistance of an interpreter if he cannot understand or speak the language used in court.

The right not to suffer punishment without legal authorization

This article articulates the right to protection from punishment, protected through the Human Rights Act 1998.

European Convention on Human Rights

Article 7

1. No one shall be held guilty of any criminal offence on account of any act or omission which did not constitute a criminal offence under national or international law at the time when it was committed. Nor shall a heavier penalty be imposed than the one that was applicable at the time the criminal offence was committed.

2. This Article shall not prejudice the trial and punishment of any person for any act or omission which, at the time when it was committed, was criminal according to the general principles of law recognised by civilised nations.

The right to respect for private and family life

This article articulates the right to respect for private and family life, protected through the Human Rights Act 1998. Note that the first paragraph sets out the right and the second explains when an interference in it can be justified.

European Convention on Human Rights

Article 8

1. Everyone has the right to respect for his private and family life, his home and his correspondence.
2. There shall be no interference by a public authority with the exercise of this right except such as is in accordance with the law and is necessary in a democratic society in the interests of national security, public safety or the economic well-being of the country, for the prevention of disorder or crime, for the protection of health or morals, or for the protection of the rights and freedoms of others.

The right to freedom of thought, conscience, and religion

This article articulates the right to freedom of thought, conscience, and religion, protected through the Human Rights Act 1998.

European Convention on Human Rights

Article 9

1. Everyone has the right to freedom of thought, conscience and religion; this right includes freedom to change his religion or belief and freedom, either alone or in community with others and in public or private, to manifest his religion or belief, in worship, teaching, practice and observance.
2. Freedom to manifest one's religion or beliefs shall be subject only to such limitations as are prescribed by law and are necessary in a democratic society in the interests of public safety, for the protection of public order, health or morals, or for the protection of the rights and freedoms of others.

The right to freedom of expression

This article articulates the right to freedom of expression, protected through the Human Rights Act 1998. Note that the first paragraph sets out the right and the second explains when an interference in it can be justified.

European Convention on Human Rights

Article 10

1. Everyone has the right to freedom of expression. This right shall include freedom to hold opinions and to receive and impart information and ideas without interference by public authority and regardless of frontiers. This Article shall not prevent States from requiring the licensing of broadcasting, television or cinema enterprises.

2. The exercise of these freedoms, since it carries with it duties and responsibilities, may be subject to such formalities, conditions, restrictions or penalties as are prescribed by law and are necessary in a democratic society, in the interests of national security, territorial integrity or public safety, for the prevention of disorder or crime, for the protection of health or morals, for the protection of the reputation or rights of others, for preventing the disclosure of information received in confidence, or for maintaining the authority and impartiality of the judiciary.

The right to freedom of assembly and association

This article articulates the right to freedom of assembly and association, protected through the Human Rights Act 1998.

European Convention on Human Rights

Article 11

1. Everyone has the right to freedom of peaceful assembly and to freedom of association with others, including the right to form and to join trade unions for the protection of his interests.

2. No restrictions shall be placed on the exercise of these rights other than such as are prescribed by law and are necessary in a democratic society in the interests of national security or public safety, for the prevention of disorder or crime, for the protection of health or morals or for the protection of the rights and freedoms of others. This Article shall not prevent the imposition of lawful restrictions on the exercise of these rights by members of the armed forces, of the police or of the administration of the State.

The right to marry

This article articulates the right to marry, protected through the Human Rights Act 1998.

European Convention on Human Rights
Article 12
Men and women of marriageable age have the right to marry and to found a family, according to the national laws governing the exercise of this right.

The right to protection from discrimination

This article articulates the right to life, protected through the Human Rights Act 1998. Note this can only be used if you can show another right has been interfered with.

European Convention on Human Rights
Article 14
The enjoyment of the rights and freedoms set forth in this Convention shall be secured without discrimination on any ground such as sex, race, colour, language, religion, political or other opinion, national or social origin, association with a national minority, property, birth or other status.

Human Tissue Act 2004

Regulation of human tissue *308*
Human tissue: consent by children *312*
Human tissue: consent by adults *314*
Prohibited activities in relation to human tissue *316*
Restrictions on donated human tissue *318*
Prohibition of commercial dealings in human material for transplantation *320*
Restrictions on donations using live transplants *322*

Regulation of human tissue

This section sets out some general principles on the regulation of human tissue.

Human Tissue Act 2004

Section 1

(1) The following activities shall be lawful if done with appropriate consent—

   (a) the storage of the body of a deceased person for use for a purpose specified in Schedule 1, other than anatomical examination;

   (b) the use of the body of a deceased person for a purpose so specified, other than anatomical examination;

   (c) the removal from the body of a deceased person, for use for a purpose specified in Schedule 1, of any relevant material of which the body consists or which it contains;

   (d) the storage for use for a purpose specified in Part 1 of Schedule 1 of any relevant material which has come from a human body;

   (e) the storage for use for a purpose specified in Part 2 of Schedule 1 of any relevant material which has come from the body of a deceased person;

   (f) the use for a purpose specified in Part 1 of Schedule 1 of any relevant material which has come from a human body;

   (g) the use for a purpose specified in Part 2 of Schedule 1 of any relevant material which has come from the body of a deceased person.

(2) The storage of the body of a deceased person for use for the purpose of anatomical examination shall be lawful if done—

   (a) with appropriate consent, and

   (b) after the signing of a certificate—

      (i) under section 22(1) of the Births and Deaths Registration Act 1953 (c. 20), or

      (ii) under Article 25(2) of the Births and Deaths Registration (Northern Ireland) Order 1976 (S.I. 1976/1041 (N.I. 14)), of the cause of death of the person.

(3) The use of the body of a deceased person for the purpose of anatomical examination shall be lawful if done—

   (a) with appropriate consent, and

   (b) after the death of the person has been registered—

      (i) under section 15 of the Births and Deaths Registration Act 1953, or

      (ii) under Article 21 of the Births and Deaths Registration (Northern Ireland) Order 1976.

(4) Subsections (1) to (3) do not apply to an activity of a kind mentioned there if it is done in relation to—

   (a) a body to which subsection (5) applies, or

   (b) relevant material to which subsection (6) applies.

(5) This subsection applies to a body if—

   (a) it has been imported, or

     (b) it is the body of a person who died before the day on which this section comes into force and at least one hundred years have elapsed since the date of the person's death.

(6) This subsection applies to relevant material if—
     (a) it has been imported,
     (b) it has come from a body which has been imported, or
     (c) it is material which has come from the body of a person who died before the day on which this section comes into force and at least one hundred years have elapsed since the date of the person's death.

(7) Subsection (1)(d) does not apply to the storage of relevant material for use for the purpose of research in connection with disorders, or the functioning, of the human body if—
     (a) the material has come from the body of a living person, and
     (b) the research falls within subsection (9).

(8) Subsection (1)(f) does not apply to the use of relevant material for the purpose of research in connection with disorders, or the functioning, of the human body if—
     (a) the material has come from the body of a living person, and
     (b) the research falls within subsection (9).

(9) Research falls within this subsection if—
     (a) it is ethically approved in accordance with regulations made by the Secretary of State, and
     (b) it is to be, or is, carried out in circumstances such that the person carrying it out is not in possession, and not likely to come into possession, of information from which the person from whose body the material has come can be identified.

(9A) Subsection (1)(f) does not apply to the use of relevant material for the purpose of research where the use of the material requires consent under paragraph 6(1) or 12(1) of Schedule 3 to the Human Fertilisation and Embryology Act 1990 (use of human cells to create an embryo or a human admixed embryo) or would require such consent but for paragraphs 16 and 20 of that Schedule.

(9B) Subsection (1) does not apply in relation to—
     (a) transplantation activities done in Wales; or
     (b) transplantation activities done outside Wales in relation to relevant material that was removed from a human body in Wales.

(10) The following activities shall be lawful—
     (a) the storage for use for a purpose specified in Part 2 of Schedule 1 of any relevant material which has come from the body of a living person;
     (b) the use for such a purpose of any relevant material which has come from the body of a living person;
     (c) an activity in relation to which subsection (4), (7), (8) or (9B)(b) has effect.

(10A) In the case of an activity in relation to which subsection (8) has effect, subsection (10)(c) is to be read subject to any requirements imposed by Schedule 3 to the Human Fertilisation and Embryology Act 1990 in relation to the activity.

(11) The Secretary of State may by order—
    (a) vary or omit any of the purposes specified in Part 1 or 2 of Schedule 1, or
    (b) add to the purposes specified in Part 1 or 2 of that Schedule.

(12) Nothing in this section applies to—
    (a) the use of relevant material in connection with a device to which Directive 98/79/EC of the European Parliament and of the Council on in vitro diagnostic medical devices applies, where the use falls within the Directive, or
    (b) the storage of relevant material for use falling within paragraph (a).

(13) In this section, the references to a body or material which has been imported do not include a body or material which has been imported after having been exported with a view to its subsequently being re-imported.

(14) In this section 'transplantation activities' has the same meaning as in the Human Transplantation (Wales) Act 2013 (which makes provision in relation to consent for transplantation activities done in Wales).

Human tissue: consent by children

Human Tissue Act 2004

Section 2

(1)   This section makes provision for the interpretation of 'appropriate consent' in section 1 in relation to an activity involving the body, or material from the body, of a person who is a child or has died a child ('the child concerned').

(2)   Subject to subsection (3), where the child concerned is alive, 'appropriate consent' means his consent.

(3)   Where—
  (a) the child concerned is alive,
  (b) neither a decision of his to consent to the activity, nor a decision of his not to consent to it, is in force, and
  (c) either he is not competent to deal with the issue of consent in relation to the activity or, though he is competent to deal with that issue, he fails to do so, 'appropriate consent' means the consent of a person who has parental responsibility for him.

(4)   Where the child concerned has died and the activity is one to which subsection (5) applies, 'appropriate consent' means his consent in writing.

(5)   This subsection applies to an activity involving storage for use, or use, for the purpose of—
  (a) public display, or
  (b) where the subject-matter of the activity is not excepted material, anatomical examination.

(6)   Consent in writing for the purposes of subsection (4) is only valid if—
  (a) it is signed by the child concerned in the presence of at least one witness who attests the signature, or
  (b) it is signed at the direction of the child concerned, in his presence and in the presence of at least one witness who attests the signature.

(7)   Where the child concerned has died and the activity is not one to which subsection (5) applies, 'appropriate consent' means —
  (a) if a decision of his to consent to the activity, or a decision of his not to consent to it, was in force immediately before he died, his consent;
  (b) if paragraph (a) does not apply—
    (i) the consent of a person who had parental responsibility for him immediately before he died, or
    (ii) where no person had parental responsibility for him immediately before he died, the consent of a person who stood in a qualifying relationship to him at that time.

Human tissue: consent by adults

This provision governs how adults consent in dealings with human tissue.

Human Tissue Act 2004

Section 3

(1) This section makes provision for the interpretation of 'appropriate consent' in section 1 in relation to an activity involving the body, or material from the body, of a person who is an adult or has died an adult ('the person concerned').

(2) Where the person concerned is alive, 'appropriate consent' means his consent.

(3) Where the person concerned has died and the activity is one to which subsection (4) applies, 'appropriate consent' means his consent in writing.

(4) This subsection applies to an activity involving storage for use, or use, for the purpose of—
  (a) public display, or
  (b) where the subject-matter of the activity is not excepted material, anatomical examination.

(5) Consent in writing for the purposes of subsection (3) is only valid if—
  (a) it is signed by the person concerned in the presence of at least one witness who attests the signature,
  (b) it is signed at the direction of the person concerned, in his presence and in the presence of at least one witness who attests the signature, or
  (c) it is contained in a will of the person concerned made in accordance with the requirements of—
    (i) section 9 of the Wills Act 1837 (c. 26), or
    (ii) Article 5 of the Wills and Administration Proceedings (Northern Ireland) Order 1994 (S.I. 1994/1899 (N.I. 13)).

(6) Where the person concerned has died and the activity is not one to which subsection (4) applies, 'appropriate consent' means—
  (a) if a decision of his to consent to the activity, or a decision of his not to consent to it, was in force immediately before he died, his consent;
  (b) if—
    (i) paragraph (a) does not apply, and
    (ii) he has appointed a person or persons under section 4 to deal after his death with the issue of consent in relation to the activity, consent given under the appointment;
  (ba) if neither paragraph (a) nor paragraph (b) applies and the activity is one to which subsection (6A) applies, the deemed consent of the person concerned;
  (c) if neither paragraph (a) nor paragraph (b) applies and the activity is not one to which subsection (6A) applies, the consent of a person who stood in a qualifying relationship to him immediately before he died.

(6A) This subsection applies to the following activities done in England unless the body is the body of an excepted adult—

    (a) the storage of the body of a deceased person for use for the purpose of transplantation;

    (b) the removal from the body of a deceased person, for use for the purpose of transplantation, of any permitted material of which the body consists or which it contains;

    (c) the storage for use for the purpose of transplantation of any permitted material which has come from a human body;

    (d) the use for the purpose of transplantation of any permitted material which has come from a human body.

(6B) The person concerned is to be deemed, for the purposes of subsection (6)(ba), to have consented to the activity unless a person who stood in a qualifying relationship to the person concerned immediately before death provides information that would lead a reasonable person to conclude that the person concerned would not have consented.

(7) Where the person concerned has appointed a person or persons under section 4 to deal after his death with the issue of consent in relation to the activity, the appointment shall be disregarded for the purposes of subsection (6) if no one is able to give consent under it.

(8) If it is not reasonably practicable to communicate with a person appointed under section 4 within the time available if consent in relation to the activity is to be acted on, he shall be treated for the purposes of subsection (7) as not able to give consent under the appointment in relation to it.

(9) In subsection (6A)—

    'excepted adult' means—

    (a) an adult who has died and who had not been ordinarily resident in England for a period of at least 12 months immediately before dying, or

    (b) an adult who has died and who for a significant period before dying lacked capacity to understand the effect of subsection (6) (ba);

    'permitted material' means relevant material other than relevant material of a type specified in regulations made by the Secretary of State.

(10) **For the purposes of the definition of 'excepted adult' in subsection (9) a significant period means a sufficiently long period as to lead a reasonable person to conclude that it would be inappropriate for consent to be deemed to be given under subsection (6)(ba).**

Prohibited activities in relation to human tissue

Human Tissue Act 2004

Section 5

(1)　A person commits an offence if, without appropriate consent, he does an activity to which subsection (1), (2) or (3) of section 1 applies, unless he reasonably believes—

　(a)　that he does the activity with appropriate consent, or

　(b)　that what he does is not an activity to which the subsection applies.

(2)　A person commits an offence if—

　(a)　he falsely represents to a person whom he knows or believes is going to, or may, do an activity to which subsection (1), (2) or (3) of section 1 applies—

　　(i)　that there is appropriate consent to the doing of the activity, or

　　(ii)　that the activity is not one to which the subsection applies, and

　(b)　he knows that the representation is false or does not believe it to be true.

(3)　Subject to subsection (4), a person commits an offence if, when he does an activity to which section 1(2) applies, neither of the following has been signed in relation to the cause of death of the person concerned—

　(a)　a certificate under section 22(1) of the Births and Deaths Registration Act 1953 (c. 20), and

　(b)　a certificate under Article 25(2) of the Births and Deaths Registration (Northern Ireland) Order 1976 (S.I. 1976/1041 (N.I. 14)).

(4)　Subsection (3) does not apply—

　(a)　where the person reasonably believes—

　　(i)　that a certificate under either of those provisions has been signed in relation to the cause of death of the person concerned, or

　　(ii)　that what he does is not an activity to which section 1(2) applies, or

　(b)　where the person comes into lawful possession of the body immediately after death and stores it prior to its removal to a place where anatomical examination is to take place.

(5)　Subject to subsection (6), a person commits an offence if, when he does an activity to which section 1(3) applies, the death of the person concerned has not been registered under either of the following provisions—

　(a)　section 15 of the Births and Deaths Registration Act 1953, and

　(b)　Article 21 of the Births and Deaths Registration (Northern Ireland) Order 1976.

(6) Subsection (5) does not apply where the person reasonably believes—
  (a) hat the death of the person concerned has been registered under either of those provisions, or
  (b) that what he does is not an activity to which section 1(3) applies.

(7) A person guilty of an offence under this section shall be liable—
  (a) on summary conviction to a fine not exceeding the statutory maximum;
  (b) on conviction on indictment—
    (i) to imprisonment for a term not exceeding 3 years, or
    (ii) to a fine, or
    (iii) to both.

(8) In this section, 'appropriate consent' has the same meaning as in section 1.

Restrictions on donated human tissue

This provision sets out restrictions on use of donated human material.

Human Tissue Act 2004

Section 8

(1)   Subject to subsection (2), a person commits an offence if he—
    (a) uses donated material for a purpose which is not a qualifying purpose, or
    (b) stores donated material for use for a purpose which is not a qualifying purpose.

(2)   Subsection (1) does not apply where the person reasonably believes that what he uses, or stores, is not donated material.

(3)   A person guilty of an offence under this section shall be liable—
    (a) on summary conviction to a fine not exceeding the statutory maximum;
    (b) on conviction on indictment—
        (i) to imprisonment for a term not exceeding 3 years, or
        (ii) to a fine, or
        (iii) to both.

(4)   In subsection (1), references to a qualifying purpose are to—
    (a) a purpose specified in Schedule 1,
    (b) the purpose of medical diagnosis or treatment,
    (c) the purpose of decent disposal, or
    (d) a purpose specified in regulations made by the Secretary of State.

(5)   In this section, references to donated material are to—
    (a) the body of a deceased person, or
    (b) relevant material which has come from a human body, which is, or has been, the subject of donation.

(6)   For the purposes of subsection (5), a body, or material, is the subject of donation if authority under section 1(1) to (3) or section 3(1) to (3) of the Human Transplantation (Wales) Act 2013 exists in relation to it.

Prohibition of commercial dealings in human material for transplantation

This section sets out the prohibition on commercial dealings with transplant material.

Human Tissue Act 2004

Section 32

(1) A person commits an offence if he—

  (a) gives or receives a reward for the supply of, or for an offer to supply, any controlled material;

  (b) seeks to find a person willing to supply any controlled material for reward;

  (c) offers to supply any controlled material for reward;

  (d) initiates or negotiates any arrangement involving the giving of a reward for the supply of, or for an offer to supply, any controlled material;

  (e) takes part in the management or control of a body of persons corporate or unincorporate whose activities consist of or include the initiation or negotiation of such arrangements.

(2) Without prejudice to subsection (1)(b) and (c), a person commits an offence if he causes to be published or distributed, or knowingly publishes or distributes, an advertisement—

  (a) inviting persons to supply, or offering to supply, any controlled material for reward, or

  (b) indicating that the advertiser is willing to initiate or negotiate any such arrangement as is mentioned in subsection (1)(d).

(3) A person who engages in an activity to which subsection (1) or (2) applies does not commit an offence under that subsection if he is designated by the Authority as a person who may lawfully engage in the activity.

(3A) The Authority may not designate a person under subsection (3) if doing so could result in the United Kingdom being in breach of—

  (a) Article 12 of Directive 2004/23/EC of the European Parliament and of the Council on setting standards of quality and safety for the donation, procurement, testing, processing, preservation, storage and distribution of human tissues and cells, or

  (b) Article 13 of Directive 2010/53/ EU of the European Parliament and of the Council on standards of quality and safety of human organs intended for transplantation.

(4) A person guilty of an offence under subsection (1) shall be liable—

  (a) on summary conviction—

    (i) to imprisonment for a term not exceeding 12 months, or

    (ii) to a fine not exceeding the statutory maximum, or

    (iii) to both;

  (b) on conviction on indictment—

    (i) to imprisonment for a term not exceeding 3 years, or

    (ii) to a fine, or

    (iii) to both.

(5) A person guilty of an offence under subsection (2) shall be liable on summary conviction—

   (a) to imprisonment for a term not exceeding 51 weeks, or

   (b) to a fine not exceeding level 5 on the standard scale, or

   (c) to both.

(6) For the purposes of subsections (1) and (2), payment in money or money's worth to the holder of a licence shall be treated as not being a reward where—

   (a) it is in consideration for transporting, removing, preparing, preserving or storing controlled material, and

   (b) its receipt by the holder of the licence is not expressly prohibited by the terms of the licence.

(7) References in subsections (1) and (2) to reward, in relation to the supply of any controlled material, do not include payment in money or money's worth for defraying or reimbursing—

   (a) any expenses incurred in, or in connection with, transporting, removing, preparing, preserving or storing the material,

   (b) any liability incurred in respect of—

      (i) expenses incurred by a third party in, or in connection with, any of the activities mentioned in paragraph (a), or

      (ii) a payment in relation to which subsection (6) has effect, or

   (c) any expenses or loss of earnings incurred by the person from whose body the material comes so far as reasonably and directly attributable to his supplying the material from his body.

(8) For the purposes of this section, controlled material is any material which—

   (a) consists of or includes human cells,

   (b) is, or is intended to be removed, from a human body,

   (c) is intended to be used for the purpose of transplantation, and

   (d) is not of a kind excepted under subsection (9).

(9) The following kinds of material are excepted—

   (a) gametes,

   (b) embryos, and

   (c) material which is the subject of property because of an application of human skill.

(10) Where the body of a deceased person is intended to be used to provide material which—

   (a) consists of or includes human cells, and

   (b) is not of a kind excepted under subsection (9), for use for the purpose of transplantation, the body shall be treated as controlled material for the purposes of this section.

(11) In this section—

'advertisement' includes any form of advertising whether to the public generally, to any section of the public or individually to selected persons;

'reward' means any description of financial or other material advantage.

Restrictions on donations using live transplants

This provision sets out restriction on use of transplants using material from live donors.

Human Tissue Act 2004

Section 33

(1) Subject to subsections (3) and (5), a person commits an offence if—
   (a) he removes any transplantable material from the body of a living person intending that the material be used for the purpose of transplantation, and
   (b) when he removes the material, he knows, or might reasonably be expected to know, that the person from whose body he removes the material is alive.

(2) Subject to subsections (3) and (5), a person commits an offence if—
   (a) he uses for the purpose of transplantation any transplantable material which has come from the body of a living person, and
   (b) when he does so, he knows, or might reasonably be expected to know, that the transplantable material has come from the body of a living person.

(3) The Secretary of State may by regulations provide that subsection (1) or (2) shall not apply in a case where—
   (a) the Authority is satisfied—
      (i) that no reward has been or is to be given in contravention of section 32, and
      (ii) that such other conditions as are specified in the regulations are satisfied, and
   (b) such other requirements as are specified in the regulations are complied with.

(4) Regulations under subsection (3) shall include provision for decisions of the Authority in relation to matters which fall to be decided by it under the regulations to be subject, in such circumstances as the regulations may provide, to reconsideration in accordance with such procedure as the regulations may provide.

(5) Where under subsection (3) an exception from subsection (1) or (2) is in force, a person does not commit an offence under that subsection if he reasonably believes that the exception applies.

(6) A person guilty of an offence under this section is liable on summary conviction—
   (a) to imprisonment for a term not exceeding 51 weeks, or
   (b) to a fine not exceeding level 5 on the standard scale, or
   (c) to both.

(7) In this section—
   'reward' has the same meaning as in section 32;
   'transplantable material' means material of a description specified regulations made by the Secretary of State.

Chapter 30

Mental Capacity Act 2005

The five key principles in the Mental Capacity Act 324
The core test for mental capacity 324
The obligation to assist a person to gain capacity 325
The best interests assessment when a patient lacks capacity 325
Non-discrimination in best interests assessment 326
Deprivation of liberty: general principles 326
Derivation of liberty: life-saving treatment 328
Protection for those wrongly assessing capacity or best interests 330
Definition of a lasting power of attorney 330
General provisions on advanced directives 331
Validity and applicability of advance decisions 332
Effect of advance decisions 333
Things that the Mental Capacity Act cannot authorize 334
Authorizing of deprivation of liberty 336

The five key principles in the Mental Capacity Act

These are the five principles underpinning the Mental Capacity Act.

Mental Capacity Act 2005

Section 1

(2) A person must be assumed to have capacity unless it is established that he lacks capacity.

(3) A person is not to be treated as unable to make a decision unless all practicable steps to help him to do so have been taken without success.

(4) A person is not to be treated as unable to make a decision merely because he makes an unwise decision.

(5) An act done, or decision made, under this Act for or on behalf of a person who lacks capacity must be done, or made, in his best interests.

(6) Before the act is done, or the decision is made, regard must be had to whether the purpose for which it is needed can be as effectively achieved in a way that is less restrictive of the person's rights and freedom of action.

The core test for mental capacity

These two provisions provide the core test for mental capacity.

Mental Capacity Act 2005

Section 2

(1) For the purposes of this Act, a person lacks capacity in relation to a matter if at the material time he is unable to make a decision for himself in relation to the matter because of an impairment of, or a disturbance in the functioning of, the mind or brain.

Section 3

(1) For the purposes of section 2, a person is unable to make a decision for himself if he is unable—

   (a) to understand the information relevant to the decision,

   (b) to retain that information,

   (c) to use or weigh that information as part of the process of making the decision, or

   (d) to communicate his decision (whether by talking, using sign language or any other means).

The obligation to assist a person to gain capacity

This is the provision which requires a person to be assisted to, if possible, make the decision for themselves.

Mental Capacity Act 2005

Section 3

(2) A person is not to be regarded as unable to understand the information relevant to a decision if he is able to understand an explanation of it given to him in a way that is appropriate to his circumstances (using simple language, visual aids or any other means).

The best interests assessment when a patient lacks capacity

Factors to be considered in deciding what is in the best interests of a patient lacking capacity.

Mental Capacity Act 2005

Section 4

(6) [Anyone making a best interests assessment] must consider, so far as is reasonably ascertainable—
  (a) the person's past and present wishes and feelings (and, in particular, any relevant written statement made by him when he had capacity),
  (b) the beliefs and values that would be likely to influence his decision if he had capacity, and
  (c) the other factors that he would be likely to consider if he were able to do so.

(7) He must take into account, if it is practicable and appropriate to consult them, the views of—
  (a) anyone named by the person as someone to be consulted on the matter in question or on matters of that kind,
  (b) anyone engaged in caring for the person or interested in his welfare,
  (c) any donee of a lasting power of attorney granted by the person, and
  (d) any deputy appointed for the person by the court, as to what would be in the person's best interests and, in particular, as to the matters mentioned in subsection (6).

Non-discrimination in best interests assessment

This provision sets out the importance of not discriminating when making a best interests assessment.

Mental Capacity Act 2005

Section 4

(1) In determining for the purposes of this Act what is in a person's best interests, the person making the determination must not make it merely on the basis of—

   (a) the person's age or appearance, or

   (b) a condition of his, or an aspect of his behaviour, which might lead others to make unjustified assumptions about what might be in his best interests.

Deprivation of liberty: general principles

The basic principles on deprivation of liberty.

Mental Capacity Act 2005

Section 4A

(1) This Act does not authorise any person ('D') to deprive any other person ('P') of his liberty.

   . . .

(3) D may deprive P of his liberty if, by doing so, D is giving effect to a relevant decision of the court.

   . . .

(5) D may deprive P of liberty if, by doing so, D is carrying out arrangements authorised under Schedule AA1 (arrangements enabling the care and treatment of persons who lack capacity).

Derivation of liberty: life-saving treatment

When a deprivation of liberty is permitted for life-sustaining treatment or a vital act.

Mental Capacity Act 2005

Section 4B

(1) If Conditions 1 to 4 are met, D is authorised to take steps which deprive P of liberty.

(2) Condition 1 is that the steps—
   (a) are wholly or partly for the purpose of giving P life-sustaining treatment or doing any vital act, or
   (b) consist wholly or partly of giving P life-sustaining treatment or doing any vital act.

(3) A vital act is any act which the person doing it reasonably believes to be necessary to prevent a serious deterioration in P's condition.

(4) Condition 2 is that the steps are necessary in order to give the life-sustaining treatment or do the vital act.

(5) Condition 3 is that D reasonably believes that P lacks capacity to consent to D taking the steps.

(6) Condition 4 is that—
   (a) subsection (7) applies, or
   (b) there is an emergency.

(7) This subsection applies if—
   (a) a decision relevant to whether D is authorised to deprive P of liberty is being sought from the court, or
   (b) a responsible body is carrying out functions under Schedule AA1 with a view to determining whether to authorise arrangements that give rise to a deprivation of P's liberty.

(8) In subsection (7) it does not matter—
   (a) whether the decision mentioned in paragraph (a) relates to the steps mentioned in subsection (1);
   (b) whether the arrangements mentioned in paragraph (b) include those steps.

(9) There is an emergency if D reasonably believes that—
   (a) there is an urgent need to take the steps mentioned in subsection (1) in order to give the life-sustaining treatment or do the vital act, and
   (b) it is not reasonably practicable before taking those steps—
      (i) to make an application for P to be detained under Part 2 of the Mental Health Act,
      (ii) to make an application within subsection (7)(a), or
      (iii) to secure that action within subsection (7)(b) is taken.

Section 4C

(1) This section applies to an act that a person ('D') does in carrying out arrangements authorised under Schedule AA1.

(2) D does not incur any liability in relation to the act that would not have been incurred if the cared-for person—
  (a) had had capacity to consent in relation to D doing the act, and
  (b) had consented to D doing the act.

(3) Nothing in this section excludes a person's civil liability for loss or damage, or a person's criminal liability, resulting from that person's negligence in doing the act.

(4) Paragraph 31 of Schedule AA1 applies if an authorisation ceases to have effect in certain cases.

(5) 'Cared-for person' has the meaning given by paragraph 2(1) of that Schedule.

Protection for those wrongly assessing capacity or best interests

This provision provides a defence to legal liability where a professional has incorrectly assessed a patient is lacking mental capacity.

Mental Capacity Act 2005

Section 5

(1)   If a person ('D') does an act in connection with the care or treatment of another person ('P'), the act is one to which this section applies if—

    (a) before doing the act, D takes reasonable steps to establish whether P lacks capacity in relation to the matter in question, and

    (b) when doing the act, D reasonably believes—

        (i) that P lacks capacity in relation to the matter, and

        (ii) that it will be in P's best interests for the act to be done.

(2)   D does not incur any liability in relation to the act that he would not have incurred if P—

    (a) had had capacity to consent in relation to the matter, and

    (b) had consented to D's doing the act.

(3)   Nothing in this section excludes a person's civil liability for loss or damage, or his criminal liability, resulting from his negligence in doing the act.

Definition of a lasting power of attorney

The following sections define a LPA.

Mental Capacity Act 2005

Section 9

(1)   A lasting power of attorney is a power of attorney under which the donor ('P') confers on the donee (or donees) authority to make decisions about all or any of the following—

    (a) P's personal welfare or specified matters concerning P's personal welfare, and

    (b) P's property and affairs or specified matters concerning P's property and affairs, and which includes authority to make such decisions in circumstances where P no longer has capacity.

Section 11

(1)   A lasting power of attorney does not authorise the donee (or, if more than one, any of them) to do an act that is intended to restrain P, unless three conditions are satisfied.

(2)   The first condition is that P lacks, or the donee reasonably believes that P lacks, capacity in relation to the matter in question.

(3)   The second is that the donee reasonably believes that it is necessary to do the act in order to prevent harm to P.

(4)   The third is that the act is a proportionate response to—

    (a) the likelihood of P's suffering harm, and

    (b) the seriousness of that harm.

General provisions on advanced directives

The following provides a definition of an advance directive.

Mental Capacity Act 2005

Section 24

(1) 'Advance decision' means a decision made by a person ('P'), after he has reached 18 and when he has capacity to do so, that if—

    (a) at a later time and in such circumstances as he may specify, a specified treatment is proposed to be carried out or continued by a person providing health care for him, and

    (b) at that time he lacks capacity to consent to the carrying out or continuation of the treatment, the specified treatment is not to be carried out or continued.

(2) For the purposes of subsection (1)(a), a decision may be regarded as specifying a treatment or circumstances even though expressed in layman's terms.

(3) P may withdraw or alter an advance decision at any time when he has capacity to do so.

(4) A withdrawal (including a partial withdrawal) need not be in writing.

(5) An alteration of an advance decision need not be in writing (unless section 25(5) applies in relation to the decision resulting from the alteration).

Validity and applicability of advance decisions

The following describes the validity and applicability of an advance directive.

Mental Capacity Act 2005

Section 25

(1) An advance decision does not affect the liability which a person may incur for carrying out or continuing a treatment in relation to P unless the decision is at the material time—
   (a) valid, and
   (b) applicable to the treatment.

(2) An advance decision is not valid if P—
   (a) has withdrawn the decision at a time when he had capacity to do so,
   (b) has, under a lasting power of attorney created after the advance decision was made, conferred authority on the donee (or, if more than one, any of them) to give or refuse consent to the treatment to which the advance decision relates, or
   (c) has done anything else clearly inconsistent with the advance decision remaining his fixed decision.

(3) An advance decision is not applicable to the treatment in question if at the material time P has capacity to give or refuse consent to it.

(4) An advance decision is not applicable to the treatment in question if—
   (a) that treatment is not the treatment specified in the advance decision,
   (b) any circumstances specified in the advance decision are absent, or
   (c) there are reasonable grounds for believing that circumstances exist which P did not anticipate at the time of the advance decision and which would have affected his decision had he anticipated them.

(5) An advance decision is not applicable to life-sustaining treatment unless—
   (a) the decision is verified by a statement by P to the effect that it is to apply to that treatment even if life is at risk, and
   (b) the decision and statement comply with subsection (6).

(6) A decision or statement complies with this subsection only if—
   (a) it is in writing,
   (b) it is signed by P or by another person in P's presence and by P's direction,
   (c) the signature is made or acknowledged by P in the presence of a witness, and
   (d) the witness signs it, or acknowledges his signature, in P's presence.

(7) The existence of any lasting power of attorney other than one of a description mentioned in subsection (2)(b) does not prevent the advance decision from being regarded as valid and applicable.

Effect of advance decisions

The following states the effect of an advance directive if it is binding.

Mental Capacity Act 2005

Section 26

(1)   If P has made an advance decision which is—
    (a) valid, and
    (b) applicable to a treatment, the decision has effect as if he had made it, and had had capacity to make it, at the time when the question arises whether the treatment should be carried out or continued.

(2)   A person does not incur liability for carrying out or continuing the treatment unless, at the time, he is satisfied that an advance decision exists which is valid and applicable to the treatment.

(3)   A person does not incur liability for the consequences of withholding or withdrawing a treatment from P if, at the time, he reasonably believes that an advance decision exists which is valid and applicable to the treatment.

(4)   The court may make a declaration as to whether an advance decision—
    (a) exists;
    (b) is valid;
    (c) is applicable to a treatment.

(5)   Nothing in an apparent advance decision stops a person—
    (a) providing life-sustaining treatment, or
    (b) doing any act he reasonably believes to be necessary to prevent a serious deterioration in P's condition, while a decision as respects any relevant issue is sought from the court.

Things that the Mental Capacity Act cannot authorize

There are several acts that cannot be authorized under the best interests test in the Mental Capacity Act. These are listed in the following section.

Mental Capacity Act 2005

Section 27

(1) Nothing in this Act permits a decision on any of the following matters to be made on behalf of a person—

   (a) consenting to marriage or a civil partnership,
   (b) consenting to have sexual relations,
   (c) consenting to a decree of divorce being granted on the basis of two years' separation,
   (d) consenting to a dissolution order being made in relation to a civil partnership on the basis of two years' separation,
   (e) consenting to a child's being placed for adoption by an adoption agency,
   (f) consenting to the making of an adoption order,
   (g) discharging parental responsibilities in matters not relating to a child's property,
   (h) giving a consent under the Human Fertilisation and Embryology Act 1990 (c. 37),
   (i) giving a consent under the Human Fertilisation and Embryology Act 2008.

Authorizing of deprivation of liberty

The following provisions set out when a deprivation of liberty can be authorized.

The Act only applies if these three conditions are satisfied.

Mental Capacity Act 2005, schedule 1

Paragraph 1

(2)   The first condition is that a person ('P') is detained in a hospital or care home—for the purpose of being given care or treatment—in circumstances which amount to deprivation of the person's liberty.

(3)   The second condition is that a standard or urgent authorisation is in force.

(4)   The third condition is that the standard or urgent authorisation relates—

 (a) to P, and

 (b) to the hospital or care home in which P is detained.

The following qualifying requirements need to be met to justify the interference in liberty.

Mental Capacity Act 2005, schedule 1

The qualifying requirements

12(1) These are the qualifying requirements referred to in this Schedule—

 (a) the age requirement;

 (b) the mental health requirement;

 (c) the mental capacity requirement;

 (d) the best interests requirement;

 (e) the eligibility requirement;

 (f) the no refusals requirement.

(2)   Any question of whether a person who is, or is to be, a detained resident meets the qualifying requirements is to be determined in accordance with this Part.

(3)   In a case where—

 (a) the question of whether a person meets a particular qualifying requirement arises in relation to the giving of a standard authorisation, and

 (b) any circumstances relevant to determining that question are expected to change between the time when the determination is made and the time when the authorisation is expected to come into force, those circumstances are to be taken into account as they are expected to be at the later time.

The age requirement

13   The relevant person meets the age requirement if he has reached 18.

The mental health requirement

14   (1) The relevant person meets the mental health requirement if he is suffering from mental disorder (within the meaning of the Mental Health Act, but disregarding any exclusion for persons with learning disability).

(2)   An exclusion for persons with learning disability is any provision of the Mental Health Act which provides for a person with learning disability not to be regarded as suffering from mental disorder for one or more purposes of that Act.

The mental capacity requirement

15   The relevant person meets the mental capacity requirement if he lacks capacity in relation to the question whether or not he should be accommodated in the relevant hospital or care home for the purpose of being given the relevant care or treatment.

The best interests requirement

16(1) The relevant person meets the best interests requirement if all of the following conditions are met.

(2)   The first condition is that the relevant person is, or is to be, a detained resident.

(3)   The second condition is that it is in the best interests of the relevant person for him to be a detained resident.

(4)   The third condition is that, in order to prevent harm to the relevant person, it is necessary for him to be a detained resident.

(5)   The fourth condition is that it is a proportionate response to—
    (a) the likelihood of the relevant person suffering harm, and
    (b) the seriousness of that harm, for him to be a detained resident.

The eligibility requirement

17(1) The relevant person meets the eligibility requirement unless he is ineligible to be deprived of liberty by this Act.

(2)   Schedule 1A applies for the purpose of determining whether or not P is ineligible to be deprived of liberty by this Act.

The no refusals requirement

18   The relevant person meets the no refusals requirement unless there is a refusal within the meaning of paragraph 19 or 20.

19(1) There is a refusal if these conditions are met—
    (a) the relevant person has made an advance decision;
    (b) the advance decision is valid;
    (c) the advance decision is applicable to some or all of the relevant treatment.

(2)   Expressions used in this paragraph and any of sections 24, 25 or 26 have the same meaning in this paragraph as in that section.

20(1) There is a refusal if it would be in conflict with a valid decision of a donee or deputy for the relevant person to be accommodated in the relevant hospital or care home for the purpose of receiving some or all of the relevant care or treatment—
    (a) in circumstances which amount to deprivation of the person's liberty, or
    (b) at all.

(2)   A donee is a donee of a lasting power of attorney granted by the relevant person.

(3)   A decision of a donee or deputy is valid if it is made—
    (a) within the scope of his authority as donee or deputy, and
    (b) in accordance with Part 1 of this Act.

Mental Health Act 1983

The definition of mental disorder under the Mental
Health Act *340*

Criteria for admission under section 2 *341*

Criteria for admission under section 3 *342*

Criteria for emergency admission under section 4 *343*

Brain tissue treatment *344*

Electro-convulsive therapy *346*

The definition of mental disorder under the Mental Health Act

The following section defines a mental disorder for the purposes of the Mental Health Act 1983.

Mental Health Act 1983

Section 1

(2)   In this Act—
'mental disorder' means any disorder or disability of the mind; and 'mentally disordered' shall be construed accordingly;
and other expressions shall have the meanings assigned to them in section 145 below.

(2A)   But a person with learning disability shall not be considered by reason of that disability to be—
(a) suffering from mental disorder for the purposes of the provisions mentioned in subsection (2B) below; or
(b) requiring treatment in hospital for mental disorder for the purposes of sections 17E and 50 to 53 below, unless that disability is associated with abnormally aggressive or seriously irresponsible conduct on his part.

(2B)   The provisions are—
(a) sections 3, 7, 17A, 20 and 20A below;
(b) sections 35 to 38, 45A, 47, 48 and 51 below; and
(c) section 72(1)(b) and (c) and (4) below.

(3)   Dependence on alcohol or drugs is not considered to be a disorder or disability of the mind for the purposes of subsection (2) above.

(4)   In subsection (2A) above, 'learning disability' means a state of arrested or incomplete development of the mind which includes significant impairment of intelligence and social functioning.

Criteria for admission under section 2

The following provision sets out one of the circumstances in which a patient can be admitted for treatment under the Mental Health Act 1983.

Mental Health Act 1983

Section 2

(1)   A patient may be admitted to a hospital and detained there for the period allowed by subsection (4) below in pursuance of an application (in this Act referred to as 'an application for admission for assessment') made in accordance with subsections (2) and (3) below.

(2)   An application for admission for assessment may be made in respect of a patient on the grounds that—
  (a) he is suffering from mental disorder of a nature or degree which warrants the detention of the patient in a hospital for assessment (or for assessment followed by medical treatment) for at least a limited period; and
  (b) he ought to be so detained in the interests of his own health or safety or with a view to the protection of other persons.

(3)   An application for admission for assessment shall be founded on the written recommendations in the prescribed form of two registered medical practitioners, including in each case a statement that in the opinion of the practitioner the conditions set out in subsection (2) above are complied with.

(4)   Subject to the provisions of section 29(4) below, a patient admitted to hospital in pursuance of an application for admission for assessment may be detained for a period not exceeding 28 days beginning with the day on which he is admitted, but shall not be detained after the expiration of that period unless before it has expired he has become liable to be detained by virtue of a subsequent application, order or direction under the following provisions of this Act.

Criteria for admission under section 3

The following provision sets out one of the circumstances in which a patient can be admitted for treatment under the Mental Health Act 1983.

Mental Health Act 1983

Section 3

(1) A patient may be admitted to a hospital and detained there for the period allowed by the following provisions of this Act in pursuance of an application (in this Act referred to as 'an application for admission for treatment') made in accordance with this section.

(2) An application for admission for treatment may be made in respect of a patient on the grounds that—

    (a) he is suffering from mental disorder of a nature or degree which makes it appropriate for him to receive medical treatment in a hospital; and

    (c) it is necessary for the health or safety of the patient or for the protection of other persons that he should receive such treatment and it cannot be provided unless he is detained under this section; and

    (d) appropriate medical treatment is available for him.

(3) An application for admission for treatment shall be founded on the written recommendations in the prescribed form of two registered medical practitioners, including in each case a statement that in the opinion of the practitioner the conditions set out in subsection (2) above are complied with; and each such recommendation shall include—

    (a) such particulars as may be prescribed of the grounds for that opinion so far as it relates to the conditions set out in paragraphs (a) and (d) of that subsection; and

    (b) a statement of the reasons for that opinion so far as it relates to the conditions set out in paragraph (c) of that subsection, specifying whether other methods of dealing with the patient are available and, if so, why they are not appropriate.

(4) In this Act, references to appropriate medical treatment, in relation to a person suffering from mental disorder, are references to medical treatment which is appropriate in his case, taking into account the nature and degree of the mental disorder and all other circumstances of his case.

Criteria for emergency admission under section 4

The following provision sets out the circumstances in which a patient can be admitted for emergency treatment under the Mental Health Act 1983.

Mental Health Act 1983

Section 4

(1)　In any case of urgent necessity, an application for admission for assessment may be made in respect of a patient in accordance with the following provisions of this section, and any application so made is in this Act referred to as 'an emergency application'.

(2)　An emergency application may be made either by an approved mental health professional or by the nearest relative of the patient; and every such application shall include a statement that it is of urgent necessity for the patient to be admitted and detained under section 2 above, and that compliance with the provisions of this Part of this Act relating to applications under that section would involve undesirable delay.

(3)　An emergency application shall be sufficient in the first instance if founded on one of the medical recommendations required by section 2 above, given, if practicable, by a practitioner who has previous acquaintance with the patient and otherwise complying with the requirements of section 12 below so far as applicable to a single recommendation, and verifying the statement referred to in subsection (2) above.

(4)　An emergency application shall cease to have effect on the expiration of a period of 72 hours from the time when the patient is admitted to the hospital unless—

(a)　the second medical recommendation required by section 2 above is given and received by the managers within that period; and

(b)　that recommendation and the recommendation referred to in subsection (3) above together comply with all the requirements of section 12 below (other than the requirement as to the time of signature of the second recommendation).

Brain tissue treatment

This provision sets out when brain tissue treatment can be performed under the Mental Health Act.

Mental Health Act 1983

Section 57

(1)   This section applies to the following forms of medical treatment for mental disorder—

    (a) any surgical operation for destroying brain tissue or for destroying the functioning of brain tissue; and

    (b) such other forms of treatment as may be specified for the purposes of this section by regulations made by the Secretary of State.

(2)   Subject to section 62 below, a patient shall not be given any form of treatment to which this section applies unless he has consented to it and—

    (a) a registered medical practitioner appointed for the purposes of this Part of this Act by the regulatory authority(not being the responsible clinician (if there is one) or the person in charge of the treatment in question) and two other persons appointed for the purposes of this paragraph by the regulatory authority(not being registered medical practitioners) have certified in writing that the patient is capable of understanding the nature, purpose and likely effects of the treatment in question and has consented to it; and

    (b) the registered medical practitioner referred to in paragraph (a) above has certified in writing that it is appropriate for the treatment to be given.

(3)   Before giving a certificate under subsection (2)(b) above the registered medical practitioner concerned shall consult two other persons who have been professionally concerned with the patient's medical treatment but, of those persons—

    (a) one shall be a nurse and the other shall be neither a nurse nor a registered medical practitioner; and

    (b) neither shall be the responsible clinician (if there is one) or the person in charge of the treatment in question.

Electro-convulsive therapy

This provision sets out the circumstances in which electro-convulsive therapy can be offered.

Mental Health Act 1983

Section 58A

(1)   This section applies to the following forms of medical treatment for mental disorder—
- (a) electro-convulsive therapy; and
- (b) such other forms of treatment as may be specified for the purposes of this section by regulations made by the appropriate national authority.

(2)   Subject to section 62 below, a patient shall be not be given any form of treatment to which this section applies unless he falls within subsection (3), (4) or (5) below.

(3)   A patient falls within this subsection if—
- (a) he has attained the age of 18 years;
- (b) he has consented to the treatment in question; and
- (c) either the approved clinician in charge of it or a registered medical practitioner appointed as mentioned in section 58(3) above has certified in writing that the patient is capable of understanding the nature, purpose and likely effects of the treatment and has consented to it.

(4)   A patient falls within this subsection if—
- (a) he has not attained the age of 18 years; but
- (b) he has consented to the treatment in question; and
- (c) a registered medical practitioner appointed as aforesaid (not being the approved clinician in charge of the treatment) has certified in writing—
  - (i) that the patient is capable of understanding the nature, purpose and likely effects of the treatment and has consented to it; and
  - (ii) that it is appropriate for the treatment to be given.

(5)   A patient falls within this subsection if a registered medical practitioner appointed as aforesaid (not being the responsible clinician (if there is one) or the approved clinician in charge of the treatment in question) has certified in writing—
- (a) that the patient is not capable of understanding the nature, purpose and likely effects of the treatment; but
- (b) that it is appropriate for the treatment to be given; and
- (c) that giving him the treatment would not conflict with—
  - (i) an advance decision which the registered medical practitioner concerned is satisfied is valid and applicable; or
  - (ii) a decision made by a donee or deputy or by the Court of Protection.

(6) Before giving a certificate under subsection (5) above the registered medical practitioner concerned shall consult two other persons who have been professionally concerned with the patient's medical treatment but, of those persons—
  (a) one shall be a nurse and the other shall be neither a nurse nor a registered medical practitioner; and
  (b) neither shall be the responsible clinician (if there is one) or the approved clinician in charge of the treatment in question.

(7) This section shall not by itself confer sufficient authority for a patient who falls within section 56(5) above to be given a form of treatment to which this section applies if he is not capable of understanding the nature, purpose and likely effects of the treatment (and cannot therefore consent to it).

(8) Before making any regulations for the purposes of this section, the appropriate national authority shall consult such bodies as appear to it to be concerned.

(9) In this section—
  (a) a reference to an advance decision is to an advance decision (within the meaning of the Mental Capacity Act 2005) made by the patient;
  (b) 'valid and applicable', in relation to such a decision, means valid and applicable to the treatment in question in accordance with section 25 of that Act;
  (c) a reference to a donee is to a donee of a lasting power of attorney (within the meaning of section 9 of that Act) created by the patient, where the donee is acting within the scope of his authority and in accordance with that Act; and
  (d) a reference to a deputy is to a deputy appointed for the patient by the Court of Protection under section 16 of that Act, where the deputy is acting within the scope of his authority and in accordance with that Act.

(10) In this section, 'the appropriate national authority' means—
  (a) in a case where the treatment in question would, if given, be given in England, the Secretary of State;
  (b) in a case where the treatment in question would, if given, be given in Wales, the Welsh Ministers.

Suicide Act 1961

Suicide *350*

Suicide

These provisions set out the law on suicide and assisting suicide.

Suicide Act 1961

Section 1

The rule of law whereby it is a crime for a person to commit suicide is hereby abrogated.

Section 2

Criminal liability for complicity in another's suicide.

(1)   A person ('D') commits an offence if—

    (a) D does an act capable of encouraging or assisting the suicide or attempted suicide of another person, and

    (b) D's act was intended to encourage or assist suicide or an attempt at suicide.

(1A)   The person referred to in subsection (1)(a) need not be a specific person (or class of persons) known to, or identified by, D.

(1B)   D may commit an offence under this section whether or not a suicide, or an attempt at suicide, occurs.

(1C)   An offence under this section is triable on indictment and a person convicted of such an offence is liable to imprisonment for a term not exceeding 14 years.

(2)   If on the trial of an indictment for murder or manslaughter of a person it is proved that the deceased person committed suicide, and the accused committed an offence under subsection (1) in relation to that suicide, the jury may find the accused guilty of the offence under subsection (1).

(3)   The enactments mentioned in the first column of the First Schedule to this Act shall have effect subject to the amendments provided for in the second column (which preserve in relation to offences under this section the previous operation of those enactments in relation to murder or manslaughter).

(4)   No proceedings shall be instituted for an offence under this section except by or with the consent of the Director of Public Prosecutions.

Surrogacy Arrangements Act 1985

Surrogacy *352*
Prohibition of commercial surrogacy *354*

Surrogacy

This provision makes it clear that surrogacy contracts are not enforceable.

Surrogacy Arrangements Act 1985

Section 1A

No surrogacy arrangement is enforceable by or against any of the persons making it.

Prohibition of commercial surrogacy

This provision prohibits commercial surrogacy.

Surrogacy Arrangements Act 1985

Section 2

(1) No person shall on a commercial basis do any of the following acts in the United Kingdom, that is—

(a) initiate any negotiations with a view to the making of a surrogacy arrangement,

(aa) take part in any negotiations with a view to the making of a surrogacy arrangement,

(b) offer or agree to negotiate the making of a surrogacy arrangement, or

(c) compile any information with a view to its use in making, or negotiating the making of, surrogacy arrangements;

and no person shall in the United Kingdom knowingly cause another to do any of those acts on a commercial basis.

(2) A person who contravenes subsection (1) above is guilty of an offence; but it is not a contravention of that subsection—

(a) for a woman, with a view to becoming a surrogate mother herself, to do any act mentioned in that subsection or to cause such an act to be done, or

(b) for any person, with a view to a surrogate mother carrying a child for him, to do such an act or to cause such an act to be done.

(2A) A non-profit making body does not contravene subsection (1) merely because—

(a) the body does an act falling within subsection (1)(a) or (c) in respect of which any reasonable payment is at any time received by it or another, or

(b) it does an act falling within subsection (1)(a) or (c) with a view to any reasonable payment being received by it or another in respect of facilitating the making of any surrogacy arrangement.

(2B) A person who knowingly causes a non-profit making body to do an act falling within subsection (1)(a) or (c) does not contravene subsection (1) merely because—

(a) any reasonable payment is at any time received by the body or another in respect of the body doing the act, or

(b) the body does the act with a view to any reasonable payment being received by it or another person in respect of the body facilitating the making of any surrogacy arrangement.

(2C) Any reference in subsection (2A) or (2B) to a reasonable payment in respect of the doing of an act by a non-profit making body is a reference to a payment not exceeding the body's costs reasonably attributable to the doing of the act.

(3) For the purposes of this section, a person does an act on a commercial basis (subject to subsection (4) below) if—

(a) any payment is at any time received by himself or another in respect of it, or

(b) he does it with a view to any payment being received by himself or another in respect of making, or negotiating or facilitating the making of, any surrogacy arrangement.

In this subsection 'payment' does not include payment to or for the benefit of a surrogate mother or prospective surrogate mother.

(4) In proceedings against a person for an offence under subsection (1) above, he is not to be treated as doing an act on a commercial basis by reason of any payment received by another in respect of the act if it is proved that—

(a) in a case where the payment was received before he did the act, he did not do the act knowing or having reasonable cause to suspect that any payment had been received in respect of the act; and

(b) in any other case, he did not do the act with a view to any payment being received in respect of it.

(5) Where—

(a) a person acting on behalf of a body of persons takes any part in negotiating or facilitating the making of a surrogacy arrangement in the United Kingdom, and

(b) negotiating or facilitating the making of surrogacy arrangements is an activity of the body, then, if the body at any time receives any payment made by or on behalf of—

(i) a woman who carries a child in pursuance of the arrangement,

(ii) the person or persons for whom she carries it, or

(iii) any person connected with the woman or with that person or those persons, the body is guilty of an offence.

For the purposes of this subsection, a payment received by a person connected with a body is to be treated as received by the body.

(5A) A non-profit making body is not guilty of an offence under subsection (5), in respect of the receipt of any payment described in that subsection, merely because a person acting on behalf of the body takes part in facilitating the making of a surrogacy arrangement.

(6) In proceedings against a body for an offence under subsection (5) above, it is a defence to prove that the payment concerned was not made in respect of the arrangement mentioned in paragraph (a) of that subsection.

(7) A person who in the United Kingdom takes part in the management or control—

(a) of any body of persons, or

(b) of any of the activities of any body of persons, is guilty of an offence if the activity described in subsection (8) below is an activity of the body concerned.

(8) The activity referred to in subsection (7) above is negotiating or facilitating the making of surrogacy arrangements in the United Kingdom, being—

(a) arrangements the making of which is negotiated or facilitated on a commercial basis, or

        (b) arrangements in the case of which payments are received (or treated for the purposes of subsection (5) above as received) by the body concerned in contravention of subsection (5) above.

(8A) A person is not guilty of an offence under subsection (7) if—
        (a) the body of persons referred to in that subsection is a non-profit making body, and
        (b) the only activity of that body which falls within subsection (8) is facilitating the making of surrogacy arrangements in the United Kingdom.

(8B) In subsection (8A)(b) 'facilitating the making of surrogacy arrangements' is to be construed in accordance with subsection (8).

(9)   In proceedings against a person for an offence under subsection (7) above, it is a defence to prove that he neither knew nor had reasonable cause to suspect that the activity described in subsection (8) above was an activity of the body concerned; and for the purposes of such proceedings any arrangement falling within subsection (8)(b) above shall be disregarded if it is proved that the payment concerned was not made in respect of the arrangement.

Index

Notes
Tables and figures are indicated by *t* and *f* following the page number.
vs. indicates a comparison
Abbreviations used in the index
ECHR - European Convention on Human Rights
GMC - General Medical Council

A

ABC v St George's Healthcare NHS Foundation Trust [2015] 252
ABC v St George's Healthcare NHS Foundation Trust [2017] 99, 242, 254
abortion 253
  conscience and 175
  conscientious objections 285
  regulation of 284
Abortion Act 1967 175, 253, 283–5
absolute human rights 77
absoluteness, ECHR article 3 79
Accident and Compensation Corporation (New Zealand) 114–15
accomplice liability 112
act, duty to 110
active euthanasia 180
  duty to act 110
acute kidney injury (AKI), paracetamol overdose 274
advance decisions 158, 160–2
  effectiveness 160–1
  end of life care 178–9
  ethical issues 161
advanced directives 331
  effects of 333
  validity & applicability 332
advice, critical reasoning 60
agreement, deontology 25
Ahsan v University Hospitals Leicester [2006] 166–7
AIDS 138–9
  see also HIV infection
Aintree University Hospitals NHS Foundation Trust v James [2013] 166–7, 244, 268, 274, 275, 278
Airedale NHS Trust v Bland [1993] 180
AMCP (approved mental capacity professionals) 169

Ames v Nottinghamshire County Council [2018] 112–13
anaesthetics, child refusing treatment 232–3
anonymized information 139
answers, reasoning *vs.* 57
antibiotics, appendix masses 250
apologies 115
appendicitis, innovations 250
appendix masses 250
approved mental capacity professionals (AMCP) 169
Aristotle 10–11, 12–13, 44, 120–1
assembly, freedom of 304
assisted dying 184
assisted suicide 182–3
association, freedom of 304
assumptions, critical reasoning 61
atherosclerosis 280
authorization, Liberty Protection Safeguards 169–70
autonomy 31, 32–3
  advance decisions 161
  beneficence *vs.* 274
  consent 32
  definition 32
  euthanasia debates 190–1
  informed decision-making 33
  paternalism and 32–3
  range of 32

B

beneficence 31, 34–5, 41
  autonomy *vs.* 274
  centrality in medicine 34
  cultural values 34–5
  definition 34
  illness prevention 34
  life-saving 34
  views on 34
Bentham, Jeremy 16
best interests assessment
  mental capacity 166–7

Mental Capacity Act 2005 325
Birch v UCL [2008] 256
Bland, Anthony 186
blood donation 196
The Bolam test 100–1
  criticism of 100
  current knowledge 101
  emergencies 101
  professional guidance 101
  specialism 101
Bolam v Friern Hospital Management [1957] 100–1, 250
The Bolitho development 100
Bolitho v City and Hackney [1998] 100
bone marrow donation 196
brain tissue treatment, Mental Health Act 1983 344
brain-dead donors 195
breach of duty 100–2, 104
  'but for' tests 104
  causation 104
  disclosure of risk 102
  multiple causes 104
breast screening 36
budget management 122
'but for' tests, breach of duty 104

C

candour 132
  cardiac surgery 234–5
  duty of 204–5
  maxillofacial surgery 258–9
capacity *see* mental capacity
cardiac surgery 234–5
cardiopulmonary resuscitation (CPR) 32–3, 186–7
  patients with mental capacity 187
  patients without mental capacity 187
  refusal of 187–8
  unsuccessful/inappropriateness 187

care, duty of 99
care ethics 43–7
  definition 44
  different aspects 45
  feminine critique 45
  male bias 44
  pros & cons 45
  relationships 45
  sample questions 46, 47
carers 167
carotid endarterectomy 280
case law 68
categorical imperative,
    deontology 22
causation, breach of duty 104
cause of death
  confidentiality and 143
  death certificates 144
Chatterton v Gerson [1981]
    234, 245
Chester v Afshar [2004]
    156–7, 232
children
  cardiology 271
  consent *see* consent
  medical research 216–17
  parent consent 248
  rights of *vs.* parents'
      rights 264
  treatment refusal 232–3
choice, freedom of 126
*Christian Institute v Lord
    Advocate* [2013] 265
circumcision 248
civil cases 70, 86
clarity, confidentiality 222
Clinical Commissioning
    Groups 130
clinical photography 268
clinical questions,
    GMC 210
commercial dealing in
    tissues 320–1
commercial surrogacy 354
common law 68
communication inability,
    mental capacity 154
compassion 10
complexity, dealing with 56
conclusions, critical
    reasoning 62
confidentiality 134–5
  breaches of 134–5, 265
  death after 142–4
  Declaration of Helsinki
      (1964) 215
  definition 134
  disclosures 139
  expert witnesses 89
  explanation to patient 142
  genetics 252
  HIV infection 254

importance of 134–5
legal aspects 138–9
medical training 222
overriding of 138–9
practical limitations 137
professional guidelines 136
conflict resolution, end of life
    care 179
conscience 174–5
  abortion and 175
  definition 174
  freedom of *see* freedom of
      conscience
  psychological power of 174
  variability of 174–5
conscientious
    objections 174–5
  abortion 285
  ECHR article 9 81
consent 150–1
  adults 314–15
  autonomy 32
  children aged 16-17 172
  children under 16 172
  refusal in 172
  clinical photography 268
  Declaration of Helsinki
      (1964) 215
  deontology 25
  ENT 245
  explicit consent *see* explicit
      consent
  forms of 150
  Human Tissue Act
      2004 314–15
  implicit consent *see* implicit
      consent
  invalid types 153–4
  material risk disclosure
      156, 157
  medical training 221
  mental capacity 152–5, 158
  nature of 151
  neonatology 263
  non-obtaining of 156
  organ donation 194
  parents for children 248
  presumed consent *see*
      presumed consent
  signed consent 150
  standards of 194
  therapeutic
      exception 156–7
  time limits 154–5
  tooth extraction 236
  unconscious patients 215
  verbal consent 150
  withdrawal of 194
  see also advance decisions
consequentialism 15–20
  acts and omissions 18
  definition 16

justice 18
practice in 18–19
problems with 18
pros & cons 19
public health 19
rule utilitarianism *vs.* 19
sample questions 20
contexts
  critical reasoning 62–3
  legal principles 68–9
contraceptive advice
  Gillick competence 246
  under-age minors 246
contracts 71
  National Health Service
      (NHS) 93
  private medicine 94
core test of mental
    capacity 324
coroners 73
corporate liability 112
Corporate Manslaughter and
    Corporate Homicide
    Act 2007 112
Court of Protection
  emergency number 262
  lack of mental capacity 244
  treatment refusal 274
court orders, children's
    consent 172
courts 83–9
  Court of Protection *see*
      Court of Protection
  Crown Court 84
  European Court of Human
      Rights (ECtHR) 72
  European Court of Justice
      (ECJ) 72
  expert witnesses 88
  hierarchy of 72f, 72–3
  magistrates' court 84
CPR *see* cardiopulmonary
    resuscitation (CPR)
criminal cases 70, 84
  guilty pleas &
      sentencing 84–5
  public interest 84
criminal liability 112
critical reasoning 55–63
  advice seeking 60
  assumption identification &
      assumptions 61
  complexity and 56
  conclusions 62
  definition 56
  ethical conflicts 61
  interest identification 61–2
  issues 62–3
  mistakes 62
  moral reasoning 57
  right answers *vs.* right
      reasoning 57

sample questions 58, 60–3
value identification 61
Crown Court 84
Crown Prosecution
    Service 84
cultural circumcision 248
cultural factors
    beneficence 34–5
    doctors 253
    resource allocation 126
current knowledge, The
    Bolam test 101

D

damages
    negligences 106
    payments 108
Darnley v Croydon [2018] 99
Data Protection Act
    2018 140–1
dead donor organ
    transplants 192–3
dealing with complexity 56
death certificates 144
death & dying 177–99
    assisted dying 184
    assisted suicide 182–3
    cause of *see* cause
        of death
    deceased in medical
        training 224–5
    definition of 180
    end of life care 178–9
    euthanasia 180–1
    human rights 184
deception, mental capacity
    and 153
decisions
    consent and 32
    informed 33
    mental capacity 164
Declaration of Helsinki
    1964 214–15
degrading treatment, ECHR
    article 3 79
dementia 152–3
dentistry, Gillick
    competence 236
deontology 21–8
    consent & agreement 25
    definition 22
    dignity & human
        rights 25–6
    duties & reason 22
    lying 24
    means & ends 24–5
    pros & cons 26
    sample question 28
dependents 129
    "rationing by desert" 125

deputies 158, 162
dermatology 237
deserving patients 38
desires, resource
    allocation 124
developing world, medical
    research 217
diabetology, clinical
    records 238–9
diagnostic tests, mental
    capacity 152–3, 154
dialysis refusal 274
dignity
    deontology 25–6
    medical training
        on deceased
        patients 224–5
disciplinary proceedings 93
disclosures
    breach of duty 102
    clinical records 238
    plastics 272–3
    vascular surgery 280
discrimination 39
    mental capacity 152
    protection 305
distributive justice 127
diversity 52
do not attempt
    cardiopulmonary
    resuscitation
    (DNACPR) 255
do not attempt resuscitation
    (DNAR) 186–7
doctor–patient
    relationship 147–75
    new understanding 148–9
    paternalism 148
    trust 149
    see also consent
doctors
    cultural beliefs 253
    full registration 202
    provisional registration
        of 202
    specialist registration
        of 202
    doesn't want to know, end
        of life care 179
donation, Human Tissue
    Act 2004 318
double effect doctrine
    181, 276
Driver and Vehicle Licensing
    Agency (DVLA) 270
duty, breach of *see* breach
    of duty
duty of candour 204–5
duty of care 99
duty to act 110
Dworkin, Ronald 161

E

ECHR *see* European
    Convention on Human
    Rights (ECHR)
ECJ (European Court of
    Justice) 72
ECtHR (European Court of
    Human Rights) 72
elderly care
    resource allocations 240
    treatment refusal 240–1
elective ventilation, organ
    donors 194
electro-convulsive therapy
    (ECT) 346
electronic prescribing
    system 238
embryo research 292
emergencies, The Bolam
    test 101
emergency department
    knife crime 242
    restraint & self-
        defence 243
empathy 10
end of life care 178–9
endocrinology 244
English law 68
    Good Samaritanism 110
ENT (ear, nose and throat)
    surgery 245
Epicurus 12
equipoise, medical
    research 216
ethical issues
    advance decisions 161
    care ethics *see* care ethics
    children's consent 173
    conflict resolution 61
    critical reasoning 62–3
    debates and death
        definition 180
    decisions & theory 6
    GMC 206, 210
    questions 210
    social endeavour as 52–3
    social nature of 52–3
    virtue ethics *see*
        virtue ethics
ethical theory 6
    ethical decisions and 6
    sample questions 7
    scientific theory *vs.* 6
ethical-legal issues 229–
    59, 261–80
eudaimonia 12
European Convention
    on Human Rights
    (ECHR) 72, 76
    article 2 78

European Convention on
Human Rights (ECHR)
(Contd.)
article 3 79, 80
article 8 81
article 9 81
article 10 82
article 14 82
see also Human Rights
Act 1998
European Court of Human
Rights (ECtHR) 72
European Court of Justice
(ECJ) 72
European Courts 72
European Union (EU) 68
euthanasia 180–1
active euthanasia *see*
active euthanasia
debates over 190–1
definition 180
involuntary euthanasia 180
non-voluntary
euthanasia 180
passive euthanasia 180
types 180
voluntary euthanasia 180
Euthyphro dilemma 22
evidence
expert witnesses 88
preservation 268
expense, innovations 267
expert witnesses 88–9
confidentiality 89
duty to the court 88
giving evidence 88
independence 88
opinion changes 89
role of 88
explicit consent
confidentiality 136
confidentiality
disclosures 139
confidentiality
overriding 138–9
expression, freedom of *see*
freedom of expression

F

fair trials 302
family life
ECHR article 8 81
Human Rights Act
1998 303
family members, end of life
care 179
family planning, Gillick
competence 246
fast track cases 86
father definition 294–7

female genital mutilation
(FGM) 34–5, 287–8
Female Genital Mutilation
Act 2003 287–8
feminine critique, care
ethics 45
Fitness to Practice Rules
2004 (GMC) 207–8
forced labour
protection 300
four principles 29–41, 134–5
background 30
need for 30
practice in 38–9
pros and cons 39
sample questions 40, 41
see also autonomy;
beneficence; justice;
non-maleficence
freedom of assembly &
association 304
freedom of choice 126
freedom of conscience
ECHR article 9 81
Human Rights Act
1998 303
freedom of expression 82
Human Rights Act
1998 303
freedom of religion
ECHR article 9 81
Human Rights Act
1998 303
freedom of thought
ECHR article 9 81
Human Rights Act
1998 303
full registration of
doctors 202
functional test of mental
capacity 153, 154

G

gametes, storage & use 293
gastroenterology 247
Gender Recognition Act
2004 289–90
General Data Protection
Regulations
(GCPR) 140–1
General Medical Council
(GMC) 201–10
clinical questions 210
confidentiality
guidelines 136
death certificates 144
definition 202
duty of candour 204–5
ethical guidelines 204–5
ethical questions 210

Fitness to Practice Rules
2004 207–8
Good Medical Practice
(2012) 110, 239, 251
investigations about
doctors 206–8
legal questions 210
patient information 258
Professional and Linguistic
Assessment
Board 202
registration types 202
revalidation 202
whistle-blowing 205
General Practitioners
(GPs) 202
cultural circumcision 248
medical indemnity 92
general surgery,
innovation 250–1
genetics, confidentiality 252
germline cells 292
Gillick competence 172, 232
dentistry 236
family planning 246
*Gillick v West Norfolk Area
Health Authority* [1985]
172, 232, 236
*Gillick v West Norfolk Area
Health Authority* [1986]
246, 262, 263, 264
Gilligan, Carol 45
golden rule, legal
principles 68–9
good consequences 16
Good Medical Practice 2012
(GMC) 110, 204–5,
239, 251
Good Samaritanism 110–11
causation in omission
cases 110–11
liability for failure to
rescue 110
*Greater Glasgow Health
Board v Doogan*
[2014] 175
guilty pleas 84–5
gynaecology, abortion 253

H

*H (A Healthworker) v
Associated Newspaper
Ltd* [2002] 270
harm
confidentiality after
death 143
living organ
donation 196–7
protection from 214–15
screening programmes 36

understanding of 36
see also non-maleficence
HE v A Hospital NHS Trust
[2003] 160–1
head injuries 268
Health and Social Care Act
2008 132
Health Board v Doogan
[2014] 253
health inequalities 126
Health Protection
Agency 138–9
healthy limb amputation 36
Helsinki protocol 216
high-fidelity
simulators 224–5
Hippocratic Oath 4, 5, 134
pros & cons 5
use of 5
HIV infection
confidentiality 254
confidentiality after death
142, 143
duty of care 99
non-notifiable disease
as 138–9
see also AIDS
HL v United Kingdom [2002]
ECHR 279
homogeneous society,
illusory nature 52
*The Hospital v JJ (by his
litigation friend, the
Official Solicitor)*
[2019] 238
hospitals, suing of 107
Human Fertilization and
Embryology Act
1990 291–7
embryo research 292
father definition 294–7
gamete storage & use 293
germline cells 292
mother definition 293
human rights
death & dying 184
deontology 25–6
limited 77
positive & negative
rights 77
against state &
citizens 77
types of 77
Human Rights Act 1998
76–77, 299–305
confidentiality 138–9
discrimination
protection 305
fair trial 302
forced labour
protection 300

freedom of assembly &
association 304
freedom of
conscience 303
freedom of
expression 304
freedom of religion 303
freedom of thought 303
legal authorization 302
liberty & security 301
marriage 305
private & family life 303
protection from
torture 300
right to life 300
slavery prohibition 300
Human Tissue Act 2004
192–3, 307–22
adult consent 314–15
children consent 312
commercial dealing
prohibition 320–1
donated human tissue 318
liver transplants 322
living organ donation 196
prohibited
activities 316–17
tissue regulation 308–10
Human Tissue Authority
(HTA) 196
human tissue
regulations 308–10
humanity, importance of 24
Huntington's disease 252

I

ICHGCP (International
Council on
Harmonisation
of Technical
Requirements for
Registration of
Pharmaceuticals for
Human Use, Good
Clinical Practice) 30
illness prevention,
beneficence 34
illusory nature of
homogeneous
society 52
implicit consent 150
confidentiality
overriding 138–9
In the Matter of Charles Gard
[2017] 236, 264
in vivo fertilization (IVF) 38
independence, expert
witnesses 88
independent mental capacity
advocates (IMCA) 164

information
governance in
neurosurgery 265
omission in death
certificates 144
patient access 136
protection 136
retention and mental
capacity 153
weighing of in mental
capacity 153–4
Information Commissioner's
Office 265
informed decision-
making 33
Inglis, Francis 182–3
inhuman treatment 79
innovations
expense 267
general surgery 250–1
neurosurgery 266–7
insulin-dependent diabetes,
lack of mental
capacity 244
intensive care, do
not attempt
cardiopulmonary
resuscitation 255
interest identification,
critical reasoning 61–2
International Council
on Harmonisation
of Technical
Requirements for
Registration of
Pharmaceuticals for
Human Use, Good
Clinical Practice
(ICHGCP) 30
interventional
radiology 256
intracranial vascular
anomalies 256
involuntary euthanasia 180
isotretinoin 237
issue-specific mental
capacity 152

J

Jehovah's Witnesses 262
*Jones v Royal Devon & Exeter
NHS* [2015] 94
justice 37
consequentialism 18
definition 37
distributive justice 127
need 37
resource
allocation 37
virtue ethics 12–13

K

Kant, Immanuel 22
kidneys, living organ
    donation 196
killing 180–1
knife crime 242

L

lack of capacity
    Court of Protection 244
    end of life care 178–9
    insulin-dependent
        diabetes 244
    medical research 217
lasting power of attorney
    (LPA) 158, 161, 330
    cardiopulmonary
        resuscitation 187
    Mental Capacity Act
        2005 330
laws
    case law 68
    England see English law
    Good Samaritanism 110
    key articles 75–82
    medical practice and 91–5
    National Health
        Service 93
    private medicine 94–5
LBL v RY [2010] 153
learning difficulties 152–3
legal authorization, Human
    Rights Act 1998 302
legal principles 68–9
    dead donor organ
        transplantation 192–3
    GMC 210
    living organ donation 196
    sources of law 68
    statue interpretation 68–9
liability
    accomplice liability 112
    corporate liability 112
    criminal liability 112
    failure to rescue 110
    no-fault liability 114–15
    vicarious liability 112–13
liberty of persons
    deprivation, Mental
        Capacity Act 2005
        326, 328–9, 336–7
    ECHR article 3 80
    Human Rights Act
        1998 301
    urology and 279
Liberty Protection
    Safeguards (LPS)
    authorization
        effects 169–70

pre-authorization
    review 169
    requirements 169
    restraint/force
        use 168–70
    satisfaction decision
        of 168–9
life, sanctity of 190
life-saving treatment
    beneficence 34
    Mental Capacity Act
        2005 328–9
lifestyle choices, resource
    allocation 126
Lillywhite v UCL [2005] 250
limb amputation 36
limitation period for
    negligences 107
limited human rights 77
literal rule, legal
    principles 68–9
liver transplants 322
living organ
    donation 196–7
loss of a chance cases 106
loved ones, rationing by
    desert 125
LPA see lasting power of
    attorney (LPA)
LPS see Liberty Protection
    Safeguards (LPS)
lying
    confidentiality after
        death 143
    deontology 24

M

magistrates' court 84
male bias 44
marriage 305
material risks, disclosure of
    156, 157
maxillofacial surgery,
    candour 258–9
medical education see
    medical training
medical indemnity 92
medical need 38
Medical Practitioners
    Tribunal
    Service (MPTS)
    GMC investigations 206
    referral to 207–8
medical records
    access to 140–1
    diabetology 238–9
medical research 211–17
    Declaration of
        Helsinki 214–15
    ethics 212–13

non-therapeutic
    research 212
Nuremburg Code 214–15
participation 41
scientific validity 212–13
therapeutic research 212
types of 216–17
Medical Research Council
    (MRC) 216–17
medical training 219–25
    confidentiality 222
    consent 221
    deceased patients 224–5
    patient role 220
Medicines for Human
    Use (Clinical
    Trials) Regulations
    2004 216–17
mental capacity 152–5
    assessment 277
    assisted suicide 182–3
    best interests
        assessment 166–7
    cardiopulmonary
        resuscitation 187
    communication
        inability 154
    consent problems 158
    core test 324
    decisions that cannot be
        made 164
    diagnostic test 152–3, 154
    end of life care 178
    functional test 153, 154
    gaining 325
    general test 152
    independent mental
        capacity
        advocates 164
    information retention 153
    lack of see lack of capacity
    mistake protection 330
    overriding of
        confidentiality 138–9
    patient information
        and 252
    relative & carers views 167
    speech 277
    time specific 152
    understanding and 153
    unwise decisions 154
    weighing of
        information 153–4
Mental Capacity Act 2005
    152, 278, 323–37
    advance decisions see
        advance decisions
    advanced directives see
        advanced directives
    best interests assessment
        166–7, 325

capacity mistake
protection 330
consent 158
core test 324
elderly care 240
end of life care 178–9
five principles of 324
gaining of mental
capacity 325
independent mental
capacity
advocates 164
lasting power of attorney
see lasting power of
attorney (LPA)
liberty deprivation 326,
328–9, 336–7
life-saving
treatment 328–9
medical research 217
non-authorizable
items 334
patient's best interests 244
Mental Capacity
Amendment Act
2019 168–70
mental disorders 340
Mental Health
Act 1983 339
admission criteria under
section 2 341
admission criteria under
section 3 342
brain tissue
treatment 344
electro-convulsive therapy
346
emergency admission
criteria under section
4 343
gastroenterology 247
mental disorder definition
340
Mill, John Stuart 16, 196–7
minimum necessary
personal
information 136
Mohr v Williams 104 NW 12
(SC Minn 1905) 245
*Montgomery v Lanarkshire
Health Board* [2015]
UKSC 11 102, 148–9,
156–7, 234, 256, 258–
9, 272, 280
moral reasoning 57
mother definition 293
MPTS see Medical
Practitioners Tribunal
Service (MPTS)
multi-track cases 86
murder 180–1

N

National Health Service
(NHS) 37
contracts 93
costs of 120–1
disciplinary proceedings 93
laws within 93
medical indemnity 92
suing of 107
National Health Service
(Scotland) Act
1978 284
National Health Service Act
2006 284
National Institute for
Health and Care
Excellence (NICE)
innovation expense 267
postcode lotteries 130
rationing by desert 125
Nazi Germany 52
necessity, children's
consent 173
necrotizing enterocolitis,
neonates 262
needle phobia 269
needs, resource
allocation 124
negligence 97–108
claims 157, 266
consequences of 106–8
damage payments 108
damages 106
innovation 251
limitation period 107
secondary victims 107
see also breach of duty
neonates
consent 263
necrotizing
enterocolitis 262
surgery and Jehovah's
Witnesses 262
neurology, child's rights *vs.*
parents' rights 264
neurosurgery
evidence preservation 268
information
governance 265
innovation 266–7
New Zealand, no-fault
liability 114–15
NHS see National Health
Service (NHS)
NHS Redress Act 2006 115
NICE see National Institute
for Health and Care
Excellence (NICE)
no-fault liability 114–15
non-discrimination

best interests
assessment 326
ECHR article 14 82
non-heart-beating
donors 195
non-human materials 258
non-maleficence 31, 36, 41
definition 36
scope of 36
see also harm
non-regenerative tissue
donation 196
non-therapeutic medical
research 212
non-voluntary
euthanasia 180
Northern Ireland, laws 68
notifiable diseases 138–9
Nuremberg trials 4
Nuremburg Code 214–15

O

obstetrics, needle
phobia 269
omission case
causation, Good
Samaritanism 110–11
ophthalmology 270
opinion changes, expert
witnesses 89
Organ Donation (Deemed
Consent) Act
2019 192–3
organ donor shortages 193
organ transplantation 192–5
case study 195
dead donors 192–3
donor shortages 193
non-heart-beating
donors 195
presumed consent 193
recipient decisions 193
standards of consent 194
orthopaedic trauma 278

P

*P v Cheshire West and
Chester Council* [2014]
UKSC 19 279
paediatric cardiology 271
paracetamol overdose
247, 274
paranoia 152–3
parents' rights, child's rights
vs. 264
part 7 claim form 86
passive euthanasia 180
paternalism 148
autonomy and 32–3

patient information 156–7
confidentiality 136
GMC 258
mental capacity and 252
non-human materials 258
patients
autonomy 237
banning from emergency
department 243
deserving patients 38
disclosure of treatment
risks 272
doctor relationships see
doctor–patient
relationship
explanations to 142
identity confidentiality 134
information see patient
information
medical training 220
safety concerns 242
teaching hospitals 41
unconscious patients 215
Patterson, Ian 149
people, liberty of see liberty
of persons
percutaneous endoscopic
gastrostomy (PEG) 240
persistent vegetative state
(PVS) 186
death & dying 180
personal data, Data
Protection Act
2018 140–1
pharmacists 92
photography, clinical 268
pig-based material,
maxillofacial
surgery 258
pinnaplasty 245
pitfalls, critical reasoning 60
plastics 272–3
Plato 22
police 242
Police and Criminal Evidence
Act 1984 268
postcode lotteries 38
resource allocation 130
pre-authorization review,
Liberty Protection
Safeguards 169
pregnancy, treatment
refusal 269
presumed consent
organ donation 194
organ
transplantation 193
private life
ECHR article 8 81
Human Rights Act
1998 303

private medicine
contracts 94
laws 94–5
medical indemnity 92
Professional and Linguistic
Assessment Board
(GMC) 202
professional guidance, The
Bolam test 101
prohibited activities,
Human Tissue Act
2004 316–17
promises, confidentiality
after death 143
protection from harm,
Declaration of Helsinki
(1964) 214–15
protection from torture,
Human Rights Act
1998 300
provisional registration of
doctors 202
public health 19
public interest
confidentiality
overriding 138–9
criminal cases 84
purpose rule, legal
principles 68–9
PVS see persistent
vegetative state (PVS)

Q

qualified human
rights 77
qualifying relationships,
organ
transplantation 192
quality of life, euthanasia
and 190
quality-adjusted life years
(QALYs) 129

R

R v Adams 181
R v BM [2018] 154–5
R v East London and the
City mental Health
NHS Trust exparte
von Brandenburg
[2003] 247
R (Burke) v General Medical
Council [2005] 150,
237, 266, 271
R v Gladstone Williams
[1984] 243
R (Ferreira) v HM Coroner
for Inner London South
[2017] 168

R (Nicklinson) v Ministry of
Justice [2014] 184
R v Tabassum [2000] 153
radiology 256
randomized clinical trials
(RCTs) 216
rationing by desert,
resource allocation 125
Re A (conjoined twins)
[2001] 276
Re A (A Child) [2015] 180
Re B (Adult: Refusal Medical
Treatment) [2002] 240
Re F (Mental Patient
Sterilisation) [1990] 245
Re J (A Minor) (Medical
Treatment) [1992] 262
Re L and B (Children: Specific
Issues: Temporary Leave
from the Jurisdiction:
Circumcision)
[2016] 248
Re MB (Medical Treatment)
[1997] 2 FLR 426 269
Re S (Child as Parent:
Adoption: Consent)
[2017] 263
Re W (A Minor) (Medical
Treatment: Court's
Jurisdiction) [1992]
236, 246
Re X (A Child) [2014]
EWHC 1871
(Fam) 246
Re X (A Child) [2020]
EWHC (Admin)
1958 264
Re Y [2018] 186
reasoning, answers vs. 57
receptionists, duty of
care 99
records see medical records
rectal examinations 60
regenerative tissue
donation 196
relationships, care ethics 45
relative risks, interventional
radiology 256
relative views, mental
capacity 167
relativism &
subjectivism 49–54
definition 50
limits to 52
pros & cons 53
sample question 54
tolerance & diversity 52
relevant information
sharing 136
religion
deontology and 22

freedom of see freedom
of religion
renal disease 274
res ipsa loquitur 101
research see medical
research
resource allocation 119–30
budget management 122
cake slices 120–1
case study 124
elderly care 240
freedom of choice 126
health inequalities 126
justice 37
needs & desires 124
postcode lotteries 130
rationing by desert 125
retributive & distributive
justice 127
social values 128
taxes 122
triage 123
respiratory medicine 275
responsibilities
confidentiality 136
rationing by desert 125
restraint/force use 168–70
definition 168
emergency department 243
retributive justice 127
rheumatology 276
right to life
ECHR article 2 78
Human Rights Act
1998 300
right to treatment 237
risk disclosure 256
risks, patient disclosure 272
risk-taking
resource allocation 126
types of 128
Roaccutane® 237
Royal College of
Physicians 214–15
rule utilitarianism,
consequentialism vs. 19

S

safety concerns, patient
trust 242
sanctity of life 190
scientific theory, ethical
theory vs. 6
scientific validity, medical
research 212–13
Scotland
Good Samaritanism 110
legal principles 68
screening programmes,
harm 36

secondary victims,
negligences 107
security of persons
ECHR article 3 80
Human Rights Act
1998 301
sedation 168
self-defence, emergency
department 243
self-employed
practitioners 92
sentencing, criminal
cases 84–5
Shipman, Harold 149
signed consent 150
Simms v Simms [2004]
266, 271
simulations 224–5
Singer, Peter 18
slavery prohibition 300
small claims cases 86
smoking cessation
refusal 275
social endeavour 52–3
social nature 52–3
social values, resource
allocation 128
specialism, The Bolam
test 101
specialist registration of
doctors 202
speech, mental capacity 277
St George's Healthcare NHS
Trust v S [1992] 277
St George's Healthcare NHS
Trust v S [1998] 240
statutes
interpretation 68–9
legislation 68
statutory disclosures 270
subjectivism 50
see also relativism &
subjectivism
suicide 350
assisted suicide 182–3
Suicide Act 1961 350
suing 107
Surrogacy Arrangements
Act 1985 352
commercial surrogacy
prohibition 354

T

taxes 122
teaching hospitals 41
terminal disease subjects,
medical research 216
Terrorism Act 2000 268
therapeutic medical
research 212

thought, freedom of see
freedom of thought
time limits
abortion 284
consent 154–5
mental capacity 152
tolerance 52
tooth extraction 236
tort 71
vicarious liability 112–13
torture 79
Tracey v Cambridge
University Hospital
NHS Foundation Trust
[2014] 255
training see medical training
trauma, orthopaedics 278
treatment refusal
elderly care 240–1
pregnancy 269
renal disease 274
treatment withdrawal/
withholding 186–8
triage 123
trust, doctor–patient
relationship 149

U

UK legislation 68
unconscious patient
consent 215
under-age minors,
contraceptive
advice 246
understanding, mental
capacity and 153
unlicensed equipment 271
unsound mind 80
unwise decisions
mental capacity 154
respiratory medicine 275
urology 279
utilitarianism 44, 134–5

V

value identification, critical
reasoning 61
value to society 125
vascular surgery 280
verbal consent 150
vicarious liability 112–13
virtue ethics 10, 12–13
eudaimonia 12
justice 12–13
pros & cons 13
sample questions 14
wisdom 12
voluntary erasure 206
voluntary euthanasia 180

W

Wales
  Good Samaritanism 110
  legal principles 68
weighing of information 153–4
whistle-blowing, GMC 205

Winspear v City Hospitals
  Sunderland NHS
  Foundation Trust
  [2015] 255
wisdom 12
witnesses. expert *see* expert
  witnesses

World Medical Association 5
Wye Valley NHS Trust v Mr B
  [2015] 244, 275, 278

Z

zidovudine 217